GLORIOUS SHADE

# GLORIOUS SHADE

# Dazzling Plants, Design Ideas, and Proven Techniques for Your Shady Garden

**JENNY ROSE CAREY**

**TIMBER PRESS**
PORTLAND, OREGON

Frontispiece: A stunning *Rhododendron* collection growing at the
Royal Horticultural Society Garden Wisley in Surrey, England.
Page 6: Raindrops glisten on the young leaves of *Cercis canadensis*.

Published in 2017 by Timber Press, Inc.

The Haseltine Building
133 S.W. Second Avenue, Suite 450
Portland, Oregon 97204-3527
timberpress.com

Printed in China

Text design by Laura Shaw Design, Inc.
Cover design by Debbie Berne

Library of Congress Cataloging-in-Publication Data

Names: Carey, Jenny Rose, author.
Title: Glorious shade: dazzling plants, design ideas, and proven techniques
  for your shady garden / Jenny Rose Carey.
Description: Portland, Oregon: Timber Press, 2017. | Includes
  bibliographical references and index.
Identifiers: LCCN 2016036949 | ISBN 9781604696813 (pbk.)
Subjects: LCSH: Gardening in the shade. | Shade-tolerant plants.
Classification: LCC SB434.7 .C37 2017 | DDC 635.9/543—dc23 LC record available at
    https://lccn.loc.gov/2016036949

A catalog record for this book is also available from the British Library.

To my husband, Gus, and my daughters, Meade, Janet, and Emily, all of whom have shared in the development of our shade garden.

# CONTENTS

Preface    9

## SHADES OF SHADE  15
*Observing Shifting Patterns in Your Garden*

## THE GARDENER'S CALENDAR  37
*Seasonal Changes in the Shade Garden*

## DOWN AND DIRTY  61
*The Intertwined, Underground World of Soil and Roots*

## PLANTING FOR SUCCESS  77
*Techniques and Maintenance*

## DESIGNING IN THE SHADOWS  105
*Bright Ideas for Shady Spaces*

## THE PLANT PALETTE  149
*Choosing Plants for Your Shade Garden*

Metric Conversions and Hardiness Zones    310
Suggested Reading    311
Garden and Photography Credits    313
Acknowledgments    314
Index    315

# PREFACE

My journey to shade gardening came about through my early love of trees and natural areas. Growing up in a village in rural England, we took long walks beneath trees, through shady lanes, and along hedgerows. With my botanist father as a guide, we'd stop at each plant and he would tell me its name. I learned from a young age that certain plants could only be found in the partial shade at the base of a hedge, while others only grew well in the full shade of woodlands.

I loved the cycles of the year and the dramatic changes that happened in shaded areas. In spring, we strolled through woods carpeted with scented English bluebells of an ethereal blue that no photograph could ever capture. In fall, we walked through crunchy, fallen leaves that emitted their characteristic bittersweet smell when crushed beneath our feet. Years later, I still love to walk through woods wherever I am, including around my Pennsylvania home. The woodlands here are carpeted with Virginia bluebells in spring and shaded by soaring oaks, spreading beech trees, and wonderful flowering dogwoods and redbuds. The natural layers of the wild places that I love to explore inspire my garden designs. I tuck plants into every garden corner—tall trees, smaller understory trees and shrubs, and an herbaceous layer at ground level.

When I first moved to the United States, I had to adapt to the new climate, different soils, and a whole new set of plants. My garden, Northview, was then extremely overgrown; choked with vines and invasive plants. The first thing that I set out to do after arriving was to identify which plants would stay and which should be removed. After clearing out the unwanted vegetation,

An English bluebell wood is the essence of springtime.

I reached out to gardening friends and neighbors for advice on making smart plant choices. They then generously offered me plant divisions and seeds that were suited to this region, helping me on my way.

The shaded areas of my garden look very different today than they did when I first moved in—they now offer a retreat. There are cool, refreshing places to sit away from the heat of the sun and paths that entice visitors to explore. The garden is plant-packed and personal and it suits my house, the area where I live, and the needs of my family.

My shade garden is a constant source of joy to me. I walk around my garden paths as often as I can to see what has happened since I last looked. Close observation is always coupled with anticipation: what flower buds have opened since yesterday? Have the fern fronds unfurled? The growing cycles of the year give me things to look forward to in every season: a profusion of spring blossoms followed by summer greenery, colored fall leaves, and then the subtle joys of winter.

I understand that gardening in shade is a long-term process. I have learned to wait and have patience while saplings grow, bulbs emerge from the soil, and shrubs become big enough to flower. I garden at an unhurried pace. I appreciate and enjoy the gradual transformations that occur year after year. I would never want my garden to be "finished"—gardens are all about growth and change, after all.

*Ulmus americana*, American elm, is one of the most majestic canopy trees.

opposite In the shade garden at Northview, Virginia bluebells mingle with other charming, pastel spring flowers.

I have designed the garden to encourage a diversity of plants and animals because I am aware of the role it plays in the larger ecosystem that surrounds me. I have included as many native plants as possible and am committed to making the space a haven for pollinators, birds, and other wildlife. There are water features to provide fresh water and plants where food, shelter, and places to nest can be found.

No garden stays the same for long. I plan for the succession of shade in my garden by planting young trees of all shapes and sizes that will grow up and take the place of older, declining specimens. I have the benefit of gardening beneath majestic, shade-providing trees that were planted here over a century ago. I am just one in a long line of caretakers that have gardened and will continue to garden in this space. I encourage you to view the process the same way; planting new trees will provide you and future gardeners with all of the benefits of a shaded area.

As you develop your own shade garden, choose trees that you love, fill your space with plants that inspire you, and arrange them in ways that please you. Your garden will be an outdoor place that is as unique as you are, and will provide pleasure for you, your family, and your guests.

The ever-changing beauty of the shade garden is a celebration of life; a multifaceted ecosystem full of a diverse community of plants and animals. The lush greenness of the vegetation provides a cool, soothing place to relax, protected by the enclosure of the sheltering trees or walls. Rather than stress over your shady spaces, it is time to celebrate them and revel in the benefits that a glorious shade garden will bring to your life.

This beautiful space shaded by walls, hedges, and *Magnolia* trees at the Sissinghurst Castle Garden in Kent, England, brings back happy memories of my childhood.

# SHADES OF SHADE

## OBSERVING SHIFTING PATTERNS IN YOUR GARDEN

Shade in a garden is not a tangible thing; it is a fragile, ephemeral, will-o-the-wispy shape-shifter, hard to define because it changes with the path of the sun. Because of its transient nature, it is difficult to describe and even harder to comprehend. Try explaining shadows to a young child. I remember watching one of my daughters, at age two, discovering her shadow. She saw it, bent down to touch it, but then it changed; she stood up, walked toward it, and carried on along the path trying to figure it out. In our own gardens, watching shadows is fun and fascinating. Learning about our shade patterns is an interesting process, but well worth the effort, because it makes us better gardeners.

Ever-changing shade patterns along an azalea walk at Jenkins Arboretum and Gardens in Devon, Pennsylvania.

Trees cast shadows on high enclosing walls, providing additional shade and relief from summer heat in this garden at the Real Alcázar de Sevilla in Spain.

**above right** A thrilling combination of shade-loving plants, including *Gentiana*, *Begonia*, and *Athyrium*, at the Royal Horticultural Society Garden Rosemoor, in Devon, England

Shade is described as the absence of light, but the lack of something is rarely so beautiful and so useful. The objects that block the sun's direct rays and prevent them from hitting the ground also provide character and structure to a garden. The trees, buildings, and other large objects are the permanent framework of a garden; they define spaces both on the ground and in the air.

Shade, whether from structures, trees, or even tall perennials, reduces light levels and also lowers the temperature for both plants and people. Shady areas are where we seek relief from the heat on a hot summer day. Instead of seeing these areas of lower light as ones to be avoided in your garden, I encourage you to relish the pleasures to be found there.

Developing these spaces in your garden adds to the diversity and interest of the plants that you can grow. All plants need some sunlight to grow, but not all plants require full sun. Each plant has a range of light conditions where it will grow successfully. The plants that thrive in shade gardens are those whose natural habitat is the floor of forests and woodlands. Learn through observation about the shade in your garden so that you can select plants that will flourish. Recognizing patterns and types of shade is a key to successful shade gardening.

# TYPES OF SHADE

By its nature, shade shifts daily and seasonally. The number of hours of shade, the time of day that it occurs, and the intensity of the light falling on a garden are the major factors used to describe types of shade. Shade definitions can be made objective by using light meters to record the number of hours of sunlight a garden receives, but this is unnecessary for the home gardener. I prefer to use an observational approach to assess shade levels.

Generally speaking, full shade areas of the garden receive fewer than two hours of light, while an area in part shade receives between two and six hours of sunlight and is shaded for the rest of the day. For comparison, a garden in full sun receives direct sunlight for more than six hours a day.

It is helpful, however, to be specific about shade conditions in our gardens, as this allows us to make intelligent plant choices. The following categories can be used to describe garden shade more accurately.

## FULL SHADE

Areas of full shade receive little direct sunlight, but some ambient light will reach plants by being bounced around and reflected off nearby surfaces. Such areas are often found on the darker side of houses, walls, or buildings, under coniferous trees, and beside dense hedges.

In full shade, plants grow steadily but slowly. They tend to flower less profusely than they would with more light, but the individual flowers last longer as temperatures are lower. Shade-loving plants tend to increase vegetatively, often by runners, called stolons. This is a type of asexual reproduction that produces a patch of plants that grows and spreads steadily out from the parent plant.

The darkest areas of full shade are described as deep shade, and they receive almost no direct sunlight. These areas of low light intensity are often coupled with dry soil, so plants have to be carefully selected to suit these conditions.

## PART SHADE

An area in part shade is shaded for a portion of the day and receives between two and six hours of sunlight. This type of shade is the most common in the garden. Part shade can occur under or beside trees and shrubs, or next to hedges, walls, fences, and other garden structures.

The classification of part shade is elusive because it has so many variables. The shade-providing object, the direction of the sunlight with respect to the shade producer, and the intensity of the shade all affect what classification of part shade a garden receives.

Solid walls and other built structures are uniform barriers that block light from one direction. Plants growing near walls are shaded on one side, but not necessarily on others. Additional light may reach plants from above if they are open to the sky. Trees or other organic objects provide irregular shade. Those under the tree canopy are in dappled shade. Plants at the edge of the canopy receive more light, but are still shaded by the tree for part of the day.

Part shade can also be described by the time of day that an area is shaded—morning or afternoon. If any of these shaded situations receives additional indirect light, they can also be

A multilayered tree canopy provides full shade to the garden below.

right This partly shaded suburban garden, enclosed by trees and shrubs as well as by the solid walls of a house, has a colorful and exciting selection of plants.

qualified as bright shade (for example, bright afternoon shade). All of the following descriptions are categories of part shade that can be used to more accurately describe specific garden shade conditions.

EDGE SHADE The site around the perimeter of a deciduous woodland is where you will find edge shade. In a home garden, it can even be found around individual trees, typically below the perimeter of the tree canopy. Edge shade provides some of the best growing conditions in the garden. It is an ideal situation because the light that reaches the plants is sufficient for growth and flowering, but there is enough shade so that plants do not burn during hot summer days.

DAPPLED SHADE Dappled shade is a type of part shade provided by trees, especially deciduous ones. The size of the leaves and the height and extent of the canopy influence the amount of light that reaches the ground. Trees with a higher canopy or smaller leaves allow more light to the ground below, while a low canopy and large leaves provide a more dense shade.

The tree leaves block much of the sun's light but do not form a complete cover, allowing areas of sun to reach the ground below in a constantly moving pattern. As trees shift in the wind and the sun passes overhead, the "puddles" of light move and change in shape. Many shade-loving plants were originally from wooded areas, so they do best in dappled shade. Plants in this type of shade can receive significant light but it is unpredictable and highly seasonal.

BRIGHT SHADE An area in bright shade is near reflective objects that bounce light around. Bright shade might be found near lakes, ponds, or other water features. In urban gardens, bright shade is often located near windows and white or light-colored walls. The amount of light that reaches these areas may vary considerably according to the time of day and the season of the year. There is a wider range of plants that can be grown in bright shade than in full shade due to the increased light intensity.

MORNING AND AFTERNOON SHADE Planting areas that are to the west of a shade producer are in morning shade. These areas stay cool in the mornings but heat up in the hot rays of afternoon sun.

Plants that benefit from morning shade are those that bloom early in the year, as their delicate flower buds need to warm up gradually after a frosty night. Plants such as *Rhododendron*, *Magnolia*, and fruit trees have delicate flower buds that do well in morning shade. In summer, these west-facing plants receive the hottest sun of the day, so choose tough plants that can cope with the afternoon heat. Try drought-tolerant plants to prevent leaf desiccation.

Late day sun can easily scorch fragile leaves and flowers, so site plants that need protection from heat as well as sun in afternoon shade. The hotter your climate, the better afternoon shade is for the health of your plants. A planting bed situated to the east of a shade producer will receive morning sun and afternoon shade.

Plants such as *Clematis* and *Lonicera* are perfect on an east-facing wall, which receives afternoon shade. Shade plants that thrive in moist soil, or that tend to dry out, should also be situated in afternoon shade. Plants with large, fleshy leaves that desiccate easily, such as *Rodgersia*, *Hosta*, and *Astilbe*, are suited to this type of shade.

Informally arranged trees create a variety of partly shaded conditions in this diverse garden at the Pennsylvania Horticultural Society's Meadowbrook Farm in Jenkintown, Pennsylvania.

A beautiful planting bed at the edge of a woodland.

right *Betula* branches and leaves filter light, casting dappled shadows onto *Aquilegia* and *Digitalis* in a Worcestershire country garden in England.

opposite The water in this pond reflects light into a shaded section of the Coastal Maine Botanical Gardens in Boothbay, Maine.

Trees and shrubs shelter this garden from the heat of the late afternoon sun.

opposite *Magnolia*, *Acer*, and other trees block the morning sun in this partly shaded hillside garden.

## HOW SHADE SHIFTS THROUGHOUT THE YEAR

Shade changes with the seasons. In all gardens, except those at the equator, there is a predictable progression of seasonal shade that affects plants. The closer to the earth's poles that you garden, the greater the difference will be between the shade patterns of summer and winter. At the equator, day length is consistent throughout the year, and seasonal change is minimal.

The three factors that affect shade seasonally in the garden are the length of the day, the height of the sun above the horizon, and the intensity of the sunlight. We all know that the shaded areas in our gardens change from month to month, but we may not realize how much.

During winter, the weather is cooler or cold, depending on where you live. There is more shade, as the sun is only up for a short time and its path across the sky is low. Some areas of the garden are in full shade for days or weeks at a time. Plants slow their rate of growth or retreat into winter dormancy. Evergreen plants retain their leaves and so are the only ones affected by the low light intensity of the winter sun.

In spring, the days lengthen and there are fewer hours of shade. The sun is higher in the sky, the days become longer, and the patterns of shade change. Plants emerge from dormancy and begin to grow.

By the summer equinox, the day is at its longest. The path of the sun is high, allowing light to filter into unexpected places. The plants need the extra light because they are in active growth. As summer progresses, the days get shorter again but the sun is at its strongest intensity and temperatures are at their highest.

Shadows cast by the bare branches of a deciduous tree fall on pristine snow.

opposite  By early summer, the leaves of this deciduous tree have formed almost a full canopy.

Autumn brings shorter days and a decrease in shade as the deciduous trees drop their leaves. The colder weather brings on dormancy in most plants, so the change in shade level does not impact their growth. Taking time to observe the seasonal shade changes in your garden will make you a better and more knowledgeable gardener.

The key to successful shade gardening is being aware of the changing daily and seasonal shade patterns. To garden effectively in shaded places, it is important to look at how long areas are shaded and the type of shade that is present. Once you understand your garden's shade, you can make good plant choices.

Gardens have many different plants and structures that can provide shade, so examine every area and notice when it is shaded and by how much. Walk around your garden and study the shadows cast by nonliving objects, such as hills, rocks, buildings, fences, and walls. Look at any plants that provide shade, especially the more permanent woody plants—the trees, shrubs, and hedges.

Familiarize yourself with how much shade is produced in the morning, at midday, and later in the afternoon. Carefully observe the levels of shade in each area of your garden. Are they dappled, bright, or full? Repeat this exercise throughout the year to see how the patterns change seasonally. Deciduous trees and shrubs produce shade that varies during the year, whereas evergreen plants like coniferous trees cast consistent shade in every season. Sections of your garden will have different amounts of shade, giving you more planting opportunities. Use this diversity of gardening conditions to expand your plant palette.

Study your garden at different times of the day and throughout the year to see how the shade patterns change.

# CHANGING THE SHADE LEVELS IN YOUR GARDEN

Shade gardening is a process and not an end result. Sometimes, shade disappears suddenly if a limb falls off a tree or a tree dies, leaving a hole in the canopy. Successful gardeners know that the amount and location of shade they have in their garden today will be altered in a few years' time as the trees and shrubs grow.

The shade in our gardens can be changed to suit our needs. The most important aspect of shade management is to think both short- and long-term. Think about what you need for shade this year, while also keeping in mind that if you want a tree in your garden in the future, you should be planting it now. Many older gardeners will say, "I wish I had planted more trees when I started my garden." The trees that you plant do not have to be huge; small understory flowering or fruit trees add beauty and shade to the garden but on a smaller scale.

Objects that produce shade in the garden can either be built structures or plants. For more immediate shade, build garden structures; for shade in the future, plant trees.

## TREES

Trees are the largest plants in the shaded ecosystem; they play a dominant role because they set the scene for the garden underneath. Trees can either be evergreen or deciduous. Evergreen trees provide part to full shade year-round, while deciduous trees provide shade from spring to fall. Beneath the largest trees, understory trees and shrubs add additional layers of shade.

A tree or shrub of any size will contribute more shade if planted on the sunniest side of the garden. In a garden of established trees, plan ahead to ensure the succession of shade. Continue to plant young trees that will eventually take the place of the older, mature trees in the canopy.

There are three tree qualities to consider when you are thinking about adding a tree to your garden for shade purposes. The first thing to remember is that the ultimate height and width of the tree will determine the amount of shade that it will provide. Think ahead to the eventual size of each tree when siting it. Large trees are often planted to shade the house and garden, and are sometimes called shade trees. Smaller trees may grow beneath these large trees as part of the understory layer. In a small garden, these shorter trees may be the primary shade producers. Think ahead to the ultimate size of each tree when siting it.

The next consideration is the eventual shape of the tree: vase-shaped, upright, weeping, or spreading. Each shape produces a different pattern and extent of shade. Weeping and spreading trees have an area of full shade beneath their canopy when mature. Vase-shaped and columnar trees allow more light at their base, even at maturity. Other tree forms produce shade levels that range from bright to full shade, depending on the species.

The final aspect to think about is the size and abundance of the tree's leaves, which determine the amount of light that filters down to the understory below. In general, a tree with large leaves produces more shade, whereas trees with smaller leaves are more likely to produce a brighter or dappled shade.

There are shapes and sizes of trees that suit gardens of every size, even tiny ones. In a smaller space, the type of tree that you choose should be short or narrow in profile. There are plenty of small trees that provide shade and seasonal interest. Shrubs can be used to add additional

top *Camellia* and *Azalea* add depth to the shade produced by a live oak covered in Spanish moss in the historic gardens at Middleton Place in Charleston, South Carolina.

bottom left The ovular shape of this magnolia allows light to penetrate to the ground plane of the garden.

bottom right The heart-shaped leaves of *Cercis canadensis* capture any available sunlight that reaches the understory.

An elegant pergola at Badminton Estate in Gloucestershire, England.

shade, or may be the sole shade provider in a very compact area. If you are in doubt about how a tree will grow in your area, visit local public gardens and arboreta to observe the size and forms of mature specimens.

## GARDEN STRUCTURES

Walls, fences, pergolas, and arbors all provide some shade. The amount produced depends on the height, breadth, and density of each structure. Some produce a solid shade that will block out most direct light. Others allow some light to pass through, producing a lighter, less shady area for the plants beneath.

WALLS AND FENCES  Adding a fence to your garden can create shaded areas. The amount of shade produced by a wall or fence depends on its orientation with respect to the sun, and how it is constructed. Solid stone walls, for instance, produce a dense shade. Look for plants that require full shade if you are planting on the shaded side of stone walls.

An arbor covered with vines increases shade levels at Wyck Historic House in Philadelphia, Pennsylvania.

above left Walls and trees both contribute to the shade levels in this garden in the southern United States.

Slatted fences or open brickwork, produce less shade, and that shade changes throughout the day. For the shady side of these structures, choose plants for part shade.

GARDEN STRUCTURES These are often introduced to make a shady sitting or walking area. Especially in hot regions, where shade is at a premium, arches, arbors, pergolas, and ramadas provide necessary shelter from the sun. Vines can be grown up the sides of these structures to increase the depth of shade. Nearby beds are often great areas to fill with shade-loving plants.

## REDUCING SHADE

If there is too much shade in your garden, there are ways to reduce it: add light-reflective surfaces to your space, or reduce the amount of tree cover.

Painting walls or fences near your plants a light color is a quick and easy way to illuminate darker spaces. Sunlight bounces off of any reflective surface. The lighter and brighter that you make the surroundings, the more reflected light will reach your plants. Light-colored paving,

mulching materials, garden accessories, and plant pots can all brighten up a space. Adding water features such as a birdbath, reflecting pool, or pond will help bounce light into the area. Even the plant choices you make can help bring more light into the understory of your garden. Trees with light-colored trunks, such as some *Betula* species, and plants with shiny leaves, like *Bergenia*, can have this effect.

Selectively removing a few branches from a tree can open up the canopy, letting more light through to the plants below. Limbing-up a tree (by removing its lower branches) can also reduce shade. Homeowners can do some of this work themselves, but should call in professionals for the removal of large branches, those that are high off the ground, or those near power lines. Take some time to plan where you will prune and be cautious when removing limbs. It is best to remove a few branches at a time. Then, stand back and observe the effect from all angles before continuing to prune. Never remove more than a quarter of the branches of one tree in a year, as doing so will weaken the tree and cause unhealthy stress growth.

Removing a whole tree is a quick but irreversible way to reduce the shade in your garden. Think carefully before you take this drastic step. Call in a professional arborist for help with most tree removals, as it is a difficult and dangerous job.

opposite The brilliant white bark of *Betula* brightens the surrounding area.

below At Middleton Place, a gentle breeze ripples the Azalea Pool as it reflects the last rays of the setting sun.

# THE GARDENER'S CALENDAR

## SEASONAL CHANGES IN THE SHADE GARDEN

Shade gardens have a cyclical rhythm to them, with a predictable parade of plants that emerge at about the same time each year, flower, set fruit, and retreat from center stage until the following year. Light levels, day length, and weather conditions dictate the timing and duration of these seasonal plant pictures. For a successful and satisfying shade garden, it is important to include a variety of plants that will provide interest in every season.

The long-awaited blooms of *Crocus* provide tiny splashes of color in early spring.

## SPRING PROFUSION

The spring shade garden is a pleasure for winter-deprived senses. As the early sunshine begins to warm the soil, the garden shows the first signs of life. Spring is the start of the growing season (which extends until the onset of winter).

The first plant tips to emerge from the still-cold earth are those of the tiny bulbs. Energy stored belowground fuels their rapid growth. The blue, pink, and purple blooms of *Crocus, Chionodoxa, Puschkinia,* and *Scilla* follow snowy white *Galanthus.* The longer and colder the winter has been, the more we appreciate this colorful early show.

The next plants to show signs of growth are the wildflowers of temperate woodland habitats, often called spring ephemerals. The earliest ones, like *Sanguinaria* and *Jeffersonia,* bloom at the same time as *Scilla.* They, too, have energy stored in their roots that allows them to grow and flower quickly before the deciduous tree canopy closes overhead.

Above the bulbs and woodland wildflowers, some of the earliest-blooming trees and shrubs, including *Prunus mume, Cornus mas,* and *Magnolia stellata,* come into flower on naked branches. Even one specimen of any of these woody plants has a huge impact at this time of year, and it becomes a dramatic focal point.

In mid-spring, as the ground warms up, more plants start popping up out of the earth. The early spring sunshine that falls through gaps in the bare branches has enough power to energize these developing plants. Look for fleeting but worthwhile ephemeral flowers such as *Dodecatheon, Mertensia,* and *Trillium.* A small patch of any one of these becomes an eagerly anticipated annual treat.

As spring days lengthen, there is an exhilarating rush of growth. It occurs so quickly that every day brings new surprises with a variety of spring flowers blooming one after another. This time of year is one of the truly breathtaking moments in the shade garden, as the herbaceous flower colors are so brilliant when set against their fresh, spring green leaves. Flowering perennials that perform well at this time of year include *Primula, Narcissus, Aquilegia,* and *Epimedium.* Plant these in drifts, but also intermingle them to show off your favorite color combinations. I love the enchanting pastel mixture of pink, yellow, white, and blue provided by *Lamprocapnos, Stylophorum, Leucojum,* and *Mertensia.*

Some understory trees and shrubs, such as *Cercis, Cornus florida, Fothergilla,* early blooming *Rhododendron,* and *Viburnum,* flower before their leaves emerge, producing a spectacular color pop in the garden. The flowers of *Iris cristata,* woodland *Phlox,* and *Pulmonaria* carpet the ground beneath them.

Another spring joy is the profusion of animal life that returns to your shaded space. Insects appear from their winter hiding places. The early bumblebees and honeybees are out pollinating spring flowers, grateful for nectar and pollen. Birds are returning from their winter locations, ready to build nests and raise their young.

Deciduous tree leaves begin to emerge from their buds as the rising sap reaches the top of the tallest canopy trees. At first, a light haze of soft spring green is all that is visible in the treetops, and an abundance of sunlight still reaches the ground. Gradually, the tiny, translucent tree leaves begin to expand. The garden below takes on an ethereal, greenish hue as light passes through the new canopy.

top  The soft spring colors of *Dicentra*, *Polemonium*, and *Stylophorum* intermix at ground level beneath the branches of a decidious tree.

bottom left  The early tips of variegated *Polygonatum* are blushed with pink as they push their way up through leaf litter.

bottom right  Fresh white *Sanguinaria* and bright blue *Scilla* bloom together in a woodland garden.

The bright blooms of *Rhodo-dendron mucronulatum* are a stunning, early spring accent in the shaded garden at the Ambler Arboretum of Temple University in Pennsylvania.

above right Cowslip, *Primula veris*, blooms among the little blue flowers of forget-me-not, *Myosotis*, in an English garden.

right A light green haze of emerging leaves in the treetops.

Along with this greening from above is the continued foliar growth at ground level, with the unfurling of the fern fronds and the steady growth of *Hosta* leaves. The tiny spring ephemerals on the woodland floor are well into their life cycle by this time. They have flowered, set fruit, and, in the time before the tree canopy closes, are using the sunlight to make energy for their growth the following year.

By the tail end of spring, there are still new herbaceous shade plants flowering such as *Gillenia*, *Rodgersia*, hardy *Geranium*, and *Tiarella* that bloom in concert with woody plants like *Rhododendron*, *Kalmia*, *Chionanthus*, and *Deutzia*. Place some of these later bloomers together to produce a garden vignette. At the end of spring, tree leaves have grown in size and density, gradually forming a complete canopy.

## SPRING TASKS

I take a walk around my garden at least once a week in spring—or once a day if possible. The pace of growth is so fast at this time of year and I don't want to miss a thing! This stroll also allows me a chance to see which plants are emerging and to get an early start on weeding. There are opportunistic weeds that grow in cold weather and it is better to pull them up before they set seed. I also look for and remove slugs and snails in dark, damp places, such as underneath pots and boards.

As the temperatures rise and the days lengthen, it is time for spring-cleaning. Check for winter storm damage and do some general tidying up. Some gardeners do their garden cleaning in autumn, but I prefer to do so in spring, as many perennial plants have semi-evergreen leaves. It is better to let those plants keep their leaves over the winter to help protect against ice and frost damage and to make a habitat for ground birds.

Old shriveled leaves and stems from last year's growth can be cut off and cleared away. Do this early in the growing season, before new spring growth emerges, as it is easier to cut all the old leaves with hedge clippers than to painstakingly trim around new shoots. Cut back the old leaves of *Epimedium*, *Hosta*, ferns, and hybrid hellebores. As you trim back and clean up plants, reward them with a light layer of ground-up leaves or compost. Start a new compost heap for your soft trimmings and a stick pile for your woody waste. Do not compost weeds that have gone to seed or any diseased foliage.

New trees, shrubs, and perennials can be planted, and old ones moved, as soon as the ground is workable. If you garden in a cold climate, wait until the soil has thawed and warmed up before digging. Be sure to get new woody plants in the ground before their leaf or flower buds open.

Spring is the best time to divide clump-forming perennials, such as *Hosta* or ferns. Replant the newly divided sections wherever you want them in the garden. Overcrowded groups of spring bulbs such as *Galanthus*, *Narcissus*, and *Leucojum* can be dug up and gently pried apart to form smaller clumps after they have flowered. This is an easy way to spread the bulbs around your garden for a better spring display.

Plant spring-blooming flowers in containers to bring instant color into your shady spaces. Choose hardy (cold-tolerant) plants, such as annual *Viola*, that will take the changeable temperatures at this time of year. If you planned ahead and planted bulbs in pots in autumn, now is the time to move the pots out of their protected places and into the garden. Autumn-planted

## PLANTS FOR SPRING INTEREST

*Aquilegia canadensis*, Canadian columbine
*Cercis canadensis*, eastern redbud
*Claytonia virginica*, spring beauty
*Cornus florida*, flowering dogwood
*Digitalis purpurea*, common foxglove
*Dodecatheon meadia*, shooting star
*Epimedium* ×*youngianum* 'Niveum',
   snowy barrenwort
*Fritillaria meleagris*, guinea hen fritillary
*Hyacinthoides non-scripta*, English bluebell
*Jeffersonia diphylla*, twinleaf
*Lamprocapnos spectabilis*, common bleeding heart
*Mertensia virginica*, Virginia bluebells
*Narcissus* 'Thalia', daffodil 'Thalia'
*Primula vulgaris*, primrose
*Trillium grandiflorum*, large-flowered trillium

above Tiny dangling flowers of *Epimedium* 'Amber Queen' are visible once the old foliage has been cleared away.

right *Trillium grandiflorum* in bloom is one of the delights of the spring shade garden.

bulbs will flower in any light conditions for one year. This is because the flower bud was formed last year and is already present within the bulb.

Spring in the shade garden is the busiest time of the year, but it is also the most rewarding. There is such an explosion of life in a short time—from leafless branches to a sea of green in a few months. It is the season to celebrate life and to live in the moment.

## SUMMER LUSHNESS

By early summer, deciduous trees leaf out, bringing shade back to different areas of the garden. The summer shade garden has a quiet allure; it is a serene sanctuary from the heat of the sun. The early bulbs and spring ephemerals retreat back under the soil and spend summer in a semi-dormant state until their burst of new growth the following spring.

The next understory shade plants to unfurl are those that can take advantage of low light conditions. These plants will be the backbone of your shade garden all summer long. The beauty of the garden at this time of year is in the prevalent abundant green growth.

Perennials provide the fresh foliage that is the mainstay of the understory layer in summer. Plants such as ferns, *Hosta*, *Helleborus*, *Pulmonaria*, *Brunnera*, and *Asarum* continue to look cool and refreshing in spite of the mounting heat. The flowers of some perennials, like *Digitalis*, *Thalictrum*, and *Actaea*, add height and color against this green backdrop.

By the height of summer, the tree canopy has completely filled in. Fully pigmented tree leaves reduce light to the plants beneath. A number of understory trees and shrubs flower during summer, including some of the deciduous azaleas, *Philadelphus*, *Itea*, and *Clethra*. These shrubs have the benefit of sweet, enticing fragrance and many of them have bright, white blooms that catch

The canopy of this magnificent oak tree, *Quercus*, has filled in by summer.

A tussock of *Hosta* topped with scented purple flowers makes a great addition to this mossy area.

opposite Shades of green prevail in this lush and tranquil garden at Mill Fleurs in Point Pleasant, Pennsylvania.

The yellow and burgundy leaves of tender *Solenostemon* 'Pineapple' brighten a dark garden corner.

above right Hot pink *Impatiens* adds a punch of color to this highly textured composition in a private garden.

right The blooms of *Hydrangea macrophylla* are one of the most colorful features of a summer shade garden.

the eye in the increased shade. The stars of the shade garden in summer are the various species and cultivars of *Hydrangea*. By careful selection, you can have *Hydrangea* in bloom for months.

Once the weather warms, you can add a tropical look to your garden beds or containers. Tropical plants add a punch of bright color and large, lush foliage. In temperate areas, tender specimens are often planted in containers so that it is easier to bring them inside at the end of the growing season.

The large and glossy leaves of *Alocasia*, *Colocasia*, and *Philodendron* reflect light around the summer shade garden and are a good addition in pots or bordering a terrace or path. When combining plants in containers, include colorful foliage for long-lasting drama. Some of the best for this are *Caladium*, *Solenostemon*, *Strobilanthes*, and *Hypoestes*. Another way to add color to summer containers is with the addition of long-blooming flowers like *Nicotiana*, *Torenia*, *Impatiens*, and *Begonia*.

## SUMMER TASKS

All season long, trim back container plants to keep them compact, and remove spent blooms to encourage more flowers. Containers grouped together have a greater impact and make watering easier. Pots filled with tropicals or annuals can also be placed on top of the withered spring bulb foliage to fill in the "hole" that the bulbs leave in the summer border.

To keep the soil in beds and borders moist, and to protect plants from summer heat, check that your beds are well mulched. When you water, water deeply. This means that the water should penetrate the soil to a depth of at least 6 inches. If you are unsure, dig up some soil around the plants to gauge how far the water has infiltrated. By watering deeply and less often, you are encouraging roots to grow down into the soil rather than toward the soil surface. This is a good, basic gardening practice that conserves resources and makes plants self-sufficient.

Newly planted trees, shrubs, and herbaceous perennials need watering at least once a week, unless there has been about an inch of rain. Water shade gardens in the early morning so that leaves are dry by nighttime, which will help to reduce slug damage and fungal problems.

I continue my weekly walks and keep my eyes open for weeds, removing them before they set seed. These weeds are then thrown into galvanized weed buckets that I have tucked around the garden. When the buckets fill up, I empty them into the compost pile.

I also deadhead the spent flowers of desirable plants to encourage them to rebloom. Prune or deadhead shrubs like *Hydrangea* and *Philadelphus* only after they have finished flowering so that you do not cut off the flowers that are forming for next year. Other pruning tasks include shaping hedges and trimming back straggly shrubs.

The shade garden in summer is not only a pleasant place for active gardening; it is also a peaceful green oasis. The trees block sunlight, reducing temperatures and creating a cool retreat from the glare of the sun. This environment is an attractive place for people, plants, and wildlife. Take time to enjoy the season outside in your shady space, whether by reading a book, watching the birds, or having a meal. It is a wonderful place to relax.

## PLANTS FOR SUMMER INTEREST

*Actaea racemosa*, black snakeroot
*Aesculus pavia*, red buckeye
*Agastache foeniculum*, anise hyssop
*Dicentra eximia*, fringed bleeding heart
*Digitalis lutea*, straw foxglove
*Gentiana andrewsii*, bottle gentian
*Geranium macrorrhizum*, bigroot geranium
*Hosta* 'Royal Standard', hosta 'Royal Standard'
*Hydrangea macrophylla*, bigleaf hydrangea
*Kirengeshoma palmata*, yellow wax bells
*Lilium martagon*, martagon lily
*Lycoris squamigera*, magic lily
*Nectaroscordum siculum*, Sicilian honey garlic
*Thalictrum rochebruneanum*, lavender mist
    meadow rue
*Veratrum nigrum*, black false hellebore

The vibrant orange flowers of shade-tolerant *Lilium superbum* tower above other herbaceous perennials in midsummer.

This tropical-looking Ashe magnolia, *Magnolia macrophylla* subsp. *ashei*, was watered in for several summers but now needs little additional irrigation to produce magnificent fragrant flowers in summer.

This yellow *Hemerocallis* seems to glow in the shade of a variegated *Cornus florida*.

**opposite** Nestled between groupings of *Hydrangea*, this colorful spot is the perfect place for lunch in the shade.

# AUTUMN BOUNTY

Autumn is a fabulous time to enjoy the delights of the shade garden. The days get shorter and the sun is lower in the sky; its rays penetrate the canopy, lighting up unexpected corners of the garden. Gradually cooling temperatures entice gardeners outside to enjoy the changing colors and textures of the season.

Each layer of the garden has its own fall treats—the tall canopy trees begin to turn color, fruit becomes apparent in the understory layer as it matures, and fall-blooming herbaceous perennials add beauty to the late season garden. The color palette in the garden shifts from shades of green to rich hues of orange, yellow, red, and burgundy. These bright colors enliven the garden scene and remind us that the gardening year is not quite finished.

The golden autumnal sunlight and the cool, crisp air intensify the changing leaf colors. Some trees and shrubs, unremarkable in the landscape for most of the year, become focal points with their fiery fall hues. *Acer*, *Aronia*, *Enkianthus*, *Fothergilla*, and *Hamamelis* are all grown for their especially brilliant fall color.

Foliage changes are not the only admired feature of the autumn garden; many trees and shrubs have decorative fruits that ripen at this time of year. *Cornus*, *Ilex*, and *Viburnum* are all grown for their attractive autumn fruit. Birds flock to berried bushes, devouring the tastiest ones first. Migratory birds are especially drawn to swaths of fruiting plants, so when planting, choose bird-attracting shrubs and cluster them together for impact.

When choosing plants for your garden, include herbaceous perennials that bloom in autumn. These plants continue the colorful display at ground level, extending the season of interest. They flower in tones of purple, pink, yellow, and white that harmonize charmingly with the autumn color of the woody layers above them. Popular choices include *Anemone* ×*hybrida*, *Colchicum*, *Tricyrtis*, *Begonia grandis*, and *Aconitum*. Foliage plants such as the autumn fern, *Dryopteris erythrosora*, and the grasslike *Chasmanthium*, *Carex*, and *Hakonechloa*, add textural interest.

## AUTUMN TASKS

Autumn is a great time to evaluate your plantings and update your beds. Congested clumps of perennials like *Asarum* and *Epimedium* can be dug up and split with a clean, sharp shovel. Replant these divisions where needed. Trees and shrubs can be planted once the weather cools. Plan to get your autumn plantings done at least four weeks before the first expected frost date so that plant roots can begin to develop. Gardeners in areas with mild climates can continue to plant late into the season. Water in new plants thoroughly and add a few inches of mulch to the top of the soil.

Growth of overeager plants like vines and shrubs can easily overwhelm a shaded garden. Fall is a good time to keep aggressive plants under control by pruning or by digging them out. More desirable understory shrubs can be lightly trimmed to remove old blooms and to gently shape the plant if needed.

Walk around your shade garden and remove unruly branches that overhang your paths. Dig unwanted plants out of the path that have crept over the edge or seeded in. Some of these volunteer plants may be relocated back into beds, given away, or composted.

**top** Split-leaf *Acer palmatum* illuminated by the low light of the autumn sun.

**bottom left** The colors of *Dryopteris erythrosora* intensify in autumn.

**bottom center** The luminous red foliage of *Cornus florida* adds another season of interest to this classic shade garden tree.

**bottom right** The bright red seeds of *Magnolia virginiana* are devoured by songbirds.

If your garden design contains plants that are not hardy in your area, dig them up before the first frost. Annual plants can be composted and tropical plants, such as *Colocasia* and *Caladium*, can be brought inside for winter. As you are emptying your containers, it is a good time to plant them up with a selection of bulbs that will bloom next spring. Try *Tulipa*, *Narcissus*, and *Muscari* for a splash of lively color. In a frost-free area, buy pre-cooled bulbs that have been given an artificial winter cooling to prompt them to bloom. In a cold climate, store your pots in a protected place like an unheated garage, shed, or basement and bring them outside in spring.

It is also time to plant spring-blooming bulbs in the ground. Dig the planting hole to a depth of two to three times the height of the bulb and sprinkle in a little bone meal. Once you have placed your bulbs in the holes, backfill with loose soil containing compost and sand or grit to accelerate drainage. Cluster bulbs together for maximum impact and consider planting them so that they will pop up between low-growing groundcovers like *Chrysogonum* or *Asarum*.

As the leaves fall from the trees, choose a management strategy. Mulching with leaves slowly releases nutrients into the soil and insulates roots for the winter. In a naturalistic garden, leaves

The lustrous brown buckeyes of *Aesculus pavia* ripen in autumn.

above left  The white blooms of hybrid *Anemone* stand out against the blue of *Aconitum* in a shaded border.

opposite  A tree tunnel beneath the horizontal branches of *Nyssa sylvatica* needs occasional pruning to keep the path accessible.

## PLANTS FOR AUTUMN INTEREST

*Acer palmatum*, Japanese maple
*Aconitum carmichaelii*, monkshood
*Allium thunbergii*, Japanese onion
*Anemone ×hybrida*, Japanese anemone
*Begonia grandis*, hardy begonia
*Carpinus caroliniana*, American hornbeam
*Colchicum cilicicum*, colchicum
*Cornus florida*, flowering dogwood
*Cyclamen hederifolium*, fall-blooming hardy cyclamen
*Dryopteris erythrosora*, autumn fern
*Heuchera villosa*, hairy alumroot
*Hydrangea quercifolia*, oakleaf hydrangea
*Iris domestica*, blackberry lily
*Maianthemum racemosum*, false Solomon's seal
*Tricyrtis formosana*, toad lily

The speckled flowers of *Tricyrtis* 'Sinonome'. *Tricyrtis* is best divided in spring because it blooms in autumn.

can be left *in situ*. In a more manicured garden, rake or blow the leaves out of the beds and compost them to make leaf mold. My leaf strategy is to gather and shred them, and then return them to the beds.

Autumn is a more peaceful time in the garden, with less of a rush to get things done, so make sure that you take time to sit and enjoy the progression of the season. I love to take leisurely walks, crunching leaves underfoot as I stroll beneath the trees, observing the last joys of the growing season.

## WINTER DELIGHTS

The garden is at its least active during the coldest period of the year, but there is always something wonderful to find and enjoy. Winter is the best time of the year to examine your existing design and plan future improvements. Deciduous plants have lost their leaves, exposing the framework of woody trees and shrubs. You can clearly see the layout of your garden and determine if there are areas that will need additional plantings or other changes next year.

The best winter shade gardens have plants with beautiful details like evergreen foliage, attractive bark, persistent berries, or winter blooms. Many gardens can be improved by adding structural woody evergreen plants. They provide habitat for wildlife, shelter the garden from strong winds, and provide a good backdrop for deciduous understory trees and shrubs. My favorites to use are *Buxus*, *Ilex*, and *Taxus*.

The color and texture of the bark of deciduous woody plants becomes an ornamental feature in winter. *Acer*, *Betula*, and some species of *Cornus* and *Prunus* trees have distinctive bark that stands out, especially against snow or an evergreen background. While this may seem like a subtle detail, such small pleasures in the shade garden add to your year-round enjoyment.

Branches of *Diospyros virginiana*, American persimmon tree, outlined with snow.

left Snow-covered *Ilex opaca* with brilliant red berries, a food source for birds.

The fruit of crabapple *Malus* 'Donald Wyman' encased in ice following a winter storm.

left The narrow, curving, red petals of *Hamamelis ×intermedia* 'Rubin' stand out against a fresh dusting of snow.

opposite The exfoliating, copper-colored bark of *Acer griseum* is backlit by the low winter sun.

## PLANTS FOR WINTER AND EARLY SPRING INTEREST

*Acer griseum*, paperbark maple
*Camellia japonica*, common camellia
*Chionodoxa sardensis*, glory-of-the-snow
*Crocus tommasinianus*, tommies
*Cyclamen coum*, hardy cyclamen
*Eranthis hyemalis*, winter aconite
*Galanthus nivalis* 'S. Arnott',
    common snowdrop 'S. Arnott'
*Galanthus elwesii*, giant snowdrop
*Hamamelis* ×*intermedia* cultivars, hybrid
    witchhazel cultivars
*Helleborus foetidus*, stinking hellebore
*Helleborus* ×*hybridus*, hybrid hellebore
*Ilex aquifolium*, English holly
*Ruscus aculeatus*, butcher's broom
*Sarcococca orientalis*, Chinese sweetbox
*Scilla siberica*, Siberian squill

It is a surprise to many gardeners to learn that there is a selection of winter-flowering trees and shrubs, such as *Mahonia*, *Sarcococca*, some *Camellia*, and hybrid *Hamamelis*, which have the added benefit of enticing scents. Since you are less likely to be sitting out in the garden during winter, it is good idea to place these plants where you will walk by them and enjoy their wafting fragrance. I like to underplant my winter-flowering trees with the small bulbs of *Galanthus* and *Eranthis* that bloom at the same time.

## WINTER TASKS

Winter is a time for minor upkeep and thinking ahead to next year. Depending on the severity of your climate, you may have opportunities to get outside into the garden. If you can, walk around your space, and envision how you can improve it for the coming year. When there are no leaves on deciduous trees, the "bones" of your garden are apparent. Without the distraction of foliage and colorful flowers, you can see where you might need additional plantings in the coming year. Take a notebook out with you to jot down ideas.

Identify any damaged garden structures like pergolas or fences and repair them. Check for crossing branches, water sprouts, and suckers that should be removed from woody plants. This is also a good time to trim back evergreen *Ilex* trees and hedges to keep them neatly in shape. In mild climates, if the ground has not frozen, you can keep spreading leaf mold or compost on top of your beds. Be sure to clear leaves and mulch away from *Galanthus*, *Eranthis*, and other herbaceous winter flowers.

In climates with harsh winters, protect your delicate trees from damage by gently shaking heavy snow loads off of branches. If you have ice, let it melt naturally so that you do not damage leaf and flower buds. Clean up storm-damaged woody plants by neatly trimming back broken branches.

With fewer activities to occupy you outside during the winter, take time to assess the highs and lows of your gardening year and make plans for the coming seasons. Research plants and make a wish list of ones that you would like to add to your garden. Review any garden notes and photographs, thumb through catalogs, and dream of spring.

top *Acer palmatum* in a snowy landscape.

bottom The dangling white and green flowers of *Galanthus nivalis* 'Viridapice'. Snowdrops are one of the earliest bulbs to bloom in winter.

# DOWN AND DIRTY

## THE INTERTWINED, UNDERGROUND WORLD OF SOIL AND ROOTS

The soil beneath a shade garden is a crowded place. In the same way that there are multiple layers of leaves and branches above the ground competing for light, the soil contains countless roots at different depths competing for water and nutrients below the ground. Each plant needs to find what it requires in the soil so that it can grow well.

Because the soil is packed with roots, it must be able to support the nutritional needs of all of the plants that grow there. A key to successful shade gardening is the addition of organic matter to the soil, which encourages good root growth, promoting healthy plants.

In a wooded Maine garden, abundant leaf litter and fallen logs contribute to the accumulation of organic matter in the soil.

# SOIL

Shade-loving plants generally come from natural areas of forest or woodland that have deep, rich soils. In our gardens, we need to mimic these natural soils to promote strong plant growth.

Soil is not inert but is a complex web of inorganic particles, organic material, living organisms, water, air, and nutrients. All of these factors should be in balance to enhance the growth of your plants.

If you were to dig a deep hole in the ground, you would be able to see soil layers visible as differing colors. At the very bottom of the soil profile, you would see the bedrock from which your soil was formed. This rock is the key factor that determines the pH of your soil: whether it is acidic, neutral, or alkaline. The middle layer, of a slightly different color, would be made up of a combination of the unalterable geological material below and organic additions from above.

The remaining layer at the surface is called topsoil. Topsoil is heavily influenced by the yearly addition of fallen leaves and other organic matter. It is dark in color, crumbly in texture, and high in organic content. In a shade garden, the topsoil is the most important layer for plant growth and the one that gardeners can most easily amend.

## IMPROVING YOUR SOIL

Great soil is a precious resource. Soil that is ideal for plants is slow to develop, but vital for their healthy growth. The best soils share the following qualities: adequate nutrients, a loose, airy texture that allows for extensive growth of plant roots, and the ability to hold moisture without becoming waterlogged.

The oldest woodlands have soils that have formed over the course of many decades. If you visit a mature woodland and examine the soil, you'll see it is packed full of organic matter—fallen twigs, leaf litter, and anything else that was once alive. Over time, all of this material is broken down and incorporated into the soil structure.

Organisms that carry out this process are called decomposers. They consume the broken-down organic matter and release minerals back into the soil in a chemical form that plants can use. These nutrients are taken up by the roots and used as the plants grow. The soil must be fertile enough to provide adequate nutrients for the growth of the many plants that are living together in your garden. Some well-known decomposers are earthworms, beetles, bacteria, and fungi. Earthworms also help the soil structure by digging burrows that allow air and water movement through the soil. Decomposition is integral to soil health and therefore supports vigorous plant growth.

In a shady garden, mimicking these natural processes is the best practice. Adding organic matter on a regular basis ensures the continual enrichment of your soil as decomposers break it down. Some gardeners clear the leaves away from their gardens in autumn, but doing so removes necessary organic material. This decaying organic matter in the soil will also act like a sponge, holding moisture for the roots. At the same time, excess water drains down through the soil to reach deep tree roots. This is how you find the delicate balance of having well-drained soil that is also able to retain moisture.

Leaves are beneficial soil additions whether they are whole, shredded, or fully decomposed. In a naturalistic garden, autumn leaves can be left to decay in place. In a more manicured space,

leaves can be removed, shredded with a lawnmower, and put straight back onto the beds. Alternatively, they can be composted and then added back in the following year. Small leaf fragments are incorporated more quickly into the soil than whole leaves, and composted leaves, called leaf mold, are incorporated fastest of all. Other helpful ammendments for clay soil are grit, gravel, or sand, which have large, irregular particles that do not stick together, giving the soil increased aeration and better drainage.

To make fabulous, friable, or crumbly leaf mold, compost your leaves using a simple fenced structure or bin to hold the leaves. An even simpler way, for smaller gardens, is to gather deciduous leaves into a large black plastic bag. Punch a few holes in the bag and then set it out of the way for a couple of years to allow the leaves to rot down. Once you start making your own leaf mold, you will wonder how you ever gardened without it. You may even beg your neighbors for their leaves!

Making better soil is a continual and worthwhile process. In your garden, every time you dig a planting hole, add some compost or broken-down leaves. Each year, scatter compost on the

A shelf fungus is actively breaking down this log, but the only visible sign is its layered fruiting body.

above left These fallen leaves will decompose and become a vital component of healthy soil.

## HUMUS

Organic material is an important component of excellent topsoil. Humus is the most highly decomposed matter. It has been broken down so much that it is unrecognizable as plant material. At this advanced level of decay, the nutrients are freely available to plant roots.

If you rub some soil between your fingers and it leaves a dark brown stain, it is a great sign. It means that there is humus in your soil. Humus holds 80–90 percent of its weight in water, so it really benefits your plants, especially those that grow in dry shade.

Freshly fallen *Acer*, *Quercus*, and *Gingko* leaves.

left A fallen branch provides a habitat for moss and will eventually be decomposed, adding nutrients back into the soil.

opposite At the New England Wild Flower Society's Garden in the Woods in Framingham, Massachusetts, deep, fertile soils allow luxuriant, layered plant growth.

surface of the soil around your plants. This will gradually become incorporated into the soil, improving the soil structure.

You may not notice much of a difference at first, but over time you will observe your soil becoming darker in color and moist without being soggy. One of my garden mentors used to say that I could take seedlings from her garden so long as I left her soil—she had been working on it a long time and did not want to part with it.

There is no instant way to create good garden soil, but by adding small amounts of organic matter, little and often, it will improve over time. This gardening practice is key to making a healthy, self-sustaining, low-maintenance shade garden.

## SOIL pH

Soil pH influences what plants you can easily grow in your shade garden. The pH scale measures whether a soil is acidic, neutral, or alkaline. Most woodland and forest ecosystems have acidic to neutral soils due to the yearly dropping of acidic deciduous leaves such as oak, or evergreen needles like pine, which decompose, increasing acidity. For this reason, some of the most desirable shade plants thrive in acidic soils.

Some plants, including those that grow best in acidic soil, cannot access certain nutrients unless the soil is at a specific pH level. For example, if you are growing a *Rhododendron* and the soil pH is alkaline, your plant may not grow well; and may look yellow-leaved and unhealthy. In alkaline soils, its roots are unable to take up the iron needed to make green chlorophyll in the leaves. It is possible to modify the soil pH, but it is much easier to grow plants that flourish in your existing conditions.

The soil near to the foundations of a house is often alkaline due to concrete or cement building waste or leaching from walls. Choose plants that are suitable for neutral to alkaline soils for this area of the shade garden.

A flourishing *Rhododendron* collection growing in slightly acidic soil at Jenkins Arboretum.

## PLANTS FOR ACIDIC SOILS

Some of the most iconic and desirable shade plants grow best in humus-rich, acidic soil. If some of the following plants grow well in your garden or neighborhood, you probably have a relatively acidic soil, so choose others from the list to complete your plantings.

*Acer palmatum*, Japanese maple
*Adiantum pedatum*, northern maidenhair fern
*Camellia japonica*, common camellia
*Clethra alnifolia*, summersweet
*Cornus* species, dogwood
*Cyrtomium falcatum*, holly fern
*Dryopteris* species and cultivars, wood fern
*Enkianthus campanulatus*, redvein enkianthus
*Kalmia latifolia*, mountain laurel
*Leucothoe* species, leucothoe
*Maianthemum racemosum*, false Solomon's seal
*Osmunda* species, osmunda
*Pieris japonica*, Japanese pieris
*Podophyllum peltatum*, May apple
*Rhododendron* species and cultivars, rhododendron or azalea

## PLANTS FOR NEUTRAL TO ALKALINE SOILS

There are fewer shade-loving plants that are adapted to a high pH. If you garden in an area with neutral to alkaline soil, choose plants that are adaptable, or that come from chalky or limestone areas.

*Aconitum carmichaelii*, monkshood
*Adiantum capillus-veneris*, southern maidenhair fern
*Anemone* ×*hybrida*, Japanese anemone
*Asplenium scolopendrium*, hart's tongue fern
*Bergenia cordifolia*, pigsqueak
*Brunnera macrophylla*, heartleaf brunnera
*Buxus sempervirens*, common box
*Daphne* ×*burkwoodii*, hybrid daphne
*Eranthis hyemalis*, winter aconite
*Galanthus nivalis*, common snowdrop
*Geranium macrorrhizum*, bigroot geranium
*Helleborus foetidus*, stinking hellebore
*Jeffersonia diphylla*, twinleaf
*Philadelphus coronarius*, sweet mockorange
*Viburnum rhytidophyllum*, leatherleaf viburnum

## MODIFYING SOIL pH TO INCREASE ACIDITY

Many shade-loving plants have evolved to grow in the humusy soil of wooded ecosystems. These soils tend to be slightly acidic. If you have alkaline to neutral soil and want to grow, for instance, *Rhododendron*, *Enkianthus*, *Kalmia*, and some *Ilex* plants, you will need to use chemical amendments that will slightly acidify the soil. Keep in mind that it is extremely difficult to permanently change your soil pH, and it is more sustainable to choose plants that suit your native conditions. If there are plants that you crave for your garden that would not naturally do well there, consider growing them in pots where you can easily control the soil pH.

Variegated *Pieris japonica* is grown in a terracotta pot containing acidic soil because the surrounding soil is too alkaline.

Plants growing together in this understory compete with each other and the canopy trees for soil moisture and nutrients.

above left  Trees growing along an elevated bank prominently display their moss-covered roots.

# ROOTS

Plant roots function silently, buried away below the soil, and we only see or touch them during planting or when digging them up. Despite being hidden from view, however, they are essential for the functioning of the garden ecosystem. Understanding how plant roots interact with soil will help you to maximize plant health in your garden.

Tree roots grow down into the soil and spread out to cover a large area. They set the tone for the whole shade garden. Understory trees, shrubs, and herbaceous plants have shallower roots that contribute to the vast underground root network. There are many roots growing together in a shaded area that compete for water and nutrients. If each plant receives adequate resources from the soil, it will grow healthy roots and will flourish.

It is important to foster the growth of extensive, healthy root systems that perform three essential functions: to anchor the plants, store energy for their growth, and supply them with water, nutrients, and oxygen.

This massive old live oak, a species of *Quercus*, supports its large top growth with an extensive root system.

**above right** Bald cypress tree, *Taxodium*, can grow in swamps using root adaptations called pneumatophores. The knobbly pneumatophores rise out of the water, allowing the plant to obtain oxygen from the air.

## MARVELOUS MYCORRHIZAE

Mycorrhizae are microscopic fungi that have a mutually beneficial relationship with plant roots. It is a symbiotic relationship where both the plant and the fungus benefit. The fungus obtains its food from the host plant and in return it helps the plant obtain more water and nutrients than it could do by itself, even if the nutrients are in short supply in the environment.

A strongly established mycorrhizal relationship may also help to protect a tree against fungal root problems like root rots. Mycorrhizae exist in conjunction with the majority of land plants. They are found in woodlands, forests, wetlands, and even in arid ecosystems.

Encourage mycorrhizae to thrive in your soil by not applying high rates of fertilizer. A soil that is full of organic matter, such as decomposing leaves, old sticks, and wood, is more likely to promote this beneficial relationship.

These fuzzy young fern fronds unroll in early spring. Many plants, including ferns, have mycorrhizal associations with the microscopic fungi in the soil.

left Nutrients move from the roots to help in the formation of leaves and fruit, such as the berries of this *Mahonia*.

ANCHORING One of the first jobs of a strong set of roots is to keep a plant firmly anchored into the ground. Root width and depth need to match the size of the aboveground growth. Deep roots prevent the plant from blowing over in the wind. Plants also rely on the anchoring effect of their roots to resist being pulled out of the ground by herbivore browsing.

STORAGE Roots store energy, which is used to jumpstart plant growth. During the growing season, excess energy is sent to the roots and stored as food. It is mobilized when the plant requires energy, for instance after a plant is damaged, or in spring, when new buds are growing.

ABSORPTION OF WATER AND NUTRIENTS Most plants obtain their water from the soil using their roots. Roots push their way through the soil, growing from their tips. They absorb water and nutrients just behind the tip through root hairs. They are aided in this absorption by a symbiotic relationship with mycorrhizae, which are beneficial, microscopic fungi. Both the root hairs and the mycorrhizae increase the surface area of the roots to maximize absorption. The larger the tree or shrub, the more water is needed. In order to find adequate water, roots grow into the soil, forming an extensive system. Necessary nutrients also enter the plant through the root system. From the roots, nutrients travel to the parts of the plant that are actively growing, such as flowers, fruit, and new leaves.

OBTAINING OXYGEN A well-aerated soil is important for healthy root and plant growth. Plant roots obtain oxygen from air spaces in the soil. For wet shady areas, it is important to choose plants that are adapted to these low soil oxygen conditions. In a waterlogged soil, water displaces the air spaces.

## TREE ROOTS

Tree roots are the dominant player in the underground ecosystem. It is important to understand the structure and form of the roots when making plant placement and maintenance decisions.

The roots begin at the trunk and spread out to stabilize the tree. The base of the trunk widens just above the ground. This sloped area of the trunk is called the root flare and is an important part of the tree's structure.

Roots continue to spread out farther as the tree grows. The root growth keeps pace with the top growth. When it rains, water cascades off the tips of the branches onto the soil beneath. This ring around the tree is called the drip line. The drip line contains abundant roots because of the higher availability of water. In an established tree, roots will be found in the soil beyond the drip line. There may even be some tree roots that spread out two or three times the width of the tree's canopy.

The depth and extent of the tree roots influences what other plants will be able to grow within its root zone. The root zone is the area of soil occupied by the roots of a tree or other plant.

Some trees have taproots or other deep roots. These taproots grow down into the soil to provide anchorage for the tree and access to groundwater. Trees with deep roots have additional surface roots, but are some of the easiest to plant beneath.

At the other extreme are trees whose root network is fibrous and close to the soil surface. Fibrous roots spread out from the tree in all directions, forming a mesh in the topsoil. Trees make new fibrous roots to seek out sources of water and nutrients. These trees, for example many trees in the genus *Acer*, make gardening beneath them a challenge, as there is so much competition for water and nutrients in the topsoil. Many trees fall somewhere in the middle of this spectrum, with some surface roots, but not so many as to prevent underplanting.

Once you understand root functions, you can garden effectively beneath trees without damaging their important roots. There are three main gardening activities that affect tree root health: digging, compacting, and smothering.

DIGGING When you are working in your garden and find large roots, remember how important they are for anchorage and stability, and do not cut them. Roots that are less than about half an inch in diameter can be cut cleanly. Make as small a wound as possible, as the tree has to heal the cut. Damaging roots lessens their ability to supply the tree with water and nutrients.

COMPACTING Compaction of soil occurs when heavy objects run over the ground, displacing air spaces. In a shade garden, it is hard to re-aerate soil once it has been squashed because of the plethora of existing roots. Without soil air, the growth of all plants is restricted. The heavier the object on the soil, the more air is displaced. Driving anywhere under a tree may affect its health. You may not see an immediate impact, but over the next few years the outer limbs will begin to die back and the whole tree may decline.

Even stepping on the ground will compact the soil. To prevent compaction, when you design your space, create designated paths or stepping stones for you and your guests to walk on. This keeps the soil in the planting beds more aerated and fluffy, because you are not trampling on them every time you want to reach a plant.

The root flare at the base of this tree helps to stabilize its trunk.

Trees like this red oak, *Quercus ruber*, have deep enough roots to allow easy planting around the base of their trunks.

**above right** Minimize compaction in your planting beds by including a designated path.

**SMOTHERING** Adding soil around a plant can smother its roots and kill it. If the roots are covered with a thick, impervious layer such as clay soil, they may not get enough oxygen. If you want to raise the soil level in your garden, use the shallowest depth possible and keep the added soil light and aerated with organic matter and grit or sand. Around most trees, you can add from two up to a maximum depth of four inches.

If there must be a significant change in soil level, one solution is to build a tree pit. A tree pit keeps the soil around the tree roots at its original ground level, while farther away the soil level is raised and held in place by a retaining wall. The farther from the trunk that the wall is built, the fewer roots will be impacted. Ideally, the wall should be no closer to the tree trunk than the line of its outer branches.

## ALLELOPATHY

Certain plants like black walnut, *Juglans nigra*, produce a substance from their roots and other parts of the tree that can interfere with the growth of neighboring plants. The process is called allelopathy, and it gives plants a competitive advantage in the struggle for resources.

The chemical that is produced by the black walnut tree is called juglone. Some plants are more sensitive to the effects of juglone than others. If you are gardening under a black walnut, and you see a plant that is yellowing and looking sickly or stunted, it may be affected by juglone. The best solution is to move the plant to another location. Despite these problems, walnut trees are great shade producers and their fruit is a fabulous food source for wildlife. If you have a black walnut tree, underplant it with plants that can tolerate juglone, such as *Helleborus*, *Hosta*, *Mertensia*, *Viburnum*, and many ferns and spring bulbs.

*Hyacinthoides* will grow happily beneath *Juglans nigra*.

# PLANTING FOR SUCCESS
## TECHNIQUES AND MAINTENANCE

Your shade garden is a long-term commitment, full of plants that grow for decades. Because of this, it is important to adopt practices that support the slow, steady, and healthy growth of your plants. Sensible clearing, simple planting, and smart maintenance techniques are key practices that can be used to produce a successful garden that grows more beautiful each year.

This once-overgrown area has been transformed into a flourishing shade garden.

## CLEARING THE AREA

The first step in starting a new garden is to assess and remove unwanted and unhealthy existing vegetation to make way for more desirable plants.

Whether you are planning a new shade garden, or renewing an existing one, you should first take stock of the plants that are present. Determine what trees, shrubs, and herbaceous plants are in your garden space, then decide what plants will stay and what should go. There are several factors to take into account when deciding whether a plant should be removed.

The first things to identify and remove are any hazardous plants that are dead, diseased, or damaged—the "three Ds." Look at your trees for obvious damage like missing bark, leafless branches, or branches that are hanging. Any of these signs may indicate that the branch or entire tree is unhealthy and so should be pruned or cut down. Also prune away branches that cross and rub against each other. For projects that you can tackle yourself, consult a good pruning guide and be sure to follow strict safety precautions. For large projects such as a full tree health inspection or the removal of a big branch or tree, consult a professional arborist.

Next, find out if any plants in your garden are locally invasive. Invasive plants are those that come from other areas of the world and that reproduce too successfully in your environment, out-competing native vegetation. Invasive plants vary by locality, and there are lists that itemize them for each geographic area. Many public gardens and state extensions have regional resources to consult. They will help you to decide which plants you should remove. Finally, you may want to consider eliminating plants that are irritating or toxic, such as poison ivy and poison oak.

Invasive plants should be totally removed. Start by chopping the top growth to the ground and then dig up the roots. Invasive plants are very vigorous, so you may not be able to remove all of the plant on your first try. Dispose of these plants carefully so that they do not become a problem in other areas.

Vines are some of the worst invasive plants, as they scramble over and smother all other vegetation. They grow quickly and aggressively in the shade garden because many of them are found naturally in woods or forests and are adapted to grow in shade. Removal of vines requires persistence because they grow back from roots and seed themselves into the garden. If vines are attached to tree bark, do not rip them down. Instead, cut vines off at the base and dig up their roots. After a few months, you should be able to remove the dead vine from the tree without damaging its bark. Use caution when removing poison ivy or poison oak—wear protective clothing and clean anything that comes into contact with them.

In many existing gardens, there are overgrown shrubs that you may want to keep. If they are too large for the space, prune them back from the tips by about a third, or take out some of the oldest branches by cutting them at the base. The shrub will grow back from the bottom. Take out no more than a third of the shrub in a year to conserve its energy for future growth. In following years, take out a few more old branches. After three or four years, you will have a regenerated shrub with new growth that can then be shaped to your liking.

Herbaceous plants that are unwanted should be dug up. The use of general herbicides is not recommended in a shade garden, as existing vegetation will be killed along with the undesirable

Certain plants, such as this *Wisteria*, are considered invasive in some parts of the world and should be removed where they are a problem.

above left  It is important to analyze existing vegetation before beginning the removal process in a new garden. There may be wildflowers to keep or trees that should be removed, as was the case in this grove of quaking aspens, *Populus tremuloides*, in Wyoming.

left  Poison ivy, with its characteristic three leaflets, causes skin irritation and should be removed with care.

# SIMPLE PRUNING TECHNIQUES

When pruning a woody plant, there are a few simple guidelines to remember. In general, use clean and sharp tools to prevent the spread of disease. To clean your tools, wipe them with an antiseptic liquid, like rubbing alcohol, to kill pathogenic bacteria and fungi.

When you make a cut, do not trim too close to the trunk, as it will not heal well. Cut neatly just above a node, where the leaves come out of the branch, or where a smaller branch emerges from a larger branch or trunk. Make the cut just outside the slightly lumpy ring at the base of the branch where it joins the trunk. This raised ring is called the branch collar—be sure not to cut into it!

When trimming a branch, first take off most of the length of the branch to reduce its weight. If necessary, have somebody hold it steady while you make your cuts. Never stand under a branch while it is being pruned, and always be cautious when using sharp tools. The next step is to make a small cut on the underside of the remaining stub so that the weight of the branch does not rip the bark down the trunk when it falls. The final cut is the neatest one, just outside of the branch collar. Large-scale tree work should always be performed by a reputable professional.

To maintain a shrub at a specific size or shape, prune it soon after it has flowered. This allows woody plants time to develop their flower buds for the following year. For example, summer-flowering shrubs like *Hydrangea macrophylla* sometimes will not bloom if they are pruned in spring, as doing so removes this year's flower buds. To increase the bushiness of a shrub or to reduce lanky growth, trim back branch tips to encourage a fuller branching pattern.

Other pruning jobs to tackle at any time of year are the removal of suckers and water sprouts. Suckers grow straight up from the base of woody plants and look dissimilar from the main plant. Water sprouts grow vertically out of normal branches. Neither of these types of growth is desirable and both should be removed.

The area of crinkled bark between the trunk and the branch indicates the branch collar.

**opposite**  This border next to a private residence in Wyoming is filled with *Aquilegia*, *Hosta*, and other shade-loving perennials.

plants. Herbicides negatively affect the long-term health of your garden as they linger in the soil, destroying the beneficial microbes that help to break down valued organic matter.

Once you have removed hazardous, diseased, and invasive plants, the final step is to make sure that the remaining plants are all ones that you like and will be happy to live with. You want your shade garden to be a pleasant place for you and your family for years to come.

## PLANTING TECHNIQUES

After you have cleared the area of any unwanted plants, locate your planting bed and amend the ground for planting. There are several strategies that can be used, depending on whether your space is already tree-shaded, you are starting a new shade garden from scratch, or your shade garden will be next to a building.

### WORKING UNDER TREES

If you are starting your new shade bed or garden under trees, it is important to find an area without too many large structural tree roots. Such roots are physically in the way and the competition between roots will rob the soil of water and nutrients that your new plants will need.

Dig a few trial holes in the area where you are planning the bed. If you find they are full of roots, then you may have to adjust the placement of the bed, usually by moving it away from the trunk. The larger the tree's diameter, the farther away you will have to move your planting area. Examine the tree and look at the location and direction of the large roots as they emerge from the trunk. Look for possible planting pockets in the V-shape between these roots. Do not dig up the bed with a mechanical cultivator or tiller, as you will destroy too many roots. Only dig where you are going to plant.

If you are working around existing roots but want to make more room for the roots of the new plants, it is possible to add a few inches of a light and fluffy mixture of sand or grit and leaf mold to the surface of the soil. The inorganic particles add nothing to the fertility of the soil, but they improve drainage, aeration, and root growth.

There is no set ratio for the planting mixture, as it depends on what your soil already contains. If your garden soil is sandy, just use lots of leaf mold. If you have a clay soil, add as much grit and sand as you like to the mixture; it will gradually move down into the soil and open up its texture.

### WORKING IN AN OPEN AREA

Starting a shade garden when you have no trees, or only small ones, is in some ways easier than gardening under a mature canopy, as you do not have to deal with large tree roots. When you plant everything at the same time, the roots of the trees, shrubs, and herbaceous perennials will all find their own spaces in the soil as they grow together. However, you will have to be patient, as the trees and shrubs will take some time before they can completely shade your new beds.

## HERBACEOUS PLANTS TO TRY AROUND TREE ROOTS

Smart plant choices are the solution to the challenge of selecting plants that will grow among tree roots. There are two main groups of herbaceous plants that will work well in this situation. Bulbs are the first. Small bulbs, like *Chionodoxa*, *Crocus*, *Cyclamen*, *Galanthus*, and *Scilla*, are great tucked in the gaps between tree roots. The dry root zone around trees is perfect for these little bulbs as it mimics the dry summer mountain conditions where they are native.

The second group is made up of plants that naturally spread by runners, rhizomes, or by seeding in from an original, parent plant. Many of these plants can be described as groundcovers. When you plant them around a tree, place the parent plants away from the trunk in areas with fewer roots. Over time, they will spread out to completely cover the ground, including areas close to the trunk that contain many roots. This list includes my favorite herbaceous groundcovers for filling in around trees.

*Asarum* species, hardy ginger
*Brunnera macrophylla*, heartleaf brunnera
*Carex* species and cultivars, sedge
*Chrysogonum virginianum*, green and gold
*Convallaria majalis*, lily-of-the-valley
*Disporopsis pernyi*, dwarf Solomon's seal
*Epimedium ×versicolor* 'Sulphureum', bishop's hat 'Sulphureum'
*Geranium ×cantabrigiense* 'Biokovo', cranesbill 'Biokovo'
*Heuchera villosa*, hairy alumroot
*Iris cristata*, dwarf crested iris
*Ophiopogon* species and cultivars, mondo grass
*Pachysandra procumbens*, Allegheny spurge
*Phlox stolonifera*, creeping phlox
*Pulmonaria* species and cultivars, lungwort
*Tiarella* species and cultivars, foamflower

More aggressive growers that are suited for places where little else will grow include *Ajuga*, *Dennstaedtia punctilobula*, *Euonymus fortunei* var. *radicans*, *Hedera helix*, *Lamium*, *Pachysandra terminalis*, and *Vinca*.

To start your new garden, choose the location carefully; any tree you plant today will eventually shade a large area. Think about the route of the sun across the sky and which side of your garden receives more sun. To create the most shade, plant the trees on the sunniest side of your planting beds.

If you have chosen an area that has turf grass, there is a simple procedure to smother the grass in order to make your shade garden. Start with about five or so layers of paper; it can be

Spreading perennials like
*Carex* can be planted away
from a tree trunk and allowed
to fill in over time, as seen in
this serene sloped section of
the garden at Mill Fleurs.

**opposite** This bed beneath
a mature oak was created by
tucking small plants between
established tree roots.

newspaper, or any other biodegradable, nontoxic paper. The paper acts as a barrier to kill the grass, which slowly rots down in the dark. Wet the paper and overlap it on top of the entire area of the new bed or border. If necessary, weigh down the edges of the paper with large stones or logs. This also helps to delineate the planting area. On top of the paper, spread two to four inches of a light and fluffy sand and leaf mold mixture. If you are certain that there are no tree roots beneath your planting beds, you can add more of your mixture.

At this point, the bed is ready to be planted or it can be left for a few months to allow the paper and turf to decompose. If you can, prepare your bed in autumn, research your new plants over winter, and plant them in spring. Depending on your winter weather conditions, you may find that the first leaf and sand mix has already rotted down and you can add another layer to your new bed just before spring planting.

For large root balls, you may have to cut through the paper to plant, but for most small plants, you will be able to plant directly into your soil mixture. Add a mulch of leaf mold or compost after planting, and water the plants in thoroughly. Keep this bed well watered until the roots of the new plants have worked their way through the paper and into the soil below.

## WORKING NEXT TO BUILDINGS

When planting on the shady side of buildings, you may find that the soil is not ideal for plants that require moist, humus-rich soil. Instead, the soil near foundations may be dry, compacted, and full of construction rubble, rocks, or other debris. If this is the case, the easiest thing to do is to pull the planting area away from the house and bring in good topsoil and compost to raise the planting bed. It is amazing how a couple of inches of loose, organic-rich soil will help the growth of shade-loving plants.

A garden bed next to the foundation of the house, especially if it is close to paving, may stay just a few degrees warmer in winter, allowing you to grow plants that are borderline hardy in your area. Tuck your precious but slightly tender plants in the planting beds near the house. Such beds may also be dry due to overhanging eaves. Dry soil sometimes helps plants to survive during a cold, wet winter, as their crowns (the part of the plant where the roots meet the stems) stay dry. In summer, however, you may need to water the plants.

If your soil is particularly bad and it does not seem possible to plant directly in the ground, use containers. This gives you the opportunity to work with whatever soil you like and also to move the pots around to change your display.

## CHOOSING PLANTS WITH SMALL ROOT BALLS

There are several reasons to start with plants that have small root balls, such as those you have dug and divided or purchased as small plants. The most important of these is that it is easier to dig small holes between existing tree roots. Additionally, small, young plants will be more vigorous as they grow.

Youthful plants, especially those raised in a nursery, have never faced a shortage of resources. They quickly push their roots out into the surrounding area once they are in the ground. If their roots meet an obstacle, such as a big tree root, they grow around it, under it, or away from it. The advantage of a young plant is its ability to get its roots down and to adapt to its new site easily.

An exquisite combination of colorful foliage plants grown in a bed that is tucked next to a house in a private suburban garden.

left Borderline hardy plants thrive in a sheltered area next to this Tudor house in England.

Emerging from its immature leaf, the delicate flower of *Sanguinaria canadensis* is on the verge of opening in spring sunlight. *Sanguinaria* is often sold as a small plant, perfect to tuck between tree roots.

above right  This early spring clump of *Hosta* could easily be dug up and divided to make more plants.

## DIVIDING PLANTS

An easy way to increase the number of plants for your garden is to dig up large clumps of perennials and divide them into several pieces. Many shade plants can be propagated in this way including *Asarum*, *Hosta*, and ferns. Using a large spade, garden fork, or shovel, dig in a circle around the clump. Gradually ease the shovel under the plant and lever it out of the ground. Gently shake and scrape the soil off the roots. Look for obvious places where it might be possible to separate the plant into sections. Using your hands or the shovel, break or slice the root ball into several portions. Make sure that each part has some leaves and some roots. Replant the divisions and add more leaf mold to the planting hole. Firm the soil around the crown to hold the plant upright. Water the plant well and then inspect it weekly to see if it needs more water.

If there are no plants with small root balls available, purchase a large plant—*Hosta* is just one example—that can be divided into two or three pieces. Choosing little plants requires patience while you wait for them to grow and fill the space, but with good care these plants may surprise you and grow quickly.

## PREPARING, PLACING, AND PLANTING

Before digging any holes, lay out the plants on your prepared bed and make adjustments until you are happy with their placement. Keep in mind that as the plants grow, they will shade each other, so space them accordingly. Try to copy the layered look of a natural woodland by incorporating trees, shrubs, and herbaceous layers in your design. In a small garden, a shrub might be your tallest layer, but it adds needed height and interest to your composition.

When you select your plants, be sure to obtain each species or cultivar in odd numbers and to group them together to make a cluster—doing so looks better than individual specimens dotted around and has a greater visual impact. It also makes it easier for you to look after them.

Once you have located and prepared your site, dig a planting hole that is about as deep as the plant's root ball and just a little wider. Most root balls, once they have been divested of their potting soil, can be gently molded to fit into your hole. Planting in a compact hole allows newly developed roots to form a beneficial relationship with the soil mycorrhizae.

If you are working around mature tree roots, it may be easiest to dig a hole that is the shape of a slice of pie instead of a traditional round one. The pointed end of the hole will point toward the trunk and the wider part of the hole will point away from it. This allows you to plant closer to the tree, as the plant's roots will radiate out from the trunk. If the tree roots that you encounter are smaller than approximately half an inch, it is possible to cut some of them to make the planting hole. Use sterilized pruners to cut roots cleanly.

Before you install the new plant, place a few decomposing leaves or a little compost in the bottom of the hole to provide slow-release nutrients for the growing plant. If you have acquired your plants from a nursery, remove each from its pot and examine the root ball, which consists of the combined roots and potting soil. Most of the potting soil, if it is lightweight peat moss, perlite, vermiculite, or another soilless mix, must be gently shaken or combed out of the roots with your fingers. If this potting mix is left in place, the plant will struggle because the commercial potting mixture will repel water and the plant's roots will not get down into the natural garden soil. Peat moss is particularly challenging, because once it dries out, it is extremely difficult to rewet.

Now examine the roots. If they are root-bound, meaning they are tightly packed, they will need to be loosened. With your fingers or a garden tool, gently break the root ball apart. If the roots are in a solid mass, it may be necessary to cut the root ball vertically in several places with a clean garden knife. The aim is to encourage new roots to grow out into the surrounding soil. Cutting roots may seem scary, but if the roots stay in their container-sized configuration, they will not get the necessary water and nutrients they need from the surrounding soil. If you are planting into dry soil, soak the root ball in a tub of water before planting.

Place the root ball into the hole and situate the crown of the plant so that it is flush with the soil surface. Spread the roots out into the hole so that they will grow in all directions. Refill

the hole halfway with the soil that you took out mixed with a little sand and compost or leaf mold mixture. Pour water into the hole and let it sink into the soil. The water flowing around the roots helps to fill in any large pockets of air in the soil through which the roots cannot grow. Finish refilling the hole with your soil mix and water again. Gently settle the plant by firmly pressing the soil over the roots. Finally, add a light layer of mulch above the root area.

## PLANTING A TREE

When planting a tree, use good planting practices, and be certain to ensure that the soil meets the trunk at the correct level. Planting a tree at the wrong depth may kill it. Plant so that the widening base of the trunk, the root flare, is above soil level. If you plant the tree too high, the roots will be exposed to the air and will not be able to absorb water or nutrients. If you plant it too low in the soil, the tree may rot. This also applies to planting shrubs.

above left  A densely packed root ball that will need to be loosened before planting in order to encourage the roots to get down into the garden soil.

above right  Balled and burlapped *Corylus avellana* 'Contorta', known as the corkscrew hazel or Harry Lauder's walking stick, is situated at the correct depth for planting.

opposite  At Chanticleer in Wayne, Pennsylvania, the pleasing repetition of *Hakonechloa*, *Helleborus*, and *Hosta* underplanted with *Phlox divaricata* produces a cohesive garden picture.

# MAINTENANCE TECHNIQUES

Your established shade garden will only require a small amount of upkeep, but these maintenance tasks are vitally important to the health of your garden—the rewards will far outweigh the work. The main tasks include watering plants as needed, removing unwanted plants, and adding plenty of leaf mold or compost as soil amendments and mulch.

## WATERING

One of the first maintenance considerations you will need to make during planning is how much you want to rely on natural precipitation and whether or not you want to add additional irrigation. Personally, I try to work with the existing environmental conditions as much as possible. If you choose to grow plants that require more moisture than your natural environment supplies, you may have to irrigate them. In this instance, it is a good idea to cluster these water-loving plants together for ease of maintenance.

Remember that the soil in your shade garden is packed full of roots, so there is always high competition for moisture. New plants have a hard time competing with established plants and need a sensible watering regime to help them develop a healthy root system.

It is easy to assume the more frequently plants are watered the better, but this is not the case. The application of small amounts of water at frequent intervals means that the water often stays at the soil surface, which encourages the growth of shallow roots. Plants that develop shallow root systems are less likely to survive drought and are easier for foraging animals or wind to dislodge.

Instead, water deeply and less often to encourage new plants to "get their roots down"; in this way, they will become self-sufficient and find their own water. Plants with deep roots require less water and maintenance in the long-term. When watering your plants, aim to water the root zone and keep the foliage dry. This practice conserves water and reduces fungal problems. If you use these smart watering techniques, you will save yourself time and effort while producing healthier plants.

For new plantings, the old adage "the first year they sleep, the second year they creep, the third year they leap" applies to all perennial plants, but it is particularly pertinent when used to describe the growth of woody plants. Shade plants grow slowly and tend to have long lives, so be patient with them. Allow your plants time to develop a good root structure that will support healthy growth in future years.

During the first growing season, plants will not seem to be doing all that much aboveground; they appear to sleep. But the activity in the first year is hidden away, as the roots venture out of the root ball and into the soil. Make sure that your newly installed plants have adequate water at their root zones. Water thoroughly once a week until the moisture sinks down to the bottom of the root ball. These early years are when plants develop their root framework. Deep and widely spaced roots are the drought-survival kit of your plants in the years to come.

In the second growing season, there is visible top growth on the plant as it creeps into life. This is the year to let the plant struggle a little more. Do not water so often, but when you do water, really give the root zone a deep soaking. It is fine to let the plant wilt a little, as this will encourage the roots to extend into the surrounding soil in search of water. In the case of drought

top  Water-loving *Astilbe* grows vigorously in moist soil at Docton Mill Gardens in Devon, England.

bottom left  Rain droplets shimmer on foliage in a shade garden.

bottom center  To help newly planted trees, like decorative *Acer*, establish a good root system, it is vital to water them deeply.

bottom right  Choose plants that are native to your region to minimize additional watering. In eastern North America, a selection of *Tiarella* and ferns is appropriate.

# MICROCLIMATES

Microclimates in a garden are small areas where the growing conditions are not the same as they are only a few feet away. Variations are sometimes so localized that they should be called mini-microclimates.

Moist soil is often at a premium in shaded areas. The soil at the base of any slope or in any low area is likely to be moist. Areas near downspouts, rain barrels, and birdbaths receive splashes of water. The addition of rocks or stones will help the soil beneath them to stay moist for longer. Place flat stones next to biennial plants that you would like to overwinter, such as foxgloves; it keeps the plant crown dry and warm, but their roots moist.

## Rain Shadows

Most shade gardens contain at least one tree with a canopy that shades the plants beneath it from both sun and rain. The easiest way to visualize this is to think of the tree as being like an umbrella that keeps the rain and sun off the ground underneath it.

Just like rain rolling off an umbrella, water hits the treetops and runs down the branches to fall in a wide circle, known as the drip line, around the tree. Additional water also runs down the tree trunk. The gap where little water falls between the trunk and the drip line is a rain shadow. Another rain shadow is found in the shelter of buildings, particularly under the eaves.

Knowing that these areas are shady and dry is important for water management. The easiest way to deal with these dry sites is to choose drought-tolerant plants that will grow without additional watering. If this is not possible, give plants growing in these areas the best chance of success by adding compost to improve the soil. If your plants still look wilted, you have two options: move them or water them regularly.

**top** Ferns thrive in the shady, moist conditions found in this stone wall.

**bottom** A mature tree casts a wide rain shadow in this public garden in Texas.

conditions, however, where there has been no rain for an extended period of time, do not let your plants get beyond mild wilting. These are still young plants that need tending. Mulching over the root zone with organic matter during the second year will help retain moisture in the soil.

The third year is when the plant really seems to leap into growth. At last, the roots are able to support more aboveground expansion. If the plant does not seem to be thriving in year three or four, move it to another spot to provide it with more desirable conditions.

During later years, water less than before. If you have chosen a plant that is either native to your area, or adapted to similar climatic conditions, this plant should be able to go it alone. There are some arid or drought-prone climates where a nonnative or a more water-loving plant will always need irrigation. In areas where water is scarce, do yourself and our environment a favor and grow plants that are adapted to your climate.

In the years that follow, your plants will have their roots firmly established in your well-nourished soil. In times of drought, your plants may need an occasional resuscitation with some added water, but they have been launched into the world, well prepared for future growth.

## FERTILIZING

As many plants in your shade gardens have the potential to live for decades, the best long-term method for fertilization is to feed the soil rather than the plant. In most shade gardens, the natural fertility of the soil with additional organic matter will provide all the nutrients needed to grow healthy plants. Add organic matter to the soil surface, where, over time, physical actions and decomposers will break it down, incorporating it into the soil structure in a form that plants can use. This is a simple, slow, and steady method that has no uneven spikes in nutrient flow, so that plant growth is steady.

In shaded soils that have few roots, such as near walls or buildings, scratch the organic matter into the first few inches of soil with a trowel to help the incorporation process. In a bed near a tree, simply spread it on the ground without scratching it in, to avoid damaging the roots.

This approach to fertilizing your plants produces extensive, deep root systems that grow down through the soil in search of resources. Conversely, adding bagged chemical fertilizers to each individual plant encourages surface root formation. Shallow-rooted plants need more maintenance and are less likely to survive during times of environmental stress or severe weather.

If you do need to supplement with added fertilizers, the three main nutrients that are needed for plant growth are nitrogen, phosphorus, and potassium. These are listed on bagged chemical fertilizers in this order (N-P-K) with numbers that indicate the percentage of each contained in the mixture.

NITROGEN (N) is needed for all basic plant growth. In a well-managed shade garden, humus in the soil provides all the nitrogen that is needed by the plants. The addition of artificially high nitrogen fertilizers can spur too much leafy growth at the expense of root growth, making the plants prone to drought stress and herbivore browsing.

PHOSPHORUS (P) is needed for root and flower growth. In woodland ecosystems, phosphorus is supplied from the relationship between roots and mycorrhizae. This is a fragile symbiotic relationship. The addition of excessive chemical phosphorus destroys the beneficial fungus. However, when planting bulbs, a little bone meal (a complex source of phosphorus) is a good addition.

Shredded leaves on the soil surface gradually break down to release the necessary nutrients for woodland *Phlox*.

above right Decomposing logs and leaves provide moisture and nutrients for *Podophyllum peltatum*, shown here with its mottled leaves.

right This *Hosta* collection is grown in pots and may require low levels of added fertilizer to keep the plants healthy because their roots have access to a limited soil volume.

POTASSIUM (K), usually added as potash, is important for leaf development and for any part of the plant that is growing. Potassium-deficient plants are more prone to frost damage and disease, so it is a necessary nutrient for healthy plants. It is quite a mobile element in the soil and is easily washed away in heavy rains, so apply small amounts frequently, rather than a lot at once. A traditional way to add potash to soils is by scattering cooled wood ashes from stoves and fireplaces. Potash is alkaline, so it should not be used around acid-loving plants.

The easiest way to decide whether you need to add additional fertilizer is to assess how each plant is growing. If an established plant does not appear to be putting on new growth, or if its leaves appear to be an unnatural color, your plants may need some additional nutrients. If this is the case, choose fertilizers that are complex. A complex fertilizer like bone meal or blood meal releases nutrients gradually. These fertilizers do not give an instant jolt to the plants; they are slow-acting remedies for nutrient deficiencies.

If you do choose to add additional bagged fertilizer, select an organic product and use it at no more than half the recommended rate, as plant growth is naturally slower in the shade. Remember to let your plants work hard and get their roots deeply down into the soil for overall healthy growth.

There are other situations when you may need to use chemical fertilizers to maintain plant health. In hot, tropical climates, the rate of plant growth is fast. If you garden intensively in these conditions, you may need supplemental fertilizers. When gardening in containers in any climate, you usually need to fertilize because the plant roots can only access a finite amount of nutrients. Finally, if you garden on nutrient-poor soils, or sandy soils where nutrients wash away quickly, there is more need to fertilize.

## MULCHING

Mulch is material that is spread on top of the garden soil. There are several benefits of organic or inorganic mulch in your garden: mulch regulates soil temperature, retains moisture in the soil, and reduces weed germination.

The use of mulch mimics what happens naturally in most shady ecosystems with the autumnal addition of leaves from the trees. Using leaves as mulch has the added benefit of fertilizing the soil at a gradual and steady pace.

Above the soil, mulch acts as an insulating layer, protecting the roots from temperature extremes. Mulch keeps the soil cooler in summer and more consistently frozen in winter. In winters where the temperature fluctuates between freezing and thawing, the vulnerable crown of the plant may be forced out of the ground by frost heaving, killing the plant. Adding a layer of mulch reduces the problem of frost heaving in cold climates.

An effective organic mulching material will hold a certain amount of water within it and also prevent the evaporation of water from the soil surface. This is an important function of mulch in the summer, especially in warm climates.

Once your garden has an established tree and shrub canopy, general weeding is relatively easy because many ordinary garden weeds will not germinate in low light conditions. Until your canopy has filled in, adding a layer of mulch can cut down on weed growth. In general, it is simple to pull or hoe weeds out of loose mulch. Be sure to remove weeds before they go to

## VOLCANO MULCH

Thick layers of wood chips or shredded mulch piled against tree trunks in conical, mountain-like heaps are disparagingly known as "volcano" mulch. Creating a volcano of mulch around trunks is a sure way to kill your trees.

Volcano mulch forms when thick layers of mulch are piled on top of each other year after year. It sits against the bark of trees, covering the root flares and smothering the plants. The bark stays too wet and is then prone to damage by insects, small rodents, and rotting diseases. Remember, when mulching trees, stop two to three inches away from the base of the trunk so that you leave the root flare clear.

seed and do not add them to your compost. Pull the weeds out firmly by holding them near to the base of their stems and steadily pulling them out, including their roots.

Leaves, whole or shredded, are perhaps the ideal mulch for the shade garden. Whole leaves make great mulch when left in place where they fall, but may smother small plants. Chopped or shredded leaves do not mat down and so are preferable. This is one of the quickest and easiest ways of continually adding organic matter to your soil without the backbreaking task of hauling in mulch from an outside source. It is the ultimate in natural recycling.

Needled evergreens such as pines provide another natural mulch. Pine straw or pine needles are especially good for plants that thrive in acidic soil. They are slow to break down, but have an aesthetically pleasing look in shade gardens. Gather them from under pines and spread them on your beds, or make a soft, scented path through your garden.

If you do not have sufficient material to cover your ground, buy mulch in bags or in bulk. Another reason to buy mulch is if you prefer the look of a specific type of material to top-dress your beds.

Chipped, ground, or shredded bark or wood are also popular materials for mulch. Wood mulches lend a uniformity of appearance to beds and tend to last for a couple of growing seasons before breaking down. The scale of finely shredded or ground wood mulch is appropriate for use around small plants. In general, an inch or two of wood mulch is sufficient—too thick of a layer will prevent spring bulbs and wildflowers from emerging and may form matted crusts that have the potential to repel rain or wash away in a storm.

Large wood chips are the right scale to be used around trees and shrubs, but can smother small herbaceous plants. Be certain to keep wood mulch several inches away from the bark of

Hundreds of *Narcissus* plants push their way up through leaf mulch beneath tall trees at the Andalusia Foundation in Pennsylvania.

trees and shrubs. Wood chips are also a great choice for pathways. Look for good-quality mulch that is sourced locally. Wood transported from other areas may bring pests and diseases into your garden.

In arid regions, it is often better to use inorganic mulch for your shade garden. Many of the plants that thrive in arid climates need to have their foliage kept dry at all times. Using stone, grit, or gravel promotes rapid drainage from the surface but keeps the soil beneath moist for longer, reducing water needs. Remember in this situation that without adding leaves, there is not the added benefit of fertilizing from leaf decomposition. However, many of the plants that are grown in arid areas have slow rates of growth and require few additional nutrients.

The general rule of thumb for mulch use in the shade garden is "less is more." Keep the mulch light because heavy, matted-down mulch prevents water and oxygen flow into the soil. A copious layer of mulch in wet climates also becomes a hiding place for moisture-loving pests, such as slugs and snails. If you are unsure how much mulch to apply, the simplest method is to apply it specifically on top of the root zone of newly introduced plants, carefully pulling excess mulch away from the bark or stems.

Another very easy way to mulch is to scatter it by hand or with a pitchfork, in a light, sprinkled layer. Keep mulch off plant leaves, especially of the rosette-shaped plants like *Primula* and *Digitalis*. Remember that the whole surface of the soil does not have to be covered.

If your shade garden has a naturalistic style, where the look of the garden relies on self-sown plants to fill in between the more permanent plantings, use this technique of mulching. This is a great way to ensure that seeds can still find open soil in which to germinate. For the neater gardener, a consistent one to two inches over the whole garden area gives a cohesive look to

left  Match the size and quantity of the mulch to the plants you are mulching. Herbaceous plants, such as Japanese wood poppy, *Glaucidium palmatum*, should be lightly mulched.

top right  Applying pine straw as a mulch will gradually acidify the soil.

bottom right  The lidded seed capsule of *Jeffersonia diphylla* turns from green to brown when the seeds inside mature. Allow these plants to self-sow by using a light, scattered layer of mulch over the surrounding soil.

the shaded bed. Some gardeners love this clean, finished, and tidy look. If this is your preferred style, do not be in a hurry to mulch again if there is no bare soil showing from your previous mulching. Remember that too much mulch can be as harmful as too little for certain plants.

## PESTS AND DISEASES

You should not have too much trouble with pests and diseases in a well-managed shade garden. If you choose plants that are unattractive to herbivores and that are not disease-prone, you stand a better chance of having a garden with few issues. Additionally, you can boost plant health by using smart planting and maintenance techniques in order to increase plants' pest resistance.

That said, it is impossible to have plants that will never be eaten or affected by disease. The most relaxed approach is to tolerate a certain amount of damage, but the level that you find acceptable is up to you. I love seeing toads and birds, as I know that they are combatting the slugs and insects. In my naturalistic woodland garden, I have grown to appreciate that a few holey leaves may be the price to pay for this more low-key approach to pest control.

In general, the most frequent pest and disease problems in the shade garden are slugs and snails, mammalian herbivores like deer, and some fungal diseases such as powdery mildew.

### SLUGS AND SNAILS

Slugs and snails are voracious leaf-eating mollusks that are particularly prevalent in damp areas. The difference between the two is that snails have a hard shell and slugs do not. Telltale signs of slug or snail damage are iridescent slime trails and ragged-edged holes in tender leaves, especially on plants such as *Hosta* or hybrid *Heuchera*.

I do not use any chemical slug pellets or snail bait because I want to preserve the large population of toads, frogs, and birds that eat my mollusks. Using chemical pesticides introduces poisons into the food chain.

Both slugs and snails are more active at night, so this is the time to find them in your garden. Place traps made of halves of emptied, upside-down grapefruit or orange skin in areas of the garden where slugs or snails are a problem. During the night, the moisture underneath the fruit skin attracts them. In the morning, they will be under the citrus skin, where you can pick up and dispose of them, trap and all. Another low-impact slug trap is to put beer in a shallow can or tin set slightly above the soil surface. Overnight, the beer entices the mollusks and in the morning you can collect and remove them.

Additionally, you can surround your vulnerable plants with crushed eggshells or a ring of copper. These are physical barriers that dissuade the slugs or snails from reaching your plant. Or, for a more hands-on approach, check under stones and debris throughout the year to find hidden pests. Clean up your garden in spring to remove the translucent masses of whitish slug and snail eggs.

To control the general population of slugs and snails, try to keep your garden from becoming too wet and encourage good air circulation by removing excess foliage on the ground. If you

water your garden, do so in the morning so that plant leaves will be dry before nighttime. Ideally, the plants and the ground should dry out between waterings.

If you notice that plants tend to be eaten by slugs and snails, try growing them in containers. For added protection, raise the containers off the ground with pot feet or stones. The best control against slug damage is to choose plants with coarse, thick leaves like *Brunnera*, *Rodgersia*, and ferns.

## DEER, RABBITS, AND OTHER HERBIVORES

The herbivorous mammals that can cause damage in a shade garden vary from region to region, but the larger the animal, the more problems it may cause. Deer browsing is one of the biggest problems in many gardens, especially those that are sited next to natural areas. The over-population of deer in some places has drastically affected large areas of natural woodlands and gardens. Deer have eaten many of the wildflowers and they are preventing the natural regeneration of tree seedlings that ensure the continuation of the forest canopy. Soft, new plant growth attracts browsing from deer and other herbivores. The use of chemical fertilizers that artificially boost quick growth seems to encourage browsing.

## DEER-RESISTANT PLANTS

Deer browse many garden plants, especially in early spring when plants have tender new growth and in winter when they are hungry. In times of drought or other periods of environmental stress, deer damage may be more prevalent as the deer will stray from their normal routes and eating habits. Very few plants are entirely deer proof, but these are my favorite (generally) deer-resistant plants.

*Aconitum carmichaelii*, monkshood
*Aesculus parviflora*, bottlebrush buckeye
*Aquilegia canadensis*, Canadian columbine
*Brunnera macrophylla*, heartleaf brunnera
*Buxus sempervirens*, common box
*Cephalotaxus harringtonia*, Japanese plum yew
*Lamprocapnos spectabilis*, common bleeding heart
*Digitalis purpurea*, common foxglove
*Galanthus nivalis*, common snowdrop
*Helleborus foetidus*, stinking hellebore
*Lindera benzoin*, spicebush
*Narcissus* cultivars, daffodil
*Plectranthus* species and cultivars, plectranthus
*Pulmonaria* species and cultivars, lungwort
Most fern species and cultivars

*Cephalotaxus* and *Brunnera* are not likely to be eaten by deer.

The only real way to stop herbivore damage is to fence animals out of your garden. To exclude deer, your fences have to be at least eight feet tall. Once you have erected your fences, plant shrub borders on either side. Deer typically will not jump if they do not have a clear sightline for their landing. Some other herbivores like rabbits and groundhogs are more likely to dig under fences, so bury a portion underground when installing your barriers.

In autumn, male deer rub the velvet off their antlers using saplings with a smooth bark and a narrow diameter. A ring of metal or wooden posts inserted around a tree will limit access to the trunk. I do this for all of my newly installed saplings, and leave the rings in place for a few years. I also hang strongly scented soap hung in chicken wire cages to protect plants. Strong odors can confound deer as they find their food using their sense of smell.

There are herbivore deterrent sprays that can be used on foliage, but they need to be regularly reapplied, especially after a rain or when a plant has grown. While some people swear by the benefits of using anti-deer sprays on foliage, I personally do not use them. I just try to tuck the most vulnerable plants in secluded nooks of my garden.

To reduce browsing, choose plants that have a strong odor or fuzzy leaves that are not as delicious to eat such as *Plectranthus* and *Geranium macrorrhizum*. You can interplant these plants to camouflage tastier ones like *Trillium*.

### INSECTS

Insects can cause leaf and bark damage, but the vast majority of species do not cause major problems in the shade garden. Caterpillars, grasshoppers, and beetles may eat leaves, but this usually does not kill the whole plant. There are localized examples where an insect population decimates trees such as the emerald ash borer, which threatens ash forests in North America. More commonly, insects may eat holes in leaves and cause minor damage, but will not kill the tree, as their populations are kept in check by insect-eating birds.

If there is an insect population that invades your shade garden and causes major destruction, the best solution is generally to physically remove the insects. They can be crushed underfoot or knocked into a bucket of water that has a squirt of dish soap mixed into it. Tent caterpillars should be removed as soon as you see them. If I notice an overabundance of nonnative beetles in my garden, I go around in the cool of the morning and collect them in a jar of vinegar and dispose of them while they are still inactive.

Chemical sprays indiscriminately kill both unwanted insects and helpful ones like bees and preying mantises, which pollinate and protect your plants. Normally, natural insect predators like birds eat hundreds of thousands of pests each year and reduce their numbers, but they may be killed when they eat the sprayed pests. Regularly applied insecticides can also build resistance within insect populations, making unwanted species difficult to eradicate.

Insecticides may reduce the pest population in the short term, but they unbalance the ecosystem and cause greater problems in the future. The best long-term maintenance strategy in the shade garden is to encourage a diversity of animals like birds and other predators that will control insect populations without chemicals.

## FUNGAL DISEASES

While many of the fungi that inhabit the shade garden are beneficial, there are a few that can cause damage. In humid environments, there is a chance that your plants may suffer from a typically non-fatal disease called powdery mildew in the heat of summer. Leaves that have powdery mildew look as if they have been dusted with a white powder. To reduce the likelihood of this fungus, improve air circulation throughout your garden by removing branches and understory growth. There are not many other remedies for powdery mildew; the best solution is to choose mildew-resistant plants or cultivars.

The fungi that cause root rot can be a problem in waterlogged soils. To prevent root rots such as *Phytophthora* in moist soils, it is important to choose plants that are adapted to wet conditions. If you are over-irrigating an area, root rot is much more likely to occur. Infected plants will eventually die as their roots deteriorate. A shelf fungus growing out of the tree trunk, permanent discoloration on the root flare, and any splitting bark or die-back from the branch tips are all possible signs that the tree should be examined by an arborist. As soon as you identify a plant affected by root rot, it should be removed and thrown away. No matter which fungal disease you deal with, be sure to sterilize your tools thoroughly after dealing with infected plant material.

Tent caterpillars build characteristic webbed structures and should be removed before they defoliate trees or shrubs. Here, a tent occupies the branch of *Chaenomeles*, flowering quince.

# DESIGNING IN THE SHADOWS

## BRIGHT IDEAS FOR SHADY SPACES

When designing your shade garden, it is helpful to study existing gardens to get ideas and inspiration. You can find shade gardens around the world, and they are designed in distinctive types that are derived from various traditions. Some of these gardens emulate the informal look of naturally shaded areas, whereas others are formal and stylized.

The enclosed nature of a shade garden means that there is much more of a sense of mystery and excitement than in an open space. The structures that provide shade to the garden also block sightlines, so the entire garden cannot be seen at one glance. This gives visitors a chance to explore and investigate hidden surprises and vignettes. When designing a shady space, capitalize on these assets to produce a unique and personalized garden.

The boxwood parterre at the Heyward-Washington House in Charleston, South Carolina, is a charming example of a formal shaded city garden.

Look at inspirational images of shade gardens to get ideas. Visit existing shaded spaces and think about what you do and do not like. Make notes about what appeals to you and use those elements in your own garden. The key to success when creating a personal shade garden is making sure that the design matches your individual needs and preferred style.

## WOODLAND GARDENS

Woodland gardens are stylized versions of naturally occurring, tree-dominated landscapes and are the quintessential shade gardens. In these gardens, large trees and an assortment of understory woody plants produce the shade. The cathedral-like boughs of the largest trees arch overhead and their trunks enclose the space. The ground layer is a carefully orchestrated progression of smaller plants that provide beauty throughout the growing year.

Gardens in this style are predominately informal. Trees left to grow into their natural form give character to the design because of their height, width, form, and leaf quality. Winding paths curve between the trees to allow exploration of the garden. Along these paths, sheltered sitting areas are found in secluded nooks and wildlife features are perfectly at home. Water may either be used to enhance the gardens as a focal point or tucked away as a hidden surprise.

Gardeners who prefer a formal look can adapt this style by planting trees in parallel lines to create either an *allée* or grid pattern. In this formal setting, the paths are straight and lead directly to a focal point such as a bench, large container, or fountain at the end of the axis. Trees are still the dominant design feature in these gardens, but are often shaped by pruning. Understory plants may also be placed in straight lines to mimic the geometric configuration of the trees.

The woodland style of shade garden is one of the easiest types to implement in a home landscape because of its adaptability. For small gardens, a select grouping of trees can be the basis of a wooded scene in miniature. Choose small to medium trees as your tallest specimens and underplant them with flowering shrubs and shade-loving perennials. In larger landscapes, it is possible to emulate the scale of natural woodlands by planting layers of trees and shrubs in greater quantities. For cohesion, plant several of the same species together and match the scale of the garden.

top  The edge of this garden shows the layers that are characteristic of the woodland garden style.

bottom left  *Phlox*, *Mertensia*, and *Hyacinthoides* make a living blue tapestry on the woodland floor at the Winterthur Museum, Garden and Library in Wilmington, Delaware.

bottom right  Formally planted *Cercis canadensis* 'Hearts of Gold' underplanted with *Narcissus* 'Lemon Drops' line a shaded walk.

## MOSS GARDENS

The aesthetic charm of a moss garden lies in its enticing green simplicity. The verdant hue is soothing to the eye and the plants are soft to the touch. Most mosses thrive in shade where the conditions are cool and damp, as they require water to complete their life cycle. A water feature is often incorporated into this style of garden because splashing water keeps the moss healthy.

Buildings or walls can provide the shade for a mossy area, but the best moss gardens are found beneath the cover of trees. The artistic nature of curved tree trunks stands out against the green of the moss and makes an enchanting scene. The uniform look of moss is a fabulous foil for feathery ferns and bold *Hosta*.

To make a moss garden, choose an area where you see moss occurring naturally and encourage it by clearing away competing plants. My moss garden used to be a section of mossy lawn. I removed the grass, added a fountain, and it became a magnet for children and wildlife. If you are lucky enough to be able to grow moss easily, use it as a groundcover. It can take light foot traffic, but add a stepping stone path for well-traveled routes.

To cultivate moss in your shade garden, keep the soil moist and be sure to clear fallen debris off the surface, especially in autumn. Most mosses thrive in acidic soils, so adjust your pH if necessary. If conditions are right, moss is an easy-care plant. Moss does not flower but stays green year-round in most climates.

**below left** A collection of mosses adorns a rocky outcrop at the Coastal Maine Botanical Gardens.

**below right** A stepping stone nestled in a carpet of haircap moss, *Polytrichum*.

**opposite** Moss lines the streambanks under the shade of trees in this garden in southwest England.

# JAPANESE- OR CHINESE-INSPIRED GARDENS

Both Japanese and Chinese gardens are a fabulous source of inspiration for shade gardens. They each have their own aesthetics that are complex and rooted in history and tradition, with layers of meaning and cultural significance that are worth studying. Garden designers in other parts of the world have long been fascinated by Japanese and Chinese gardens, and have sought to emulate them in their own countries.

In these gardens, there is no rigid symmetry; balance is instead provided by picturesque asymmetrical design. Every aspect is carefully thought out and designed to fit the scale and style of the space. Carefully placed and pruned trees and shrubs, surrounding walls, teahouses, and other outbuildings provide these gardens with plenty of shade.

Nonliving elements play a large role in both garden styles. Water, rocks, and stones may be used symbolically to represent lakes, oceans, and mountains. Water can be used in koi ponds, cascading waterfalls, or as still, reflective surfaces. Large rocks may be used structurally to provide changes in level and to screen off hidden areas of the garden. Rocks may also be aesthetic objects, carefully chosen to be items of beauty and contemplation.

The Sand Garden is a dry garden that combines raked white sand with carefully placed rocks at the Asticou Azalea Garden, on Mount Desert Island in Maine.

right Stone lanterns are a popular addition to outdoor spaces inspired by the Japanese garden tradition.

A view across water in the Chinese garden at Biddulph Grange in Staffordshire, England.

At Shofuso Japanese House and Garden in Philadelphia, Pennsylvania, reflections of shaped evergreens add to the beauty of an autumnal scene.

Some of these gardens are designed to provide a place for meditation. In the "dry landscape" tradition of Japanese garden design, a group of significant rocks, often in threes or fives, is situated in a ground plane of carefully raked fine gravel.

Other gardens are used for walking or strolling and are often designed to direct the visitor on a route that may travel around a major body of water. The paths are usually winding and scenes are revealed one by one as the visitor traverses the garden. At some point, the path may cross water using stepping stones or a decorative bridge. Screens, hills, and pruned trees block objects until the visitor reaches each designated viewing place.

The color of these gardens is predominantly green, with both evergreen and deciduous woody plants that provide year-round structure. Trees and shrubs are carefully pruned into specific shapes that may take years to produce. For example, pine trees may be controlled as they grow by clipping them into stylized forms that reflect beautifully in water.

Both Japanese and Chinese garden styles have limited plant palettes that include azaleas, Japanese maples, camellias, Hinoki cypress, and flowering cherry and plum trees. The periods of spring bloom and fall color bring ephemeral drama to the landscape while the evergreens provide visual continuity through the seasons. Moss may also be used in some designs and it brings a feeling of peace and simplicity to these gardens.

Chinese and Japanese gardens each have distinct, recognizable styles with features that can be translated for a home garden. If you are attracted to either of these garden traditions, visit as many public examples as you can in order to get ideas. In your own garden, try using stepping stones to meander through a low groundcover, or include a large rock or rock grouping as a focal point. Additionally, choose plants that can be shaped by pruning, and create a succession of views around your shade garden.

## ROCK GARDENS

There are two types of shaded rock gardens: the first are those that are located on naturally rocky soil, and the second are gardens created by bringing in stone. In both of these situations, the rocks are a prominent design feature.

Naturally rocky gardens are often found on hillsides or near streambanks. These can be challenging to garden on due to shallow soil and difficult changes in level. Rocky shade gardens are often dramatic with memorable views, vistas, and twisted trees. If you have lots of rocks close to the soil surface in your garden, dig them up and use them in your design to build features like walls, seats, and planting beds. The stones tie your garden together visually and the well-drained soil between them makes a great planting environment for growing delicate bulbs and spring-blooming woodland wildflowers. It is a challenge to get large specimen trees established in the shallow soil that overlays naturally occurring rocks, but it may be possible to plant smaller saplings in soil pockets.

Many people admire the look of naturally wooded rock gardens so much that they strive to emulate them. I have visited some lovely rocky shade gardens and found inspirational ideas for my own woodland space. I incorporate stone to build paths and dry-stone walls. While this does not have the same effect as a craggy hillside garden, it does capture a bit of the spectacular character of such a place.

To imitate some of the spirit of a naturally rocky garden in your own shaded space, try surrounding a seating area or water feature with stone. Stones can also be used to create retaining walls, steps, seats, or bed edgings. Be sure to choose locally occurring stone as its color and texture will tend to blend best in your landscape.

Encircling stones surround a basin, which contains an abundance of candelabra primroses, *Primula japonica*, in the Quarry Garden at Winterthur Museum, Garden and Library.

The soft texture and muted tones of *Acer* specimens enhance a rock face in this private garden.

**bottom left** Dry-laid stone walls create an outdoor room in a private Cumbrian garden in England.

**bottom right** Afternoon sunlight illuminates an attractive stone retaining wall with a built-in bench on a hillside at the New England Wild Flower Society's Garden in the Woods.

# XERIC GARDENS

Xeric, or dry, gardens are those where water use is minimal. This style is most often chosen in areas of the world with low, erratic, or seasonal rainfall. Adding shade to xeric gardens cools the temperature at ground level and so reduces evaporation of water from the soil. In arid regions, hot weather makes shade very desirable and beneficial for plant growth. Built garden structures are the primary shade producers, because few large tree species can withstand true xeric conditions.

Many xeric garden designs incorporate an appealing area to sit in the shade under a pergola, ramada, or arbor. These can be covered with vines to increase the density of shade and add interest. Walls, boulders, shrubs, and small trees may provide additional shade. Much of the success of this kind of garden will depend on making smart design choices and choosing appropriate plants.

Even in areas with regular and plentiful rainfall, a gardener may design their shade garden to grow with no additional water. Many of the plants that grow in dry shade are native to rocky soils and require great drainage. The most drought-tolerant plants should be sited at the tops of slopes and those that require a little more water should go at the bottom because water will travel to the lowest areas of your garden. Choose plants native to your specific area because they are acclimated to your climate. Features to look for in plants that will grow in xeric conditions are silvery foliage, waxy-coated small leaves, and long taproots.

Use attractive pebbles, grit, or stones as a mulch to retain water in the soil. This has the added benefit of making your shade garden visually cohesive. Large stones or rocks can be added to create shady microclimates of their own.

This courtyard at the Lady Bird Johnson Wildflower Center in Austin, Texas, is shaded by walls and a golden ball lead-tree, *Leucaena retusa*, that naturally grows in poor, dry soils.

In hot climates, a shade-producing pergola or other structure is a welcome addition to the garden.

opposite *Nassella tenuissima*, Mexican feather grass, and *Agave havardiana*, Havard's century plant, are xeric plants that can tolerate some degree of shade. In very hot climates, more afternoon shade is beneficial.

A color-themed planting of *Solenostemon*, *Dichondra*, and a bold bromeliad, *Aechmea*, add excitement to a tropical container.

above right  *Fuchsia*, *Hypoestes*, ×*Fatshedera*, *Dracaena*, and *Philodendron hederaceum*, heartleaf philo-dendron, spill from a raised container.

opposite  Water spray from this waterfall cools the air and surrounding tropical plants.

# TROPICAL GARDENS

Tropical plants come from the understory of jungles near the equator. A true tropical climate has similar weather every day of the year, with regular precipitation and high temperatures, usually above 70°F. Tropical plants are naturally adapted to growing in low light conditions, making them perfect choices for the shade garden. One of the advantages of designing your garden using tropical plants is that their rapid rate of growth, especially in the heat of summer, quickly creates a bold display. Pair these plants with a water feature to add humidity, sound, and motion to your garden scene.

The distinctive look of tropical shade gardens comes from a wide range of plants with large, dramatic, and often colorful leaves that grow densely together. When making a tropical shade garden, design with layers of foliage. Create beds or borders with enough width so that you can accommodate the large size of these plants. Mimic junglelike, luxurious growth by massing plants together and combining different leaf sizes and colors. Try *Alocasia sanderiana* with *Philodendron xanadu*, or *Caladium* hybrids with *Hypoestes phyllostachya*.

Even if your whole garden is not tropical in design, it is easy to add a tropical feel to a patio or sitting area by combining some of these plants in pots. I like to choose a color scheme and then pick cultivars from genera including *Torenia*, *Colocasia*, and *Solenostemon*.

*Adiantum capillus-veneris* and other moisture-loving plants native to the southwestern United States grow along a gently moving stream.

**above right** Graceful branches reflect in an English millpond at Docton Mill Gardens.

**opposite** A flat rock on top of a waterfall is especially attractive to birds at the Royal Horticultural Society Garden Rosemoor.

## WATER GARDENS

There are many benefits to situating a water garden in a shaded place. Shade-producing trees or walls enclose the water feature, creating privacy, amplifying scent and sound, and keeping the water cool. The mirrored water surfaces bounce light around the shade garden, illuminating dark corners.

Plant a tree near the water's edge so that the overhanging boughs make the perimeter of the water garden a retreat for wildlife. Water features in the shade are dynamic places. Birds arrive to wash and drink, and dragonflies fly nearby. Frogs and fish swim in the water, which stays refreshing even in summer.

For humans, the allure of the water feature is that it engages our senses. Water can provide pleasing noises, fleeting reflections, and a feeling of coolness that suffuses the air. Dappled shadows add depth and dimension to the scene. Sparkling patches move and change on the water as light penetrates the tree canopy. Reflections of overhead trees give you double your enjoyment from their beauty. It is a tranquil spot to sit and relax.

Shaded water gardens can be strictly formal if the water is contained in a rectilinear pool, or informal if in a pond or wandering stream. Regardless of the formality of your design, it is important to choose appropriate plants to surround your water feature. Select plants that are adapted for growing in moist or wet soils. The dramatic foliage of *Astilboides*, *Petasites*, and *Rodgersia* look fabulous reflected in the water. Pair these bold plants with the finer-textured *Adiantum*, *Aruncus*, and *Astilbe*.

I have found that the areas of my shade garden that incorporate water are some of the most attractive to visitors and birds alike. Even a small water feature brings both peace and interest to a space. Add a birdbath under a tree to attract local birds and reflect the canopy overhead. If you have the space and resources, include a recirculating fountain or pond to bring motion and gentle sound to your garden.

This pond at Sezincote House and Garden in Gloucestershire, England, contains an island planted with *Primula* and topped with an uncommon snake ornament.

opposite Water meanders along a serpentine rill down a shaded path at Rousham House and Garden in Oxfordshire, England.

In the Levies Courtyard at the Real Alcázar de Sevilla in Spain, light reflected by the white walls and pool brightens the shaded space.

**above right** An ornate garden gate leads to a cool, vine-shaded walkway that provides respite from summer heat.

**opposite** An arched alcove containing a decorative tiled bench is surrounded by colorful orange walls.

## MEDITERRANEAN-INSPIRED WALLED OR COURTYARD GARDENS

Walled gardens are common in urban areas where they are often in full shade due to the tall surrounding buildings that cast shadows throughout the day. If you are looking for formal garden ideas, especially in a walled space or courtyard, then you may be inspired by gardens that have their origins in Islamic culture. These design ideas initially came from the Middle East, and were brought to southern Spain. Spaniards then took this garden style to the American continents.

This formal shade garden style, reminiscent of Mediterranean courtyards, is still favored today, especially in hot climates. Shaded outdoor patios or terraces are excellent spaces for entertaining. Elegant tiles, flagstones, or bricks are used on the ground, often in symmetrical patterns. The light-hued color palette reflects heat and light away from the space. These gardens are beautifully simple and often include a water feature to cool the air and add movement, sound, and reflection to the garden. Water may be in a tiled fountain or in a long, narrow, water-filled rill.

Gardening against a wall makes a great backdrop for vertical plantings. Grow vines up a trellis, or grow a space-saving espaliered tree on the wall. Maintain the espalier by trimming it flat and by tying back wayward branches. Walled gardens are perfect places to grow plants that provide fragrance because the enclosed space concentrates the scent.

Cool-season annuals fill a three-tiered container in this partially shaded courtyard.

**above center** Formal urns planted with shaped boxwood flank a straight path in a private plantation garden in the southern United States.

**above right** In a private garden, pots of *Hosta*, *Dodecatheon*, and *Heuchera* are combined for maximum effect against a trellis.

**opposite** A collection of containers clustered near a birdbath on a patio can be easily rearranged as the seasons change.

## CONTAINER GARDENS

Some gardens have shaded areas where it is difficult to plant directly in the ground due to hard paving, poor soil, or excessive roots. The solution for such spaces is to plant your garden above the soil in containers. Particularly in an urban environment, growing your favorite shade-loving plants in pots is an easy alternative to in-ground planting. The style and size of the containers should be chosen to suit the space.

Container gardens are simple to move and rearrange as you wish. This flexibility is an asset, allowing you to create vignettes that highlight seasonal beauty. It is simple to refresh the look of the garden by switching out faded plants and replacing them with new plants that are in bloom.

In formal gardens, place matching pots in pairs to flank a bench or a garden entrance. Pots repeated along a pathway make a strong statement. Large containers, or planted urns, can be used as focal points at the end of a garden walk.

For maximum visual effect in an informal setting, group various sizes of containers together and choose plants that complement each other, or that have a color theme. The pots can be different from each other but should still look compatible. For more impact, raise containers on risers, pot feet, or other upside-down pots.

Containers are especially useful where your soil type does not match the needs of the plants that you want to grow. For example, if you live in an area of alkaline soil, but wish to grow *Rhododendron* or other acid-loving plants, grow them in a large container with the appropriate soil pH.

# ORCHARD GARDENS

A traditional orchard is composed of spring-blooming fruit trees laid out in a formal grid. The herbaceous layer consists of rough grass interspersed with accent plants including shade-tolerant, naturalizing spring bulbs like *Camassia*, *Galanthus*, *Hyacinthoides*, and *Narcissus*. Paths are regularly mown between the trees to allow access, and the entire ground layer is cut down once or twice a year to clear the vegetation.

The major difference between an orchard and a woodland garden lies in the choice of the trees used to create the shade. In an orchard, the trees are smaller, widely spaced, and often pruned to constrain their size. Additionally, there are no understory shrubs, so there is a more open feeling among the trees.

An orchard style can easily be adapted to a home garden. By planting a collection of small to medium trees spread out from each other, you can evoke the sense of space found in a conventional orchard. Any small or medium trees with an upright or vase-shaped habit, such as *Cercis*, *Cornus*, and *Prunus*, are appropriate choices for an adapted orchard garden. The trees do not all have to be the same species, but a uniformity of size provides a pleasing regularity. Select your trees for spring bloom and other seasonal appeal.

Beneath the trees, there are dappled, edge, and bright shade conditions perfect for planting up with shade-loving herbaceous perennials. You can introduce plants for summer and fall interest such as *Digitalis*, *Eurybia*, *Lilium*, *Penstemon*, and *Thalictrum* that will grow in the shade beneath the trees.

These lightly shaded areas are attractive to wildlife because they provide nectar for pollinators, grasses for habitat, fruit and seeds for food, and branches for perching and nesting. Aesthetically, orchard-style gardens are a beautiful space for people to stroll or sit. Garden features that are appropriate for this style include a wooden bench in the shade beneath a tree, or a garden house as a focal point and gathering place.

**this page** Apples or crabapples, such as *Malus* 'Prairifire', are a traditional choice for an orchard planting.

**opposite top left** In a wild area, a fruit tree is underplanted with *Camassia* and *Anthriscus sylvestris*, cow parsley, at Bateman's in East Sussex, England, former home of the English writer Rudyard Kipling.

**opposite top right** *Prunus serrula*, Tibetan cherry, has glossy copper- and brown-colored bark, and is a medium tree that would be appropriate for an orchard-style planting.

**opposite bottom left** Wooden seats under an apple tree rest on a circular stone patio.

**opposite bottom right** Bulbs, such as this slender red and yellow tulip, are perfect for growing in the open shade of an orchard garden.

## DESIGNING YOUR SHADE GARDEN

When working out your design, decide which styles will influence your garden. Things to consider include the style of your house, the size and shape of your garden, your climate, and whether you prefer formal or informal outdoor spaces. Thinking about your design plans ahead of time will help your garden look more cohesive. If you are going to love your newly created shaded garden, it is important that it be designed to suit your needs and preferences.

Design your garden to be inviting by making it easy for people to walk around, see your favorite plants, and find places to sit. The more appealing your space, the more you will relish your time outside.

**below** An enticing stepping stone path leads to a hidden water feature in the personality-filled Yellow Garden at Ladew Topiary Gardens in Monkton, Maryland.

**opposite** This small, painted outbuilding is an attractive and useful focal point in the design of this private garden.

## PATHS WITH A PURPOSE

It is also wise during your planning to think about including pathways through the space. Paths are vital design components that provide access to the garden. There is a magical quality about walking in shade—a sense of exploration. The garden changes and unfolds as you walk among and between the shrubs and trees.

Many woodland gardens have such lush growth that they appear impenetrable from the outside. An easily visible entrance beckons visitors into your space and makes the hidden interior look inviting and accessible. Mark the beginning of the path by framing it with an arch or by flanking it with your favorite trees or shrubs.

Once you enter the shade garden, the path ahead entices you into the space. The addition of a focal point visible from the start tempts visitors to explore further. Traveling the path allows people to fully experience your garden and discover special plantings and other surprises. It is only when you engage with the garden by walking through it that you see its lovely details. Tree trunks and shrubs block sections of the garden from view until you round a corner, providing moments of surprise.

Paths should lead visitors to a seating area, water feature, or other place that you love. Remember that in a shaded garden, the placement of the paths determines the shape and size of your planting beds—all the parts that are not pathways are usually planted up.

A path curves its way around the large root flare of an ancient oak.

An appealing brick pathway delineates the planting beds around a statuesque oak tree at a plantation in South Carolina.

left A path wide enough for two people to stroll side by side curves around boulders and planting beds at the Myriad Botanical Gardens in Oklahoma City, Oklahoma.

The sinuous lines of this beautifully crafted path at the Coastal Maine Botanical Gardens are constructed with textured stone.

above right Natural-looking stones flank the millstone and gravel path at Fuller Gardens in North Hampton, New Hampshire.

In a wooded garden, trees limit where paths can go. Shrubs, small trees, and perennials can be moved, but large trees are set in place and form the basis for the design. Curvilinear paths look natural winding between mature specimens in an informal garden style. Conversely, in a formal layout, paths should be straight and intersect at angles. If you are designing your garden from scratch, lay out your paths first and then configure the beds. Think of the ultimate endpoint for your path before you begin. If possible, make the main paths broad enough for two people to walk side by side. Design enough narrower maintenance paths to allow you easy access to all areas.

Beneath the shade of trees, humid conditions can cause paths to become slippery due to the growth of moss. Therefore, it is important to choose a material that stays safe underfoot. Small-sized grit, gravel, or stone that has a rough surface for grip, all work well.

Fine gravel, used alone or to fill in between stepping stones, makes paths permeable. This allows rainwater to infiltrate into the soil. Woodchips or pine needles look appropriate in a wooded area or an informal setting, but be aware that they may become slick after a rain.

To delineate your paths, edge them with an organic or inorganic material, which also keeps feet out of planting beds. In a formal shade garden, bricks or stones buried in the soil make a clean, neat line. In a woodland setting, logs and branches blend into their surroundings and look natural. Wood edging has the additional benefit of decomposing over time to release nutrients right at the plants' root zone. When logs rot down, add others right on top.

## RAISED BEDS

Raised beds, or berms, add visual interest to your shade garden. They are used to divide one area of the garden from another and provide height in an otherwise flat area. Raised beds also increase the sense of intimacy, which is a hallmark of shade gardens. Adding woody plants on top of the berm muffles sound and helps create sheltering layers that screen secret spaces like sitting areas.

Various areas of my garden are divided up by using low berms and hillocks. I did not want to see my whole shade garden at a glance, so I added mounds of varying heights to my formerly

The delicate flowers of *Anemone nemorosa* are easily visible when raised up on a bank.

above left  A tunnel through a densely planted hill leads to a hidden area at Biddulph Grange. Raised banks are used in this eclectic garden to conceal and then reveal themed garden rooms.

Stepping stones and narrow paths traverse this wide, raised hillock, giving access to the planting beds.

flat landscape. The berms, which have different themes, divide the space into discrete sections. Hellebore Hillock is at its best in spring, and then Maple Hill takes over during summer. Neither of these areas are very large, but even a small raised bed increases the surface area available for planting. An added benefit of planting in raised beds is that many woodland plants are small or have downward-facing flowers, which can be seen up close when elevated. Additionally, fragrant plants are easier to smell if they are raised closer to your nose.

Creating raised beds is a fast way to create ideal woodland soil conditions in a garden. When you make your planting bed, you can control soil composition and add plenty of well-rotted organic matter. Many shade-loving plants thrive in soil that retains moisture, and because the bed is higher than the surrounding ground it also drains well. These beds must be situated away from existing tree roots so as not to suffocate them. The bed can be left to find its natural slope, or be edged with stone or logs. Edging material creates a microclimate for plants that is

# RAIN GARDENS

Rain gardens are designed to catch and slow water runoff from your house or paved areas and to retain it on your property. If you have an area where water puddles up after storm events, make the most of this and turn it into a rain garden. The water in the low area of the rain garden gradually sinks into the ground, reaching tree roots deep in the soil. You can grow moisture-loving plants in this situation, and add a wonderfully diverse new habitat to your shade garden.

Rain gardens may not be shady enough when they are first installed. Include a few woody shrubs like *Cephalanthus*, *Clethra*, *Itea*, and *Ilex verticillata*, as well as trees like *Betula nigra* and *Magnolia virginiana*. Underplant your shrubs and trees with herbaceous plants like *Carex*, hardy *Lobelia*, *Tiarella*, and ferns. Include plants native to your area to encourage wildlife.

Choose plants for your rain garden that thrive with their roots in wet soil, but that will tolerate drying out at other times. Locate wet-tolerant plants at the lowest point of the rain garden and more drought-tolerant ones higher up the banks.

Water-loving plants inhabit a moist spot on the side of a hill at Sezincote House and Garden.

slightly more sheltered, with a cool area for the roots. Each side of your berm will have a different shade pattern, allowing you to grow a wider variety of plants.

If the bed can be accessed from all sides, you will not have to step in it and so the soil will stay aerated. If you make a wide berm, be sure to add stepping stones for easy access. Do not block the flow of water in your garden with a berm, unless you are deliberately damming it to create a rain garden or a boggy planting area.

Another type of raised bed, known by the German term *Hügelkultur* (hill culture), can be made with a pile of logs covered by soil. As the wood rots down under the soil, it releases nutrients and moisture for the plant roots. This method accelerates the natural decomposition that happens in forests. It is an easy way to make a useful planting bed while using up extra logs that you may have in the garden.

## SHADY RETREATS: PLACES FOR PEOPLE

Walking through shade is delightful, but there is such pleasure in sitting out of the sun to enjoy the peace of the garden. Even in a small garden, it is a treat to have a quiet place to sit where you can drink your morning coffee or tea. It gives you the opportunity to admire your favorite plants and watch birds or butterflies.

A seating area in the shade garden is often a secret hideaway. Adding layers of plants for privacy may enhance this feeling of seclusion. Lush greenery muffles sounds and screens external movement. Decide whether you want your seating area to be partially or fully enclosed, keeping in mind that the more sheltered a space is, the shadier it becomes.

If you want to conceal your space from outside view, think about how you can reinforce the boundaries of your shade garden by adding plants or structures to the edges. To make a quick screen, add a trellis or fence and grow *Lonicera* or *Clematis* over it. Trees and shrubs are the longer-term solution. Choose evergreen woody plants like *Taxus* or *Cephalotaxus* to screen seating areas that will be used year-round.

Close to the house there is often an opportunity to make a terrace or patio sheltered by a pergola or arbor. Cover these structures with beautiful shade-producing vines like *Aristolochia* to make a perfect cool spot to sit. If you have established trees, find an open area, or glade, in which to create a gathering place where a small group could sit together. It is a good idea to have a dry surface underfoot, so pave the area with stone or gravel.

When you have created your space, work out where you would like to sit within it. One thing to consider is what you will see when you sit down. Be sure to situate your seats so that they are facing the best view. Selective pruning of branches can reveal sightlines to other spaces. You can create a natural bird blind by making "windows" in shrubbery that look out at a water feature, berried bush, or bird feeder. In my garden, we pruned little holes in a Japanese maple canopy to provide tantalizing views out from a shaded patio. They are not obvious from the outside, so the secret feeling of a hidden space is maintained.

Select seats or benches that are appropriate for your personal garden style. In more formal designs, metal seats or wooden carved benches are good choices. In an informal style of shade garden, consider using rough-hewn benches or log rounds. Include a hammock so that you can relax while looking up into the canopy.

top  This blue bench is sheltered by a brick wall, pergola, and shade-producing vines in the English Walled Garden at the Chicago Botanic Garden in Glencoe, Illinois.

bottom left  An Adirondack-style chair is nestled beside a beech hedge and is the perfect spot to sit with a cup of tea.

bottom center  A fern-patterned bench echoes the arching fronds behind it.

bottom right  At the Royal Horticultural Society Garden Rosemoor, a simple wooden bench is placed to provide a lovely view of the beds and borders beyond.

For a sense of fun in my children's garden, I added whimsical elements, such as this teapot water feature.

opposite A sweet sitting area for tea parties in my woodland garden at Northview.

## AREAS FOR CHILDREN

If you have young family members or visitors, include a specific area for them in your design. Shaded places are perfect for play areas as they are cool and sheltered. Think about the things you enjoyed when you were young, which might give you clues as to what to create. The area does not have to be huge, nor the spaces elaborate.

Many children love to explore secret and mysterious places, such as those hidden behind a shed or shrubs. These play areas need not be costly because you can make use of natural materials. Think about incorporating stable stones or rocks to climb on or a place to dig for worms. These are joys of childhood that will not be forgotten.

I created a space in the shade of mature trees that has been much loved by my own girls called the Fairy Garden. The centerpiece is an apple tree that was given to my eldest daughter. It is a wonderful gift that has grown alongside her. Beneath it is a simple sandbox edged with logs. To decorate it, my middle daughter painted rocks and figurines. Other favorite features for the girls were narrow winding paths for chasing and hiding and a circle of cut logs that was the place where they held teddy bear tea parties.

Many of the plants in this garden are ones that my daughters and I chose together. My youngest had a passion for bright yellow daffodils, so we planted some in autumn as an easy project. When you are designing a play space in your shade garden, encourage your children to participate by including them in the plant selection and design process.

## WATER FEATURES

Water is a beautiful and useful feature to add to a shade garden. It reinforces your chosen design aesthetic, enhances the coolness of the air, and attracts both people and wildlife.

Match the style of the water feature to the formal or informal nature of your shade garden. Formal water features have a defined geometric shape, be that a straight rill, a circular fountain, or a rectangular reflecting pool. In informal gardens, ponds or streams with irregular and naturalistic boundaries are appropriate.

No matter what style you choose, water will increase your enjoyment of the garden by adding pleasing sounds, motion, and reflections. A shaded seat near water is irresistible in the heat of summer. The water feature may be as small as a birdbath, or as large as a pond. Any size will help attract birds and other wildlife to your shaded space.

This symmetrical pool containing a fountain is the centerpiece of the formal Water Lily Garden at Ladew Topiary Gardens.

opposite A dynamic collection of moisture-loving plants surrounds this informal water feature in a private garden in Oxfordshire, England.

A narrow stream is bordered by *Asplenium*, *Alchemilla*, *Brunnera*, and *Hydrangea*, making it a welcome shelter for small creatures.

above right  This stick pile provides a place for beneficial insects to overwinter and divides a wide bed full of *Helleborus* and *Pulmonaria*.

opposite  Shallow running water at the Lady Bird Johnson Wildflower Center in Texas is attractive to birds and other wildlife, especially in the summer heat.

## ATTRACTING WILDLIFE

When planning your shade garden, there are simple and inexpensive ways to make your space ecologically diverse and welcoming to wildlife. Birds, insects, and mammals all need shelter, water, and food, which you can provide in your garden. A shade garden is well suited to wildlife as it has a multitude of plants growing together that provide many different habitats. Trees and shrubs are great places to forage for food, raise young, and provide cover from bad weather.

One way to increase the presence of small mammals, insects, and ground-dwelling birds is to provide them with protected places like log, stick, and stone piles. These piles are also a great design feature, as they can be used to separate sections of your garden. If you do not want to incorporate them into the main part of your design, you can situate them in an out-of-the-way spot. The resulting pile will still be a welcome, sheltering place for wildlife.

A little patch of shaded water becomes a magnet for fauna. Birds and insects such as dragonflies are especially drawn to it. A shady, secluded spot in your garden next to a shrub or small tree is the best location for water, as birds will hop from nearby branches to splash and drink. The water stays cooler and more refreshing in the shade. If you have a stream or waterfall, add

A European robin sits atop a bench in this garden in Devon, England.

a flat rock so that shallow water flows over it. A similar setup in my own garden is especially attractive to bathing birds. Remember that birds and predacious insects are part of your natural pest-control team. It is a smart move to encourage them!

A diversely planted shade garden contains food for wildlife year-round. Many understory shrubs bear berries, seeds, or fruit that are eaten by birds and small mammals. Plants coexist with a range of caterpillars and butterflies, bees, and other insects. Many insects are an important food source for birds, especially in spring when they are feeding their young. In general, it is best to select plants that are native to your area if you want to encourage wildlife.

A standing stump, or snag, is another idea for using existing resources to support local fauna. If a tree dies in your garden, leave a tall stump as both a garden accent and a haven for wildlife. The height of the stump should be determined by safety, aesthetics, and location. The standing stump will shelter insects and provide a hunting ground for woodpeckers and other birds. Over time, it will decompose and feed the soil in your garden. Smaller, hollow stumps can be filled with soil and planted like containers.

# STUMPERIES

Upturned roots have a sculptural quality and are a reminder of the world beneath the shade garden. Tree roots and stumps can be clustered together to make a design feature called a stumpery. This is not something that many people have heard of today, but it was a popular feature with Victorian gardeners, who used them to display their fern collections.

The stumpery in my garden came about fortuitously. During the clearing process, I dug up invasive trees that had gnarled and fascinating root systems. They seemed perfect to add some height and drama to my then undeveloped shade garden. I created a long raised bed and

topped it with the stumps to make a design feature. Then, I interplanted the upended roots and stumps with ferns and other shade-loving plants.

If a tree has been cut down, dig around the base of the stump and see if you can get it out of the ground with some of its roots intact—you may need help. If a tree blows over, the exposed root system may be left where it is. Then, the pockets of soil between the roots can be planted with shade-loving plants to make an unusual garden accent. No stump is too small; a miniature stump with a couple of tiny hostas tucked between its roots would be a great garden vignette.

High banks studded with stumps border the path through the famous stumpery at Biddulph Grange.

# THE PLANT PALETTE

## CHOOSING PLANTS FOR YOUR SHADE GARDEN

The most successful shaded spaces include a rich assembly of plants that coexist together to create a beautiful scene. The shade plants that we grow in our gardens come from shaded areas found all over the world. In their native habitats, understory plants grow together in layers and have adapted to living in the low light conditions beneath taller trees and shrubs.

Smart plant selection is key to a successful shade garden. Take your environmental conditions, physical space, and personal preference into consideration when making your plant choices.

Expanding leaves of *Fagus sylvatica* 'Tricolor', tricolor beech, catch the early morning spring sunlight. Beeches are some of the largest garden trees.

## PLANT LAYERS

A shade garden is typically composed of layers of vegetation. At the top level are the tallest trees, below them are the understory trees and shrubs, and at ground level are the lowest-growing flowering plants, ferns, and mosses. The top layer of tree branches and leaves that shade everything below is called the canopy. The trees that make up the canopy are the tallest and broadest species and the dominant plants in the garden. These large trees are the centerpiece of your garden and a wonderful source of shade and pleasure.

The understory consists of the small trees or shrubs that grow well beneath the biggest trees. The woody understory plants are small enough that you can easily enjoy the sight of their decorative features, such as flowers or fruit. They are planted for many reasons, including their textured and colorful barks, magnificent blossoms, and sheer variety of leaf styles. They are also great for wildlife, make good screens, or are themselves shade producers. In a small garden, where there is not enough space for a traditional canopy tree, the largest species may be an understory woody plant.

At the lowest level in the garden are the herbaceous species, including bulbs, ferns, mosses, groundcovers, and other plants. They receive the least light and less water because they grow beneath several layers of canopy. Plants at the ground level are especially valued for their varied leaf form, color, and texture throughout the growing season.

## UNDERSTANDING AND SUPPORTING NATURAL PROCESSES

Within the layers of a shade garden, there are complex natural processes occurring. The interactions between plants, animals, insects, bacteria, and fungi are all necessary to provide nutrients and resources for your garden. Your garden is part of a larger ecosystem that includes the gardens around you as well as natural areas. Your home garden contributes to the functioning of the region as a whole.

Becoming more aware of the benefits that natural processes confer on your shade garden makes you a better gardener. Planting a diversity of species, especially those native to your local area, supports a wide and varied array of animals and insects, which are needed in your garden as pollinators, soil aerators, and seed-dispersers. By allowing leaves and wood to rot down, you can support beneficial fungi in the soil. A functional garden food web controls pests by natural predation. Anything that disrupts natural interactions, such as the use of chemical sprays, harms the overall health of the food web.

Once you appreciate what is happening in your backyard, you can see why it is important to make planting and maintenance choices that support the food web and nutrient cycles, which in turn sustain the long-term health of your shade garden.

In the Azalea Woods at Winterthur Museum, Garden and Library, canopy trees tower over an understory of azaleas underplanted with *Trillium*.

*Jeffersonia diphylla*, a small-statured North American plant, has pristine white petals that stand out against its unusual two-parted leaf. Wildflowers like this one have intricate interactions with local fauna.

**above right**  At the Mt. Cuba Center in Hockessin, Delaware, drifts of native plants combine to produce a lovely spring picture.

## POWERING THE SHADE GARDEN

The light intensities are low in a shaded space, but the driving energy force for the shaded ecosystem is still the sun's light. Sunlight hits plant leaves and photosynthesis begins. During this chemical reaction, the energy from sunlight is turned into food energy within leaf cells. Plants manufacture energy for the whole ecosystem. Shade-loving plants are efficient energy producers, even in low light conditions. They need some light for photosynthesis, but not as much as sun-loving plants.

Herbivores consume plants, obtaining energy from them. Predators in turn may eat these herbivores, continuing the movement of energy along the food chain. When plants and animals die, they are broken down into simple, chemical parts by decomposers, such as bacteria and fungi. The chemical nutrients given off by decomposers are then recycled into the soil and used by the plants. These processes make up simplified food webs and nutrient cycles that occur continually in your garden.

## NATIVE PLANTS

If you want to encourage wildlife in your shade garden, choose native plants that provide habitat, food, and shelter for pollinators, birds, and other animals. Native plants are those that are indigenous to your region of the world. They typically require less work and fewer resources because they have adapted to grow in your local soil and climate. If you want to incorporate native plants into your shade garden, choose a wide variety of species to increase diversity. This list includes some of my favorite wildlife plants for my garden on the east coast of the United States.

*Aesculus pavia*, red buckeye
*Agastache foeniculum*, anise hyssop
*Amelanchier laevis*, Allegheny serviceberry
*Aquilegia canadensis*, Canadian columbine
*Aronia arbutifolia*, red chokeberry
*Asimina triloba*, pawpaw
*Cephalanthus occidentalis*, buttonbush
*Clethra alnifolia*, summersweet
*Cornus florida*, flowering dogwood
*Ilex opaca*, American holly
*Ilex verticillata*, common winterberry
*Lindera benzoin*, spicebush
*Magnolia virginiana*, sweetbay magnolia
*Penstemon* species, beardtongues
*Podophyllum peltatum*, May apple
*Quercus* species, oak

## ILLUMINATING COMBINATIONS

There are several important design aspects to keep in mind when choosing and combining your shade plants. Although we think of the predominant color of a shade garden as being green, dynamic plant combinations can be created by contrasting texture, size, and form. Additionally, you can play with the wide spectrum of foliage colors, as well as occasional colorful bursts from flowers and berries in order to illuminate your garden.

### PLANT FORM

When you examine a shade garden, one of the most obvious design features is the shape, or form, of the plants. Overall form should be considered when assembling your plant combinations. One of the easiest ways to successfully combine plants is to select those with different forms, such as grouping upright plants with more spreading ones. For example, the flowering spikes of *Digitalis* and *Veratrum* growing up among mounds of *Carex* provide a pleasing contrast in form. In a moist area, *Osmunda cinnamomea* can be planted to rise behind lower-growing *Hosta*.

The rounded form of clipped *Buxus* contrasts with upright *Hosta* and ribbons of burgundy *Heuchera*.

On a larger scale, be aware of form when choosing shade-producing trees. Weeping or spreading trees take up large areas that are often quite densely shaded and must be underplanted with plants that are tolerant of full shade. Columnar and vase-shaped trees allow more light at ground level. If you have enough space, consider planting two or more forms of woody plants near each other for large-scale contrast. I love the horizontally tiered branching form of *Cornus alternifolia* as a partner to the low, mounding shape of *Deutzia gracilis* 'Nikko'.

## LEAVES

When combining shade plants, consider the shape, size, and color of their leaves. Many leaves persist for the duration of the growing season, so the effects of the arrangement will be long lasting.

TEXTURE AND SHAPE When designing a shaded garden bed, use a variety of leaf textures, from fine to bold, to increase visual interest. If all leaves in a planting have approximately the same texture, they are hard to differentiate from each other. Foliage that is said to be fine textured is either highly divided or otherwise delicate in appearance. Bold foliage appears solid and is often large.

Also, think about the contrasting shapes of leaves. Leaves can be, among other things, grasslike, rounded, heart shaped, or lobed. For example, the long, thin, strap-like leaves of *Carex*, *Iris*, or *Hakonechloa* complement the rounded or kidney-shaped leaves of *Asarum* and *Brunnera*.

SIZE Another consideration when pairing foliage plants is the size of the leaves. Many shade garden plants naturally have very large leaves in order to catch as much sunlight as possible. Big, bold leaves serve

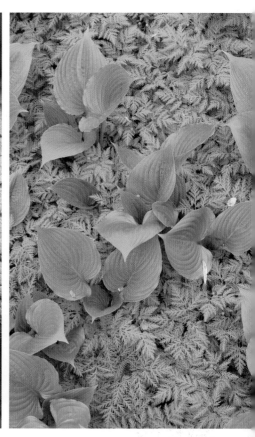

as a foil to smaller, more delicate leaves. The large leaves of plants like *Rodgersia*, *Hosta* 'Sum and Substance', *Astilboides*, or *Petasites* look good when juxtaposed with the smaller leaves of plants such as *Thalictrum*, *Phlox*, and *Polemonium*.

SURFACE The surfaces of shade plant leaves may be matte, shiny, or haired. Matte textures predominate on the forest floor—shade plants like *Aquilegia*, *Asarum canadense*, and *Lamprocapnos* belong in this group.

The glossy leaves of plants like *Asarum europaeum*, *Bergenia*, *Philodendron*, *Arum*, and *Rohdea* reflect light around the garden. Fuzzy-textured *Pulmonaria*, *Brunnera*, and *Saruma* mix well with any other leaf surfaces. Think about varying leaf surfaces when combining your plants, especially in containers where you can observe the details up close.

## FOLIAGE COLOR

During the growing season, plant compositions in the shade garden primarily consist of foliage. There is a procession of flowers during the year, but these are fleeting compared to the leaves. It is important to keep this in mind and choose foliage color combinations that appeal to you.

GREEN The predominant color of shade gardens is green of every sort. The prevalence of green is what gives a shade garden its peaceful and restful qualities. For a soothing and visually calm composition, choose foliage in similar shades of green.

above left  The thin, arching foliage of *Hakonechloa macra* 'Aureola' looks striking paired with the larger leaves of *Alchemilla* and *Hosta* at the Pennsylvania Horticultural Society's Meadowbrook Farm.

above center  The leaf surface of *Brunnera macrophylla* 'Silver Heart' is rough, with short, bristly hairs.

above right  The foliage of *Hosta* and *Adonis amurensis*, Amur adonis, intermingle to make an intense green vignette.

It is also possible to make lively garden compositions using only shades of green. Take advantage of the wide range of greens, from the dark color of evergreen needles to the verdant hues of fresh spring leaves, and pair them together. High contrast between green shades is stimulating and captivates the eye.

One of the brightest green colors is the yellow-green that is especially prevalent in early spring. Look for the chartreuse green of new *Lamprocapnos spectabilis* foliage, especially the cultivar 'Gold Heart', and pair it with dark green *Helleborus* foliage. The lime green leaves of *Acer japonicum* 'Aconitifolium' in summer contrast vibrantly with the glossy deep green leaves of *Hosta* 'Royal Standard'.

Blue-green and blue-gray, glaucous foliage read as a silvery-blue in the shade garden. Hostas such as 'Blue Cadet', 'Blue Mouse Ears', and 'Halcyon' are the primary glaucous plants in the shade garden, but *Fothergilla gardenii* 'Blue Mist' and *Carex flacca* 'Blue Zinger' are also in this color range. Blue-green foliage contrasts strongly with yellow-greens. Keep these colors apart if you like a harmonious color palette or combine them for a bold look.

VARIEGATED While green may be the dominant color in the shade garden, there are plenty of variegated leaves that can be added to brighten up the space. A variegated plant has leaves with markings of white, cream, or yellow on a green background. Sometimes the color white in leaf variegation is referred to as silver, whereas yellow may be called gold. These markings take on a characteristic form of spots, speckles, or streaks. The lighter areas are not able to photosynthesize efficiently, so the plant may be a slower grower than a nonvariegated form.

Variegated plants are a great addition to a shady garden where the long-lasting foliage patterns provide interest during the entire growing season. In fact, variegated plants grow best in bright or part shade because too much sun bleaches and dries out the leaves.

Light-colored foliage variegations are visible from a distance and can be used against a green backdrop to illuminate shaded areas. In my own garden, I find them to be very effective grouped by the color of the variegation. For example, I cluster silver-spotted *Pulmonaria* with silvery *Brunnera* cultivars. Plants with yellow in their leaves are grouped elsewhere. One of my favorite combinations is *Cornus alternifolia* 'Golden Shadows' underplanted with *Hosta* 'Pineapple Upsidedown Cake' and *H.* 'Golden Tiara'.

Some gardeners prefer a shade garden that is predominantly green and rarely use variegated plants. If they do, they carefully surround them with solid green–leaved foliage. In this way, the variegation stands out but does not overwhelm.

REDS, BURGUNDIES, AND PURPLES There is a group of shade plants that have a red, burgundy, or purple aspect to their foliage. Many tropical plants have vivid leaf coloration that may include shades of burgundy, mahogany, red, and purple. Examples include *Begonia*, *Solenostemon*, and *Plectranthus* 'Mona Lavender'. Some plants with leaves that are very deep purple or burgundy may even be described as having black foliage, such as *Colocasia esculenta* 'Black Magic'.

Some hardy plants emerge in spring with reddish foliage, such as *Pieris japonica*, *Osmanthus heterophyllus* 'Goshiki', and *Dryopteris erythrosora*. Others, like *Athyrium niponicum* var. *pictum*, *Heuchera villosa* 'Palace Purple', *Begonia grandis*, and some *Epimedium* plants maintain their red or purple tinges throughout the season. In autumn, many more temperate plants will take on these hues, providing a final, riotous display to close out the growing year.

top Glaucous, blue-gray *Hosta* next to bronze-leaved *Euphorbia*.

bottom left The white variegated foliage of *Athyrium niponicum* var. *pictum* and *Hosta* shine out in the shade.

bottom center Yellow-leaved plants look especially vibrant when grown together, such as this grouping of golden variegated *Cornus alternifolia* and *Hosta*.

bottom right Some leaves emerge in spring with a red tint or burgundy coloration that later disappears. Others, such as this *Epimedium*, retain their russet tones throughout the season.

## FLOWERS

The most persistent elements of your plant design are form and foliage, but flowers contribute seasonal color and scent to the enjoyment of your garden. The primary time for flowers in the shade garden is during spring months, but there are a variety of summer- and fall-blooming plants that should be included in your design to extend the season.

COLOR Flowers are used as accents and temporary focal points. White and other light colors are most effective as they show up best in shaded spaces. These light colors have the best contrast when paired with dark foliage, as with white-flowered *Anemone* ×*hybrida* 'Honorine Jobert' against evergreen foliage or *Galanthus nivalis* against *Ophiopogon planiscapus* 'Nigrescens'.

Shrubs or trees, when in flower, make a huge impact because of their sheer size and number of blooms. A single-flowering *Cercis canadensis* or *Cornus florida* will be the highlight of a spring garden scene. *Rhododendron* species and cultivars are widely used in shade gardens because of the stunning effect of their abundant flowers when they are in bloom. Later in the season, *Hydrangea macrophylla* cultivars add a colorful presence. To have the same sort of impact with smaller herbaceous plants, plant them in large groups or drifts. Provide additional flower color during summer months by using long-blooming annuals and tropical plants such as *Torenia*, *Browallia*, *Sutera*, *Begonia*, *Impatiens*, *Fuchsia*, and *Nicotiana*.

SCENT An important part of my personal shade garden philosophy is to design gardens that can be enjoyed using every one of my senses, including the sense of smell. If you want to include fragrance in the design of your garden, try whenever possible to select plants with scent and site them near to a path or bench so that you and your guests may enjoy them. The flowers of *Hosta* 'Royal Standard', *Chionanthus virginicus*, and *Rhododendron viscosum*, as well as many other deciduous azaleas, are all highly fragrant. Winter-blooming shrubs with fragrance include *Hamamelis* hybrids and *Sarcococca*.

Some of these fragrances, such as that of *Sarcococca*, are elusive, so you have to follow your nose. Other flowers have a much more powerful and recognizable perfume, such as *Philadelphus* or *Convallaria*.

## REPETITION

It is important to have areas of contrast in your garden to make plants stand out from each other, but excessive variety can make a garden look disjointed. The most unified gardens tend to have key plants that are repeated around the space to provide visual harmony.

Beginning shade gardeners tend to err on the side of the buy-one-of-each approach to planting design. I went through that phase myself, and my garden beds had an unattractive, dotty look. It took an older and wiser gardener to point out that my design left something to be desired. She told me that garden beds need the unity that is provided by grouping plants together in clusters.

It is best to group together odd numbers of a plant, in threes or fives, for a cohesive look. With three plants of one kind, you can arrange them together in a variety of triangular patterns that all look natural. Duplicate that same grouping further along the bed for repeated color and form. As the plants grow in and coalesce, they appear to be one clump that has visual weight in the garden.

## FRAGRANT SHADE PLANTS

Fragrant plants add another dimension of sensory delight to the shade garden. If you love fragrance, choose plants that bloom at different times of the year to extend your enjoyment. The enclosed nature of many shady spaces concentrates the scent of flowering plants.

*Calycanthus floridus*, Carolina allspice
*Chionanthus virginicus*, fringe tree
*Clethra alnifolia*, summersweet
*Convallaria majalis*, lily-of-the-valley
*Daphne* species and cultivars, daphne
*Galanthus nivalis*, especially 'S. Arnott', common snowdrop
*Hamamelis ×intermedia* 'Rochester', hybrid witchhazel 'Rochester'
*Hosta* 'Royal Standard', hosta 'Royal Standard'
*Itea virginica*, Virginia sweetspire
*Magnolia ×loebneri* 'Leonard Messel', magnolia 'Leonard Messel'
*Nicotiana sylvestris*, woodland tobacco
*Philadelphus coronarius*, sweet mockorange
*Prunus mume*, Japanese flowering apricot
*Rhododendron viscosum*, swamp azalea
*Sarcococca hookeriana* var. *humilis*, dwarf sweetbox

At the Lakeland Horticultural Society's Holehird Gardens in Cumbria, England, lovely purple *Hydrangea* frames a view across Lake Windermere.

left  Summer-blooming *Rhododendron viscosum*, the swamp azalea, has a sweet scent that travels on the air.

The strong visual impact of *Betula papyrifera*, paper birch, at the Olbrich Botanical Gardens in Madison, Wisconsin, is enhanced by its repetition along a walkway.

**above right** Large groupings of *Eurybia*, *Polygonatum*, *Helleborus*, *Carex*, and ferns form a cohesive late summer planting.

For example, instead of buying many different *Hosta* plants, choose one or two that you really like and repeat them in your beds. Over time, it is easier to have more repetition, as plants that grow well in your garden will naturally multiply. Large clumps of successful plants can be dug up, divided, and moved to new garden areas, thereby linking different sections of your shade garden together.

Creating a successful shade garden takes time. Initial ideas for plant combinations are modified as we learn more about the types of plants we like and what will grow well in our garden. Designing your shade garden is a process that takes patience and inspiration.

# HOW TO USE THE PLANT PALETTE

It is helpful to look at a wide variety of naturally shady areas for inspiration as to the types of plants that may grow in your own garden. The plants that you choose will thrive if the conditions in your garden are similar to their original habitat. This idea goes back to the tried-and-true concept of planting the right plant in the right place. By tailoring your plant selections to your own garden conditions, your plants will be healthier and more beautiful, with less effort.

When choosing plants, the hardiness of the species and its shade and moisture requirements are the first considerations.

Most gardens have a variety of spaces with different shade conditions—full or part; edge, dappled, or bright (and so on). Identify the shade levels in your space before selecting plants. After looking at your shade patterns, examine your garden soil and determine the amount of moisture available in different locations. Then, check the pH of your soil—whether it is acidic, neutral, or alkaline. Match the plants that you choose to the conditions that you have in your garden to give your plants the best chance of success. It is easier to pick plants that will thrive in the soil conditions that you have rather than trying to amend and change your soil. A steadily growing plant situated in conditions that suit it is likely to be healthy and have fewer pest and disease problems.

Some shade plants grow naturally in rocky, mountainous habitats where the soil is dry. Rocky soils are low in nutrients because they have little build-up of leaf litter. If these plants are placed into wet or boggy soils, they rot. Instead, plants from these areas are great choices if you garden in a rocky area or near house foundations where reflected heat warms and dries the soil.

Plants from evergreen or deciduous forests are also good bets for dry areas of your garden under the rain shadow of a tree or under the eaves of the house. If you garden in these situations, choose understory plants from dry woodlands.

For water-logged or otherwise damp spots in your garden, pick plants that come from wet shaded habitats in the wild, like those found naturally in low-lying places such as stream and pond banks, the bottom of valleys, and swamps. The soil in these areas has plentiful moisture and may become waterlogged for part of the year. Plants from such places are specialized to grow in wet conditions and will dessicate if planted in dry soil. These plants are particularly vulnerable to drought.

## HARDINESS

Plant hardiness, or whether a plant is hardy in your growing zone, is the first thing to consider when selecting plants for your space. Plants have a range of temperatures in which they can grow and thrive. An individual plant can only survive between certain upper and lower temperature limits. The hardiness zones that are used in this book come from the United States Department of Agriculture (USDA). To determine your zone, refer to the table at the back of this book or find your specific location on the USDA's zone map.

Some plants, like this tree fern, *Dicksonia*, are only hardy where winters are not harsh. Where they will grow, tree ferns are an impressive addition to the shaded garden, as seen here at Docton Mill Gardens.

opposite The gardens around a house have different aspects and offer opportunities to grow a wide range of shade-loving plants, as seen in this residential Maine garden.

In the garden, most areas are neither consistently wet nor dry, but vary during the year. Fortunately, many shade plants are adaptable, and can grow in a range of soil conditions.

The next decision is to choose plants that are the right size for your garden. Look at the eventual height and width of the plant and choose accordingly. In the plant descriptions included here, I have listed the typical mature size of each plant in a garden setting. When you buy a twig-like tree sapling in a pot, it is hard to remember that it may eventually grow up and tower over your house. Some gardeners control the size of large plants by regularly pruning them. If you choose to go this route, be aware that the plants will require time and effort for yearly maintenance to keep them shaped. For low-maintenance gardening, it is better to match the size and scale of the plants to your space.

It is also important to look at scale when choosing herbaceous plants. Look carefully at the dimensions and match the size of your planting bed to potential plants. A small area looks best with a choice selection of small perennials, whereas larger beds may look better filled with large and medium plants.

The last step in plant selection is to ensure that your choices fit your passions and preferences. Gardeners are opinionated and tend to know what they like. There is no point filling your personal garden with plants that you will simply walk past and ignore. Follow your heart and pick things that excite and inspire you. Plants that you love will motivate you to get outside into your garden more frequently.

## PLANTS FOR MOIST TO WET SOIL

The following shade-loving plants are all adapted to growing in moist to wet soil. Many of them require more moisture if they are planted in positions with insufficient shade.

*Astilboides tabularis*, common astilboides
*Astilbe* species and cultivars, false spiraea
*Cephalanthus occidentalis*, buttonbush
*Chelone* species, turtlehead
*Cornus sericea*, red-twig dogwood
*Filipendula rubra*, queen-of-the-prairie
*Ilex glabra*, inkberry
*Leucojum aestivum*, summer snowflake
*Lobelia siphilitica*, great blue lobelia
*Magnolia virginiana*, sweetbay magnolia
*Matteuccia struthiopteris*, ostrich fern
*Osmunda regalis*, royal fern
*Primula japonica*, candelabra primrose
*Rhododendron viscosum*, swamp azalea
*Rodgersia* species, rodgersia

## PLANTS FOR WELL-DRAINED SOIL

Certain shade-loving plants do better in soils that are well drained, such as those that are naturally found on mountains and hillsides. In a garden setting, these conditions can be found around tree roots, or in dry or rocky soil.

*Agastache foeniculum*, anise hyssop
*Alchemilla mollis*, lady's mantle
*Aspidistra elatior*, cast iron plant
*Aucuba japonica*, spotted laurel
*Brunnera macrophylla*, heartleaf brunnera
*Chasmanthium latifolium*, quaking oat grass
*Cyclamen coum* and *C. hederifolium*, hardy cyclamen
*Epimedium ×versicolor* 'Sulphureum', bishop's hat 'Sulphureum'
*Galanthus nivalis*, common snowdrop
*Geranium macrorrhizum*, bigroot geranium
*Iris domestica*, blackberry lily
*Mahonia aquifolium*, Oregon grape-holly
*Rhus aromatica*, fragrant sumac
*Sabal minor*, dwarf palmetto
*Sedum* species, stonecrop

This private horticulturist's garden has separate, low-lying wet areas and raised, dry areas that suit a wide variety of shade plants.

Developing personal preferences can be hard for beginning shade gardeners, but there are easy steps to take. As you read the plant descriptions, keep track of the species that delight you. Hang out with other gardeners and find out what they like and why. Make notes. Go to local garden centers and chat with their staff. Visit public gardens during every season and take plenty of photographs. These notes and photos will become the beginnings of your wish list. As you learn more, refine your list. Work out which plants will grow well in your conditions, suit your space, and appeal to you.

The low rays of the setting sun illuminate a richly planted spring shade garden.

opposite The blooms of *Galanthus* ×*hybridus* 'Robin Hood' and *Eranthis hyemalis* entice me outside to explore my late winter garden.

# TREES AND SHRUBS

Trees and shrubs are the ultimate shade producers, providing permanent structure and year-round beauty to the garden. These woody plants may be deciduous or evergreen. Deciduous plants lose their leaves in autumn, and evergreens retain their leaves all year. Grow deciduous trees for seasonal shade, varied leaf forms, and fall color. Choose evergreen plants for their consistent shade production and winter presence. Select trees and shrubs based on their suitability for your garden conditions, eventual size, and seasons of interest.

Once you have narrowed down your list based on whether a tree or shrub can grow well in your garden soil, decide what eventual height and width will suit your space. Then, consider the special features of each prospective species. If possible, choose plants that look good in several seasons. Woody plants can have remarkable bark, beautiful flowers, good fall color, or attractive fruit, all of which will add immensely to the enjoyment of your shady space.

Here, I have selected trees and shrubs that will grow well in the understory or in a home garden. These plants are mostly small to medium in stature, or are typically used as hedges.

## LARGE TREES

There are many other wonderful shade-producing trees that are larger in scale and that suit expansive landscapes. These are generally beyond the scope of this book, but they are very worthwhile if you have the room. When planting a large tree, it is best to start with a sapling, or young plant. While the tree is still small, plant around it with the perennials or woody species that you want to make your garden composition. All the plants will grow together, and their roots will find their own spaces in the soil.

*Carya*, *Gleditsia*, *Gymnocladus*, and *Quercus* species are some of the easiest mature trees to plant beneath. These are my favorite canopy trees for a shade garden.

*Acer saccharum*, sugar maple
*Betula nigra*, river birch
*Carya ovata*, shagbark hickory
*Cladrastis kentukea*, American yellowwood
*Fagus grandifolia*, American beech
*Fagus sylvatica*, European beech
*Gleditsia triacanthos* f. *inermis*, thornless honey locust
*Gymnocladus dioica*, Kentucky coffee tree
*Liriodendron tulipifera*, tulip tree
*Nyssa sylvatica*, black tupelo
*Quercus alba*, white oak
*Quercus phellos*, willow oak
*Quercus virginiana*, live oak
*Taxodium distichum*, baldcypress
*Tilia cordata*, littleleaf linden

opposite Woody plants, such as *Liriodendron*, *Ilex*, and *Rhododendron*, provide the framework of many shade gardens, as seen in this spring scene at the Mt. Cuba Center.

*Abelia ×grandiflora*

*Acer palmatum*

## Abelia ×grandiflora | glossy abelia

Edge or part shade | Moist, well-drained soil | Zones 6–9 | 3–10 ft. tall and wide

Plants in the genus *Abelia* are naturally found on hillsides in open woodlands. Flowers are tubular, numerous, and borne on new growth. The plants remain ornamental after flowering. Abelias perform best in humusy, acidic soil.

Abelia ×grandiflora is a vigorous, mounding, semi-evergreen shrub featuring fragrant pinkish-white flowers in midsummer. Its shiny green foliage takes on a bronze hue in fall. Cultivars are available in a variety of leaf colors. Abelias respond well to hedging and shearing, but there are cultivars that are smaller and need little to no pruning.

## Acer | maple

Maples are a group of trees and shrubs that are widely used in gardens and known for their typically excellent autumn coloration. Smaller members of this genus are good specimen trees. Maples have a shallow root system, so underplant them with plants suited for dry shade.

### ▶ Acer griseum | paperbark maple

Edge or part shade | Moist, well-drained soil | Zones 5–8 | 20–30 ft. tall, 15–25 ft. wide

*Acer griseum* is a slow-growing tree suitable for small gardens. It prefers slightly acidic soil and is intolerant of drought. Its three-parted leaves provide dappled shade during the growing season. The trunk of paperbark maple is attractive year-round, but especially in winter, when its exfoliating reddish-brown bark catches the sunlight. I love the pairing of this tree with *Tulipa orphanidea* Whittallii Group, which has a similar bronzy tone to its petals in spring.

### ▶ Acer palmatum | Japanese maple

Edge or part shade | Moist, well-drained soil | Zones 6–8; hardiness varies depending on cultivar
Size depends on cultivar, generally 15–25 ft. tall and wide

Japanese maples are extremely decorative trees that are most ornamental in spring, as their leaves emerge, and in autumn, when their foliage changes color. Even in winter, there is garden interest when their graceful bare branches are covered in snow. They grow best in part shade, which preserves their leaf color, and in moist, acidic soil. If your soil is alkaline, grow them in large containers. There are many cultivars of Japanese maple from which to choose.

I grow several cultivars and enjoy them all. Among the split-leaf maples, I like 'Waterfall' for the especially delicate texture of its leaves and its draping habit. One of my favorites in autumn is 'Hogyoku', which develops pumpkin-colored foliage. In winter, I love 'Sango-kaku', the coral-bark maple, for its brilliantly red-barked young branches. Trim off older branches from this cultivar to promote new red-twigged growth.

*Aesculus parviflora*

## *Aesculus* | buckeye

These deciduous, temperate trees and shrubs have palmate leaves. The flowers are upright and attract pollinators. Many buckeyes produce round, chestnut-like fruit that are inedible to humans but are eaten by wildlife. There are two smaller understory species, which are easily integrated into the shade garden.

### ▶ *Aesculus parviflora*
bottlebrush buckeye, dwarf buckeye

Edge to full shade
Medium to moist, well-drained soil
Zones 4–9 | 8–12 ft. tall, 8–15 ft. wide

The bottlebrush buckeye produces upright panicles of white flowers in midsummer that are butterfly magnets. This southeastern US native is intolerant of dry soil, particularly when young. When given ideal conditions, it will spread to form a large colony. Autumn color is a bright, golden yellow.

### ▶ *Aesculus pavia* | red buckeye

Edge or part shade
Medium to moist, well-drained soil
Zones 4–9 | 12–15 ft. tall and wide

Red buckeyes are native to the southern United States and are a good choice for small gardens. They tolerate clay soils and should have afternoon shade in hot summer climates to prevent their leaves from scorching. In spring, *Aesculus pavia* forms upright panicles of red-orange flowers that attract hummingbirds. I like this plant so much that I have planted three of them in my garden.

## Amelanchier lamarckii | juneberry, snowy mespilis

Edge or part shade | Medium to moist, well-drained soil | Zones 4–8
15–25 ft. tall and wide, sometimes larger

Plants in the genus *Amelanchier* are found in the wild along streambanks and in moist woodlands, where they sucker to form colonies. The different species and cultivars of *Amelanchier* vary in size and habit, and may cross with each other, making identification difficult.

    *Amelanchier lamarckii* is popular in Europe, but other plants in the genus, such as *A. canadensis* and *A. laevis*, are widely grown in North America. No matter which you choose, it will look especially beautiful in spring when its soft leaves emerge and its white, five-petaled flowers cover the plant. By summer, it will produce deep purple-black, edible fruit that can be used to make pies and jams so long as you pick them before the birds eat them. These trees are popular for their delicate appearance and integrate well into a mixed shady border.

*Amelanchier lamarckii*

*Aronia arbutifolia*

**above right** *Aucuba japonica*

*Asimina triloba*

## *Aronia arbutifolia* | red chokeberry

Edge or part shade | Medium well-drained soil is ideal, but it will tolerate boggy areas
Zones 4–9 | 6–10 ft. tall, 3–6 ft. wide

Chokeberries are deciduous shrubs that are native to eastern North America. They are adaptable plants that grow at the edges of wet woodlands in the wild, but are tolerant of both wet and dry soils. They will form colonies by suckering, so site them in naturalistic areas or away from other choice specimens.

*Aronia arbutifolia* is a fabulous shrub for a wildlife garden. In spring it blooms with white or pale pink flowers, which are followed by decorative red fruit in late summer. The red fall color of the leaves is another excellent feature. In habit, red chokeberries can be rather leggy, so surround them with ferns or other mid-height plants to cover their bare stems.

## *Asimina triloba* | pawpaw, custard apple

Edge or part shade | Moist soil | Zones 5–8 | 15–30 ft. tall, 15–20 ft. wide

Plants in the genus *Asimina* are small, deciduous trees that have large, almost tropical-looking leaves. They naturally grow in rich, moist, slightly acidic woodland soils. *Asimina triloba* is an unusual understory tree for a shade garden because of its dramatic foliage. Small, triangular, deep purple spring flowers are followed in late summer by large fruit with a custardy flesh. The fruit is edible and attractive to both humans and animals. For fruit production, it is best to plant several trees together to ensure cross-pollination, or allow the tree to form a grove by colonizing.

## *Aucuba japonica* | spotted laurel, Japanese laurel

Part to full shade | Dry to moist, well-drained soil | Zones 7–10 | 6–10 ft. tall, 5–9 ft. wide

*Aucuba* is a genus of medium shrubs that are ideal in extreme shade garden conditions. They will grow in dry shade and tolerate salty winds or air pollution. If you garden in tough conditions, they are an invaluable addition to the shade garden.

*Aucuba japonica* has shiny, thick leaves that range from dark green to speckled, spotted, or edged with yellow-gold variegation. It will grow in all soils including nutrient-poor and drought-prone but will not tolerate waterlogged soils. If you have a male and a female plant in your garden, the female plant will produce red-orange fruit that ripen in fall and often persist until spring. This is a good evergreen shrub for winter interest, but in cold climates, protect plants from icy, drying winds.

*Betula nigra* at the Ambler Arboretum of Temple University.

### *Betula* | birch

Birches are deciduous trees that often have decorative bark. The smaller birches are a great focal point for a mixed planting. Birches have shallow, fibrous roots, so pull planting beds farther away from their trunks or choose a stoloniferous groundcover. *Betula utilis* var. *jacquemontii*, *B. pendula*, and *B. papyrifera*, the classic white-barked birches, do best in cool climates and look especially dramatic in winter.

▶ **Betula lenta** | sweet birch, cherry birch

Part to full shade | Moist soil
Zones 3–7 | 40–50 ft. tall, 35 ft. wide

Sweet birch is native to eastern North America and prefers sheltered locations in moist, slightly acidic soil. The cherry-like bark is ornamental. Its leaves have a good golden-yellow fall color. The sap of *Betula lenta* was historically used to make wintergreen candy. If you nibble on the twigs, they have the same flavor. Do not prune this tree until after its sap has stopped flowing, typically by late summer.

▶ **Betula nigra** | river birch

Edge or part shade | Medium to wet soil
Zones 4–9 | 40–60 ft. or more tall, 20–40 ft. wide

Young *Betula nigra* trees have shaggy, exfoliating, blushed brown and cream bark that provides year-round interest. They are native to central and eastern North America where they are found naturally along riverbanks. This is the most heat-tolerant birch species and it also tolerates clay soil, air pollution, and deer browse. While the straight species of this tree can grow to impressive heights, many of the cultivars are clump forming and do not grow so tall. I suggest the well-regarded 'Heritage'. For the smaller garden, 'Little King' is ideal as it forms a small tree or large, rounded shrub.

## *Buxus* | box, boxwood

Part to full shade | Medium to moist, well-drained soil
Zones 5–9 | 1–10 ft. tall and wide

Plants in the genus *Buxus* are versatile garden shrubs that have been used for hundreds of years as hedges, edging, and as topiary because they respond well to trimming. Covered in small, glossy leaves, the plants are evergreen and provide winter structure in the landscape. Formal shaded gardens use boxwood to provide a symmetrical framework. Choose boxwood carefully, bearing in mind that some cultivars suffer from pest and disease problems. They tend to be deer resistant.

*Buxus sempervirens* cultivars are the traditional choices for gardens. One cultivar, 'Suffruticosa', which is slow growing, is used extensively as an edging for paths and beds. Many other *Buxus* species and cultivars are worthwhile garden plants, including *B. sempervirens* 'Vardar Valley' and 'Variegata', and *B. microphylla* var. *japonica* 'Winter Gem'. One of my particular favorites is *B. sinica* var. *insularis* 'Justin Brouwers' because it grows to form a domed mound and I rarely have to trim it.

*Buxus sinica* var. *insularis* 'Justin Brouwers' lines a shade garden path.

## *Calycanthus floridus* | Carolina allspice

Edge or part shade | Medium, well-drained soil | Zones 4–9
6–10 ft. tall, 6–12 ft. wide

*Calycanthus* is a small genus of shrubs that are perfect in a naturalistic garden. They are native to North America and bear fragrant late spring or early summer flowers.

The common name for *C. floridus*, Carolina allspice, is due to the spicy scent of its leaves and dark brownish-red flowers. Site it next to a seating area to best enjoy the fragrance. Buy a plant when it is in bloom to see if you like its individual smell. More fragrance is released from the flower when it is picked and warmed in the hand. The star-shaped flowers, when pollinated, make seed capsules that rattle when ripe. It has a suckering habit, but can be pruned to keep a more compact shape. The cultivar 'Athens' has creamy green flowers. The related hybrid 'Hartlage Wine' tends not to sucker and has bold leaves with fantastic, eye-popping fall color. Its flowers last longer than the straight species.

*Calycanthus floridus*

*Camellia japonica* 'Debutante', from the collection at Middleton Place.

**top right** *Cephalanthus occidentalis*

**below** *Carpinus caroliniana* showing fall color and persistent nutlets.

## Camellia japonica | common camellia

Bright or part shade | Medium, well-drained soil | Zones 7–9
Size varies by cultivar; typically 8–15 ft. tall and wide

Camellias are perfect fall-, winter-, or early spring–blooming shrubs for neutral to slightly acidic soil where temperatures are not too cold. Evergreen, tooth-margined, glossy leaves make a good backdrop for stunning flowers. The blooms may be single or double and come in a range of colors from white to pink and red. Camellias are immensely popular in the garden, with hundreds of different cultivars and hybrids. It is important to choose a cultivar that is hardy for your zone. I recommend that you visit a local nursery and buy them in bloom to select a specimen that appeals to you.

Camellia japonica can be used in the garden as an evergreen screen, a focal point, or in mixed plantings. It grows best when protected from cold winter winds, such as under pine trees or near houses. If temperatures fall below freezing, its flowers can turn brown. It may be slow to establish but is long-lived.

## Carpinus caroliniana | American hornbeam, musclewood

Part to full shade | Medium to moist soil | Zones 3–9 | 20–35 ft. tall and wide

Carpinus is a group of deciduous woodland trees found in northern temperate areas. Carpinus caroliniana is an understory tree that is attractive in all seasons. In spring, it has fresh green leaves, which color to yellow or peach in autumn. Clusters of its fruit, called nutlets, develop in fall. A striking winter feature is the sinuous texture of the smooth gray trunk and branches. A related species, C. betulus, is very adaptable and can be trimmed into a tall hedge as seen in some European gardens.

## Cephalanthus occidentalis | buttonbush

Edge or bright shade | Medium to wet soil | Zones 5–10 | 6–10 ft. tall, 8–14 ft. wide

Shrubs of the genus Cephalanthus flourish by water in both tropical and temperate areas. In gardens, they are grown for their spherical fragrant blooms. Cephalanthus occidentalis is a North American native and a great pollinator plant. It has funky, spiky, creamy-white round flowers that cover the shrub in summer. When in bloom, it is always a conversation plant. This wetland shrub is a great choice for a moist, shaded area of the garden.

*Cephalotaxus har-ringtonia* ‘Fastigiata’

**top right** *Chionanthus virginicus*

**below** *Cercis canadensis* ‘Appalachian Red’

## *Cephalotaxus harringtonia* 'Fastigiata'

upright Japanese plum yew

Edge or part shade | Medium soil | Zones 6–9 | 6–10 ft. tall, 3–4 ft. wide

*Cephalotaxus* is a genus of plants with dark green, needlelike leaves that resemble yew (*Taxus*) foliage. Japanese plum yews are not favored by deer, and may be used as a substitute for yews in the landscape.

*Cephalotaxus harringtonia* 'Fastigiata', upright Japanese plum yew, has an erect shape that provides a wonderful contrast to more mounding shrubs in the shaded landscape. Plant it at the back of a border or as the focal point at the end of a path. Other cultivars have different forms, including the low and spreading 'Prostrata' and the dwarf 'Nana'.

## *Cercis canadensis* | eastern redbud

Bright or part shade | Medium soil | Zones 4–9 | 12–20 ft. tall, 15–20 ft. wide

Trees in the genus *Cercis*, known as redbuds or Judas trees, are some of the most unusual-looking trees for the small garden. The flowers grow straight from the bark of the tree in spring before the emergence of the heart-shaped leaves. Their seedpods look pealike, hanging from the branches from summer through winter.

*Cercis canadensis* is an understory woodland tree that is adaptable to a variety of garden conditions. In the landscape, eastern redbuds provide good dappled shade and can be pruned to suit a small space. If I could grow just one small tree, it would either be a redbud or a dogwood—though I would probably cheat and fit them both in. The flowers of the eastern redbud bloom in some of my favorite colors, ranging from pink and purple to white. I grow many cultivars, including 'Appalachian Red', which has brighter reddish-pink flowers than the straight species. An alternative redbud for native gardens in Europe is *C. siliquastrum*.

## *Chionanthus virginicus* | fringe tree, white fringe tree

Edge or part shade | Medium soil | Zones 4–9 | 12–20 ft. tall and wide

*Chionanthus* is a genus of trees and shrubs that are grown for their decorative fringe-like flowers. *Chionanthus virginicus* is a showstopper in late spring due to its profusion of white, pendulous, fragrant blooms. For the remainder of the growing season, the ovate leaves have good substance. The shade underneath a fringe tree is quite dense by summer, so underplant it with early spring bulbs such as *Galanthus*, *Chionodoxa*, and *Scilla* that flower before the leaf canopy emerges. It tolerates clay soils and air pollution. *Chionanthus virginicus* is a small to medium North American tree. *Chionanthus retusus* is a related, slightly larger species.

*Clethra alnifolia*

## *Clethra alnifolia*
summersweet, sweet pepperbush

Edge or part shade  |  Moist soil
Zones 4–9  |  3–8 ft. tall, 4–6 ft. wide

*Clethra* is a genus of shrubs or small trees that grow naturally in woodlands that are swampy or rocky. Plants in this genus may spread by suckers when grown in ideal conditions. In gardens, they are grown for their fragrant flowers.

*Clethra alnifolia* is a great plant for wet areas, including coastal zones. It is a perfect plant for gardeners who appreciate its sweetly scented, upright panicles of white flowers in midsummer. Grow summersweet in fertile, humus-rich, acidic soil, in part shade. It will grow in full shade, but flowers less extensively. *Clethra alnifolia* is native to the east coast of the United States, and west to Texas. 'Ruby Spice' is a garden-worthy pink-flowered cultivar. 'Hummingbird' is a compact and low-growing form.

## *Cornus*  |  dogwood, cornel

This is an extremely varied genus of flowering plants that ranges in size from groundcovers to shrubs and medium-sized trees.

### ▶ *Cornus alternifolia*
pagoda dogwood

Edge or part shade
Moist, well-drained soil  |  Zones 3–7
15–20 ft. tall, 15–35 ft. wide

Pagoda dogwood has characteristic horizontal branches, tiered in arrangement. Creamy white, late spring flowers produce small blue-black fruit in summer. It is native to eastern North America and likes a cool, acidic, moist root zone. I grow a wonderful yellow variegated cultivar called 'Golden Shadows' that pairs well with yellow variegated *Hosta* 'Golden Tiara' and *H.* 'Twilight'.

### ► *Cornus florida* | flowering dogwood

Edge or part shade | Moist, well-drained soil | Zones 4–8
15–30 ft. tall and wide

*Cornus florida*

The flowering dogwood is an iconic small tree for gardens. It has four white bracts surrounding the insignificant fertile flowers. Native to eastern North America, it grows anywhere in moist, acidic soil where summers are not too hot.

*Cornus florida* has reduced in popularity due to disease problems, but if stress is minimized, it is well worth growing. Good air circulation is key for keeping the trees disease free. While there are many cultivars available, I prefer to grow specimens of the straight species that have been raised from seed to maintain genetic diversity. It is best to source locally grown dogwoods for success in your climate.

### ► *Cornus kousa* | Kousa dogwood

Edge or bright shade | Well-drained soil | Zones 5–8 | 20–30 ft. tall and wide

Kousa dogwood has late spring teardrop-shaped bracts that emerge green and become white, surrounding the true flowers. This dogwood is more drought-tolerant than *C. florida*. It has red-pink, edible fruit in autumn resembling lychees and exfoliating bark for winter interest.

### ► *Cornus mas* | Cornelian cherry

Edge or part shade | Moist, well-drained soil | Zones 4–8 | 15–20 ft. tall and wide

*Cornus mas* is grown primarily for its fluffy yellow early spring flowers, which precede tart red edible fruit that are good for jellies and jams. The fruit attracts birds, so add this to a wildlife garden. Cornelian cherry is charming in bloom above small yellow *Narcissus* or *Primula*. I grow the cultivar 'Golden Glory'. The related species *C. officinalis* is very similar; both are excellent garden plants.

### ► *Cornus sericea* | red-twig dogwood, red-osier dogwood

Edge or part shade | Medium to moist, well-drained soil | Zones 2–7 | 6–9 ft. tall, 7–10 ft. wide

The red-twig dogwood is grown for its brightly colored bark, which is most apparent in winter. It is a fast-growing, suckering shrub perfect for a naturalistic waterside, or in a moist area that requires erosion control. It produces clusters of small white flowers in late spring and is native to North America. Once plants are established, removing the oldest wood encourages bright new stems. Cultivars have bark that ranges in color from the bright yellow 'Flaviramea' to the crimson 'Cardinal'. Like all dogwoods, they prefer acidic soil. There are other *Cornus* species and cultivars that are also grown for their colored bark. I like *C. sanguinea* 'Midwinter Fire' and *C. alba* 'Sibirica'.

*Corylopsis spicata*

## *Corylopsis spicata* | spike winterhazel

Edge or part shade | Moist, well-drained soil | Zones 5–8 | 4–8 ft. tall, 5–8 ft. wide

*Corylopsis spicata* is a wonderful deciduous understory shrub for early spring interest. Its hanging chains of fluted flowers are delicately scented and a fresh, pale chartreuse. It blooms at the same time as *Rhododendron mucronulatum* and the combination is stunning. Visit Winterthur Museum, Garden and Library in Delaware to see them together on a large scale. After flowering, its foliage is attractive and remains that way through fall. The cultivar 'Aurea' has golden-yellow leaves.

*Daphne ×transatlantica*
'Jim's Pride'

## *Daphne* ×*transatlantica* | hybrid daphne

Bright or part shade | Moist, well-drained soil | Zones 5–8 | 3–5 ft. tall and wide

The genus *Daphne* contains some very desirable garden plants that are not always easy to grow. They have a reputation among gardeners for being fickle, as a plant may grow happily for a few years and then die without warning. Keep any intervention, such as pruning, to a minimum. Daphnes are primarily grown for their fragrant flowers, which are borne intermittently over a long season.

I grow *D.* ×*transatlantica* 'Jim's Pride' on a partly shaded berm with good drainage. Its white flowers appear sporadically for months starting in mid-spring. This hybrid, along with many other daphnes, should be sheltered from the worst winter winds and provided with neutral to slightly alkaline soil. If you can grow daphnes, plant a variety of different species and cultivars to extend the season of bloom.

Another group of hybrids, *D.* ×*burkwoodii*, has pink or white fragrant flowers that appear in late spring. One of the most popular is 'Carol Mackie', with leaves edged in cream and light pink flowers. *Daphne bholua* 'Jacqueline Postill' is widely grown in the United Kingdom for its scented, soft pink late winter flowers, but it is difficult to find in North America.

*Deutzia gracilis* 'Nikko'

## *Deutzia gracilis* 'Nikko' | slender deutzia 'Nikko'

Dappled or part shade | Moist, well-drained soil | Zones 5–8 | 1–2 ft. tall, 2–4 ft. wide

Deutzias are deciduous plants of scrub and woodland. Mature plants have attractive peeling brown-red bark. *Deutzia gracilis* 'Nikko' is very popular and is an excellent plant for any size of shade garden. It forms a cushion of white blooms in late spring to early summer and it grows well in the shade of larger shrubs and trees. It is often used as a decorative edging to a path or in drifts at the front of a mixed bed. The straight species has the same charming flowering habit on a larger shrub. Other cultivars include pink-blooming specimens as well as some with chartreuse foliage.

## Enkianthus campanulatus
redvein enkianthus

Edge or part shade
Moist, well-drained soil | Zones 5–8
8–12 ft. tall and wide

*Enkianthus* is a genus of deciduous shrubs
or small trees that grow best in acidic soils
in shaded conditions. Redvein enkianthus
is grown for its prolific spring display of
bell-shaped cream flowers, veined with red.
An additional attraction is its dramatic red
fall leaf color. You will only find success with
*Enkianthus* in acidic soil, and I would recommend mulching the plant with pine needles
or oak leaves to maintain pH. If you like
redder flowers, look for cultivar 'Red Bells'.

## Fagus sylvatica
European beech, common beech

Edge or part shade
Well-drained soil | Zones 4–8
50–60 ft. or more tall, 35–45 ft. or more wide

The genus *Fagus* contains many large
deciduous shade trees native to the Northern Hemisphere that are grown for their
beautiful form and smooth grey bark. Their
fruit, known as beechnuts, are a food source
for wildlife.

In the wild, *F. sylvatica* is a large tree, but
in gardens it can be sheared and kept to a
specific height and width. In this way, it is
useful as hedging. When trimmed, it retains
its leaves all winter, providing a screen
year-round. Beech cultivars are numerous.
Choose columnar or dwarf cultivars for use
as specimen plants in a partly shaded bed or
border. Beech is sensitive to soil compaction
due to its shallow roots, so be careful not to
drive heavy machinery over the root zone
and do not disturb its roots when planting
around it.

The russet-brown winter foliage of this *Fagus sylvatica* hedge separates garden
areas at the Royal Horticultural Society Garden Wisley.

*Fothergilla gardenii*

## *Fothergilla gardenii*
dwarf fothergilla

Part shade | Moist, well-drained soil
Zones 5–8 | 3–6 ft. tall and wide

Fothergillas are underused garden shrubs that have seasonal interest in both spring and fall. In spring, before the leaves emerge, the bottlebrush-like creamy white flowers bloom with a sweet scent. Autumn color of the leaves varies from bright reds, yellows, and oranges to deep maroon. Both species in the genus are native to the southeastern United States and grow best in acidic soil.

*Fothergilla gardenii* is suitable for small shade gardens, but can be massed in larger ones. When it is in bloom in late spring, it draws much attention and then it recedes into the background until it produces a final blaze of fall color. The cultivar 'Blue Mist' has eye-catching glaucous, blue-green foliage that does not color up as well in autumn. A larger species, *F. major*, grows in the same conditions but will reach 6–10 ft. tall and nearly as wide. 'Blue Shadow' is a cross between the two species, is intermediate in height, and has blue-green foliage color.

## *Hamamelis* | witchhazel

The genus *Hamamelis* includes deciduous shrubs that occur along streambanks and in the edges and understory of woodlands. They are cold hardy with strap-shaped petals. These plants work equally well as shade providers or as understory plants.

### ▶ *Hamamelis* ×*intermedia*

hybrid witchhazel

Edge or part shade
Moist, well-drained soil  |  Zones 5–8
Size varies by cultivar, generally 10–20 ft. tall and wide

*Hamamelis* ×*intermedia* 'Aurora'

Hybrid witchhazels are some of the most decorative shrubs for the late winter and early spring shade garden. They are sometimes slow to establish, but once well rooted, they require little care, and get better year after year. Flower colors vary from a bright clear yellow, through oranges, to reds. Some cultivars have fragrant blooms that vary in scent from lemony-sweet to fruity-spice. I like to buy witchhazels in bloom so that I can see the color of the flowers and smell their fragrance. As a bonus, some cultivars have good fall color.

If I could choose one witchhazel for early bloom it would be the orange 'Rochester'. For later bloom, it would be 'Aurora', with its sunrise tones. Some of the most common cultivars are 'Jelena' and 'Diane', both of which are fabulous garden plants and originate from the Kalmthout Arboretum in Belgium.

### ▶ *Hamamelis vernalis* | vernal witchhazel, Ozark witchhazel

Edge or part shade  |  Medium to moist soil  |  Zones 4–8  |  6–10 ft. tall, 6–15 ft. wide

This witchhazel has narrow petaled flowers that range in color from yellow to red in late winter or early spring. They provide a lovely surprise when they bloom because they have such a pleasant fragrance. It is native to the south-central United States, and is tolerant of a range of soil types.

### ▶ *Hamamelis virginiana* | American witchhazel

Edge or part shade  |  Medium to moist soil  |  Zones 3–8  |  12–20 ft. tall and wide

*Hamamelis virginiana* is unusual for a witchhazel in that it blooms in fall rather than winter or spring. Its small, bright yellow flowers are semi-hidden among the leaves that are still on the trees when they bloom. The flowers have a light fragrance, but not as much as some of the hybrid witchhazels. It is native to eastern North America. American witchhazel is a great choice for a wild garden where it will thrive as an understory plant. This witchhazel is used to make skincare products.

## Hydrangea | hydrangea

The genus *Hydrangea* contains many garden-worthy plants that are primarily grown for their showy flower heads. In the shade garden, hydrangeas can be used as single plants or massed for greater effect. They are easily grown in containers or planted in rich, moist soil. Prune hydrangeas right after flowering to allow next year's buds to form. Alternately, leave the heads on the shrub to provide winter interest. The old flower heads of *H. quercifolia* and *H. arborescens* can supply food for birds.

▶ *Hydrangea arborescens*
smooth hydrangea

Bright or part shade
Moist, well-drained soil  |  Zones 4–9
3–6 ft. tall and wide

*Hydrangea arborescens* produces white flowers in early to midsummer that fade to green. It is native to the eastern United States and may sucker to form colonies where conditions are ideal. You can prune it in spring because it blooms on new wood. It needs more shade in the southern United States. 'Annabelle' is one of the most popular cultivars, with very large flowers. There are also pink-flowered cultivars available.

*Hydrangea paniculata* 'Tardiva'

### ▶ *Hydrangea macrophylla* | bigleaf hydrangea

Bright or part shade | Moist, well-drained soil | Zones 6–9 | 3–5 ft. tall, 8 ft. wide

Bigleaf hydrangea is a popular shade garden plant. Its showy pink, blue, or purple flowers bloom in mid to late summer. Soil pH affects the flower color of this hydrangea. Acidic soils produce blue flowers, whereas alkaline soils make pink ones. This species is split into two main subgroups: lacecaps have delicate lacy flowers and outer decorative blooms, whereas mopheads, also known as Hortensia hybrids, have rounded flower heads. There is a cross between the two called the Teller Series. There are hundreds of available cultivars, but my favorites are 'Endless Summer', for its ability to flower on both old and new wood, and the old-fashioned lacecap 'Tokyo Delight'.

### ▶ *Hydrangea paniculata* | panicle hydrangea

Bright or part shade | Moist, well-drained soil | Zones 3–8 | 10–20 ft. tall and wide

*Hydrangea paniculata* is one of the most cold-hardy hydrangeas. White summer flowers start small and expand. Panicle hydrangea is a great garden plant, even in urban conditions. It is a large shrub and must either have plenty of room to grow or be regularly pruned. My favorite cultivar is 'Limelight', as it is easy to care for and has prolific blooms that are great for cutting. 'Tardiva' is another popular option. Look out for new, smaller-statured cultivars that are perfect for a little garden or in containers.

### ▶ *Hydrangea quercifolia* | oakleaf hydrangea

Bright or part shade | Moist, well-drained soil | Zones 5–9 | 4–8 ft. tall, 4–8 ft. or more wide

The oakleaf hydrangea is aptly named for its large-lobed leaf that resembles that of a red oak. It is native to the southeastern United States, but will grow in colder areas. Its large, creamy white conical summer flowers become tinged with pink as they age. The potent honey fragrance of the flowers is attractive to pollinators as well as people. In fall, its leaves turn a range of colors from yellow-orange to deep reds and burgundies. Plants may be evergreen or deciduous depending on the microclimate. Its wonderful exfoliating bark and persistent flower heads create winter interest.

My favorite cultivars are 'Snowflake' and 'Snow Queen', both of which have fuller-looking flowers than the straight species. For a different look in the shade garden, try 'Little Honey', which has chartreuse foliage that pairs well with any yellow variegated shade plants.

## Ilex | holly

*Ilex* is a large, versatile genus of deciduous or evergreen trees and shrubs. All hollies need both male and female plants to set fruit. Hollies can be grown as specimen plants or integrated into a woodland setting. The evergreen hollies can be used in gardens to make permanent screens, hedges, and to provide food and shelter for birds and other wildlife.

*Ilex verticillata*

### ▶ *Ilex aquifolium* | English holly

Edge or bright shade
Medium to moist, well-drained soil
Zones 6–9 | 30–50 ft. tall, 12–24 ft. wide

English hollies have decorative glossy, evergreen leaves. This holly is an understory plant, so it grows well in some shade. It is a good urban plant as it tolerates air pollution. Grow it as a specimen tree, or trim it to make hedges or other decorative topiary shapes. On female plants, white flowers in late spring yield red berries by summer. There are attractive cultivars, such as 'Ferox Argentea' with variegated spiny leaves. Remember to wear thick gloves when gardening around these hollies, as their prickly leaves are very sharp, especially when dried. Prune only as needed in late winter or early spring.

### ▶ *Ilex glabra* | inkberry

Edge or part shade | Medium to wet soil | Zones 4–9 | 5–8 ft. or more tall, 8–10 ft. or more wide

This evergreen holly is native to swampy areas in eastern North America. The inkberry is a great shrub for use in a wildlife garden or as a hedge in a more formal setting, because it responds well to pruning. It can get leggy in full shade, so ideally, place it in part shade with moist, acidic soil. Small, deep green leaves shelter its unshowy white flowers, and little black berries. There are new compact cultivars that need little, if any, pruning.

### ▶ *Ilex opaca* | American holly

Bright or part shade | Medium soil | Zones 5–9 | 30–50 ft. tall, 18–40 ft. wide

The American holly grows slowly to become a handsome pyramidal evergreen tree. This holly should be sited out of desiccating winter winds. It has dull, midgreen, spiny leaves. This is a good species for a wildlife garden, as the red berries are a great treat for birds and small mammals. There are many attractive cultivars including some with yellow berries.

▶ *Ilex verticillata* | common winterberry, winterberry holly

Bright or part shade | Medium to wet soil | Zones 3–9 | 3–10 ft. tall and wide

This North American deciduous holly is a medium shrub that suckers to make a colony in a damp or moist site. It is an ideal choice for a naturalistic wet area. Birds love to eat the red berries in autumn and winter. Certain cultivars like 'Winter Red' have berries that are eaten by birds later in the season, so the shrubs remain decorative for longer.

A favorite female cultivar, 'Red Sprite', is a compact plant for smaller gardens. 'Winter Gold' is a full size form with pumpkin-orange berries for a different look. For every six to eight female plants, include one male that you can hide toward the middle of your group. Plant the male cultivars 'Jim Dandy' and 'Southern Gentleman' to ensure a good fruit set of all female cultivars.

## *Itea virginica*
### Virginia sweetspire

Bright or part shade
Medium to wet soil | Zones 5–9
3–5 ft. tall, 3–6 ft. wide

The deciduous Virginia sweetspire is extremely adaptable and will grow in a wide range of soil conditions from fairly dry to wet and swampy. Summer flowers are elongated, white, and fragrant. Found naturally in eastern North America, this plant may sucker to form colonies that make it well suited for erosion control. The leaves turn red in autumn. The cultivar 'Henry's Garnet' has a vibrant red-purple fall color. 'Little Henry' is a more diminutive form.

*Itea virginica* in bloom.

### *Kalmia latifolia* | mountain laurel, America mountain laurel

Bright to full shade | Moist, well-drained soil | Zones 4–8 | 4–8 ft. or more tall and wide

*Kalmia* is a genus of shrubs that thrive in slightly acidic soil. The leaves of the eastern North American native *Kalmia latifolia* are an attractive, dark green. Its decorative white, pink, or dark red flowers appear in late spring or early summer. Ideal conditions for plants in this genus are cool, moist, well-drained acidic soil. In the wild, it can be large, and gorgeous, but in a garden, unless your growing conditions are just right, it is a slow grower.

### *Kerria japonica* | Japanese kerria

Bright to full shade | Well-drained soil | Zones 4–9 | 3–6 ft. tall, 6–9 ft. wide

*Kerria japonica* is an adaptable deciduous shrub that produces golden yellow flowers in spring. The straight species has delicate single flowers, but double-flowered 'Pleniflora' is more commonly grown. The bright green leaves are attractive even when this shrub is not blooming. *Kerria* suckers to form colonies in loose, loamy soil. Site this shrub in more shade for brighter-colored blooms.

### *Leucothoe fontanesiana* | drooping leucothoe

Part to full shade | Medium to moist, well-drained soil | Zones 5–9 | 3–6 ft. tall and wide

Drooping leucothoe is an evergreen shrub that is used in the landscape to provide year-round interest. The green leaves are pointed and glossy, turning a beautiful burgundy in autumn and winter. It produces clusters of slightly fragrant white, bell-shaped flowers that emerge in late spring. Native to the southeastern United States, it is typically found growing on slopes in riparian areas. In gardens, it grows best in sheltered spots with well-drained soils and adequate moisture.

All *Leucothoe* species need moist, acidic soil and form thickets by suckering. Avoid growing them in exposed or drought-prone areas. *Leucothoe axillaris* and *L. racemosa* are similar to *L. fontanesiana* and are also native to the eastern United States. *Leucothoe racemosa* is deciduous or semi-evergreen and produces flowers *en masse* in spring. It is salt and drought tolerant.

### *Lindera benzoin* | spicebush

Bright to full shade | Medium to moist soil | Zones 4–9 | 6–12 ft. tall and wide

Spicebush is so named because of the spicy fragrance that is emitted from its crushed leaves and twigs. Its bright chartreuse-yellow spring flowers are charming up close. *Lindera benzoin* is a great understory plant for a naturalistic wildlife garden. Native to eastern and central North America, male and female plants are needed to set red berries, so plant them in groups. Fall leaf color is a clear yellow. Because of its pungent smell, this plant is not preferred by herbivores such as deer. One butterfly, the spicebush swallowtail, specifically uses it as a caterpillar host plant.

*Kalmia latifolia* f. *myrtifolia* 'Elf'

*Kerria japonica* 'Pleniflora'

*Leucothoe fontanesiana*

The yellow fall leaves of *Lindera benzoin*.

*Magnolia ×loebneri* 'Leonard Messel'

### *Magnolia* | magnolia

*Magnolia* is a fabulous genus of trees that has the added bonus of dramatic, chalice-shaped flowers that range in color from white and cream to pinks and purples. Most of this group bloom in spring, but the southern magnolia and the swamp magnolia bloom in summer. Many magnolias are very large, but are well worth planting if you have the room—try *M. macrophylla* or *M. acuminata*. The species included here are suitably sized for the average home garden.

### ▶ *Magnolia virginiana*  |  sweetbay magnolia, swamp magnolia

Edge or part shade  |  Medium to wet soil  |  Zones 5–9  |  10–35 ft. tall, 10–20 ft. wide

The North American native sweetbay magnolia is a recommended tree for smaller gardens, or as an understory plant. It can take wetter soil conditions than most magnolias and can also tolerate clay soil, salt spray, and air pollution. Leaves are green and shiny above and whitish below, producing a two-tone effect when the wind blows. Its sweetly scented creamy white flowers are borne in late spring or early summer. Place it near a sitting area where the fragrance can be enjoyed. Bright red seeds in autumn are highly desirable to birds.

### ▶ *Magnolia ×loebneri* 'Leonard Messel'  |  magnolia 'Leonard Messel'

Edge or part shade  |  Medium to moist, well-drained soil  |  Zones 5–9
10–20 ft. tall, 10–18 ft. wide

There are many hybrid magnolias that are garden worthy, but one of my favorite early bloomers is *Magnolia ×loebneri* 'Leonard Messel'. I first saw this plant in full, fragrant spring flower at Wakehurst Place in Surrey, England, and it inspired me to plant two in my own garden. It has elongated white petals with a distinct pink-purple blush on the outside. It is similar to its parent species, *M. stellata* and *M. kobus*. All early blooming magnolias should be sheltered from winter weather.

## Mahonia  |  mahonia, grape-holly

Mahonias are evergreen shrubs that are grown for their handsome green foliage. They have scented winter flowers that are followed by showy fruit.

### ▶ *Mahonia aquifolium*  |  Oregon grape-holly

Bright to full shade  |  Medium soil  |  Zones 5–8  |  3–6 ft. tall, 2–5 ft. wide

Native to western North America, Oregon grape-holly is grown for year-round interest in the shade garden. Its spiky leaves are evergreen in milder climates and are sometimes tinged with red and purple in winter. In cold climates, leaves may suffer some winter damage, so plant it in a sheltered area. The fragrant yellow flowers of *Mahonia aquifolium* emerge in the late winter or early spring. The fruit that develop resemble bunches of grapes.

### ▶ *Mahonia bealei*  |  leatherleaf mahonia

Bright to full shade  |  Medium soil  |  Zones 6–9  |  3–6 ft. tall and wide

*Mahonia bealei* has stiff, divided, sharply toothed leaves and upright spikes of yellow, honey-scented flowers in late winter. Clusters of blue fruit follow the flowers. The leatherleaf mahonia can be used to make an informal hedge. In the southern United States, this plant is considered to be potentially invasive.

*Mahonia aquifolium*

*Microbiota decussata*

**right** *Osmanthus heterophyllus* 'Goshiki'

## *Microbiota decussata* | Russian arborvitae

Edge or part shade | Moist, well-drained soil | Zones 3–8 | 2 ft. tall, 10 ft. wide

*Microbiota* is a short, spreading evergreen and one of the few conifers that can grow well in part shade. This very hardy, low-growing shrub is excellent as a low-maintenance ground-cover. Situate this plant on a bank so that its branches can cascade downhill. Give each specimen plenty of room to grow, because as they mature they develop a wide spread. In winter, the color of the plant turns from green to bronzy purple.

## *Osmanthus heterophyllus* | holly osmanthus, holly tea olive

Edge or part shade | Moist, well-drained soil | Zones 7–9 | 8–10 ft. tall, 6–8 ft. wide

*Osmanthus* is a genus of evergreen shrubs that grows in woodlands and can be used to add structure to the shade garden. The holly osmanthus is an attractive plant year-round that can be used as a screen or as a backdrop for perennials. The shiny, spiny evergreen leaves look good in every season. Choose the variegated green-and-gold-leaved cultivar 'Goshiki' for some additional color interest. Its new growth has the added bonus of emerging with a pinkish tinge. I grow 'Goshiki' as well as 'Gulftide', an excellent deep green cultivar. In warmer climates, grow *O. fragrans*, the sweet osmanthus. It has deep green, shiny evergreen leaves, and flowers that can scent a whole garden.

# *Philadelphus* ×*virginalis*

sweet mockorange

Edge or part shade
Well-drained soil   |   Zones 4–8
8–10 ft. tall and wide

Mockoranges are grown for their fantastic scented orange blossom flowers. A midsummer treat, I love my mockoranges in the handful of weeks when they are in bloom. *Philadelphus* should be sited near a bench or a path to allow easy access to the source of the aroma that wafts on the air. They are especially fragrant in the evening. I grow the semi-double-flowered *P.* ×*virginalis* 'Minnesota Snowflake', which has great winter hardiness. I also grow *P. coronarius*, a taller shrub with single flowers and an excellent scent. Buy mockoranges in bloom to make sure the one you select is fragrant.

To keep your plants from sprawling, prune these somewhat gangly shrubs right after flowering. Remove the oldest branches to the ground or cut back the longest branches by a third. When these plants are not in bloom, they will be passed by, unnoticed, as they have few other redeeming features.

*Philadelphus* ×*virginalis* 'Minnesota Snowflake'

*Pieris japonica*

*Prunus mume* 'Fragrant Snow'

### *Pieris japonica* | Japanese pieris

Bright or part shade | Moist, well-drained soil | Zones 5–8 | 9–12 ft. tall, 6–8 ft. wide

Japanese pieris is grown for its glossy, evergreen leaves and its white, early spring, bell-shaped, honey-scented clusters of flowers. It is a beloved plant for woodland gardens where soil is rich, moist, and acidic. *Pieris* is a good companion to *Rhododendron* and *Kalmia*. In spring, there is often a pinkish tinge to the new leaves as they emerge, particularly in cultivars such as 'Mountain Fire'. There are also pink-flowered cultivars such as the excellent 'Dorothy Wyckoff'. *Pieris floribunda* is less showy, and is native to North America.

### *Prunus* | prunus

*Prunus* is a diverse group of garden plants including many of the stone fruits—cherries, plums, peaches, apricots, and almonds. Within this genus are a number of great understory shade garden plants.

## ▶ *Prunus laurocerasus* | cherry laurel

Edge to full shade | Moist, well-drained soil | Zones 6–9
Size varies by cultivar; may be 10–18 ft. or more tall, 20 ft. or more wide

Unlikely as it seems, the evergreen cherry laurel falls into the genus *Prunus*. It is extensively used for barriers or hedges around gardens because it can be trimmed to a particular height and will grow in all shade levels. If your climate is mild, cherry laurels are an economical way to make a screen. *Prunus laurocerasus* is a tough plant that will tolerate alkaline soils. Do not use it in areas with harsh winters as the leaves turn brown and drop. In western North America, this plant may be a problem as it escapes from gardens into natural areas. Buy cultivars according to their habit so pruning will be minimal. 'Otto Luyken' stays shorter than the species.

## ▶ *Prunus mume* | Japanese flowering apricot

Part shade | Well-drained soil | Zones 6–9 | 15–30 ft. tall and wide

*Prunus mume* is one of the earliest trees to bloom in the spring garden. It flowers at the same time as many small spring bulbs and makes an appealing companion to them. Cultivars range in flower color from white to deep pink. I pair reddish-pink-flowered 'Kobai' with bright blue *Scilla*. I also love the white-blooming 'Fragrant Snow', which has a pleasant marzipan-like scent. These and other cultivars of *P. mume* are good choices for a small garden and can be pruned to suit your space. Many cultivars of this flowering apricot originate in China and Japan, where it has been grown for hundreds of years.

## *Rhododendron* | rhododendron, azalea

*Rhododendron* is a huge genus of popular shade garden plants that contains all rhododendrons and azaleas. There are both evergreen and deciduous shrubs that bear flowers in almost every color. Plants in this group grow best in well-aerated, slightly acidic soil that is enriched with plenty of organic matter. Be sure to mulch the root zone each year. A good way to tell a rhododendron from an azalea is that rhododendrons typically have ten anthers and azaleas have five.

In temperate areas, bloom occurs primarily in spring or early summer. Look for reblooming cultivars for use in warmer climates. With so many species and hybrids to choose from, it is best to buy plants in bloom to select for flower color and fragrance. Also consider the hardiness and ultimate size. Visit local arboreta and public gardens to find rhododendrons that are suited to your region.

In addition to those described here, I especially like *R. mucronulatum*, which blooms very early in spring, *R. yakushimanum*, which has thick indumentum on the underside of its leaves, *R. luteum*, for its scented yellow flowers, *R. vaseyi*, with its fragrant flowers, and the standout floriferous performance of *R. catawbiense*.

*Rhododendron* 'Silver Slipper' at the Royal Horticultural Society Garden Wisley.

▶ *Rhododendron maximum*
rosebay rhododendron

Part shade | Moist, well-drained soil
Zones 3–7
4–15 ft. tall and 4–15 ft. wide; larger in the wild

Rosebay rhododendrons have pinkish-white flowers in early summer at a point when not much else is blooming in the shade garden. *Rhododendron maximum* is one of the largest rhododendrons and has evergreen leaves that can provide a good screen. They are native to eastern North America and thrive in cool, moist, well-drained soils.

▶ *Rhododendron periclymenoides*
pinxterbloom azalea

Bright or part shade
Well-drained soil | Zones 4–8
4–12 ft. tall, 4–6 ft. wide

*Rhododendron periclymenoides* is a deciduous azalea that has fragrant flowers in shades of pink that are delightful in spring. I like to underplant mine with pink-leaved *Heuchera* or pink-blooming *Tiarella* to echo the flower color. After flowering, the pinxterbloom azaleas' small green leaves serve as a backdrop to later-blooming plants. It is native to eastern North America. In the garden, I combine pinxterblooms with other native deciduous azaleas, such as the more wet soil–tolerant *R. viscosum* and *R. atlanticum*. Planting a variety of azaleas extends the period of bloom.

## Rhus | sumac

This genus has some larger plants that can provide shade and some lower-growing understory woody plants. They often have good fall color and are great for stabilizing hillsides because they may form massive stands.

### ▶ *Rhus aromatica* 'Gro-Low'
fragrant sumac 'Gro-Low'

Bright or part shade
Dry to medium, well-drained soil
Zones 3–9 | 2–3 ft. tall, 5–8 ft. wide

*Rhus aromatica* 'Gro-Low' is a short plant perfect for erosion control or covering a sloping bank. Its prostrate stems root as they touch the ground. This tough, pollution-tolerant plant is resistant to rabbits and will grow in dry, rocky soil. The straight species is a taller, more upright plant.

### ▶ *Rhus typhina* 'Tiger Eyes'
staghorn sumac 'Tiger Eyes'

Edge or part shade
Dry to medium, well-drained soil
Zones 4–8 | 6 ft. or more tall, 6 ft. wide

Staghorn sumac is a tough North American plant for inhospitable areas of the shade garden. It grows from underground suckers, so plant it where it can spread. *Rhus typhina* is decorative in fall with blazing autumnal color. 'Tiger Eyes' has chartreuse foliage and a persistent reddish fruit spike.

*Rhus aromatica* 'Gro-Low' at the Myriad Botanical Gardens in Oklahoma City, Oklahoma.

*Ruscus aculeatus*

*Sarcococca hookeriana* var. *humilis*

*Taxus* ×*media*

## *Ruscus aculeatus* | butcher's broom, box holly

Bright to full shade | Well-drained soil | Zones 7–10 | 1–3 ft. tall and wide

Butcher's broom is a stiff evergreen subshrub that has small red berries tucked among its foliage on female plants if male plants are present. *Ruscus aculeatus* is a good choice to add a lower-growing but more structural presence to a partially or fully shaded area, even in dry soil. This plant grows from underground rhizomes in anything but soggy soil. The foliage is a great cut green for flower arrangements. Its common name is said to derive from its use by butchers to clean their shops.

## *Sarcococca hookeriana* var. *humilis*

dwarf sweetbox, Himalayan sarcococca

Part to full shade | Medium to moist, well-drained soil | Zones 6–9
1–2 ft. tall, 1–2 ft. or more wide

*Sarcococca* is a genus of low-growing, shrubby, woody plants that are a superb addition to a shady area because of their evergreen foliage and fragrant winter flowers. Although the scent travels on the slightest breeze, grow them near to a path to allow easy access.

*Sarcococca hookeriana* var. *humilis* has fragrant pink-tinged white late winter flowers. It grows very slowly to form colonies. It can be used as a groundcover under trees in full shade and will even tolerate drought and some pollution once established. There are other worth-while species in this genus, which have similar growing requirements. I grow *S. confusa*, *S. ruscifolia*, and *S. orientalis* and enjoy them all.

## *Taxus* ×*media* | hybrid yew

Bright to full shade | Moist, well-drained soil | Zones 4–8
10–20 ft. tall and wide; size varies by cultivar

Yews have been grown in gardens for hundreds of years. They are extremely versatile plants for adding structure, screening, hedging, or topiary to a shaded landscape. Yew bushes respond well to pruning and have the added benefit of being able to sprout new shoots from old wood. Do not grow yew near farm animals like cattle, as it is toxic to them. However, the toxicity does not affect deer and they will eat what they can reach, decimating the plants.

*Taxus* ×*media* is an important evergreen garden plant because it can provide shade but can also grow in the shade of other plants. It is wonderful when used as a hedge. These plants must be grown in well-drained soil, preferably a sandy acidic loam. Cultivars vary wildly in size and form, so choose one that is appropriate to your needs. For example, in a small, narrow space pick a columnar form or a dwarf variety. A common cultivar, *T.* ×*media* 'Hicksii', is a fairly upright plant.

# Viburnum | viburnum

This group of deciduous or evergreen flowering shrubs is used in gardens for screening and structure. Many viburnums grow best in dappled or part shade. They can grow in a wide range of soil conditions but thrive in moist, well-drained soil. Their flowers may be showy and many species have decorative fruit.

## ▶ Viburnum nudum | smooth witherod

Edge or part shade | Medium to wet, well-drained soil | Zones 4–9 | 5–12 ft. tall and wide

Smooth witherod has glossy leaves and white flowers in late spring to early summer, which are followed by berries that change in color from light pink to blue, and finally black. *Viburnum nudum* is native to eastern North America and will grow in boggy soils. The cultivar 'Winterthur' is improved with a heavier fruit set, redder fall leaves, and a shorter stature.

## ▶ Viburnum plicatum f. tomentosum | doublefile viburnum

Edge or part shade | Moist, well-drained soil | Zones 5–8 | 8–12 ft. tall and wide

Doublefile viburnum has profuse nonfragrant white, lacy blooms in late spring. Its double rows of flowers are highly decorative in the landscape. In late summer, small red fruit follow the flowers. In fall, the leaves change to a wonderful deep ruby color. For optimum growth, *Viburnum plicatum* f. *tomentosum* requires well-drained, humusy soil.

## ▶ Viburnum rhytidophyllum | leatherleaf viburnum

Edge or part shade | Well-drained soil | Zones 5–7 | 10–15 ft. tall and wide

*Viburnum rhytidophyllum* can be used as a screen beneath trees. If you cannot grow rhododendrons, try this plant instead, as it looks similar in the landscape. Its creamy white flowers bloom in spring, but they are not showy. Leatherleaf viburnum has leaves that are deeply veined on the upper side and have a wooly, lighter-colored underside. The leatherleaf viburnum is evergreen in most of its range, reliably so in warmer climates. It is hardier in well-drained soil.

## ▶ Viburnum tinus | laurustinus

Edge or part shade | Medium, well-drained soil | Zones 8–10 | 6–10 ft. tall, 6–8 ft. wide

The evergreen *Viburnum tinus* blooms in winter with flat-topped white or light pink flowers. It can withstand salty air and is a great garden plant where it is hardy. Laurustinus is quite shade-tolerant and grows well beneath live oaks in the southern United States. In English gardens, it is often used as an informal hedge.

*Viburnum plicatum* f. *tomentosum*

# VINES

Vines make shade, form screens for privacy, and add textural interest to the shade garden. Some vines use tendrils to climb over structures, and others stick themselves to vertical surfaces, aiding their upward growth. They are fast growing and sometimes invasive plants. Some can be planted to scramble up through trees and shrubs, adding another season of interest to the supporting plant.

Vine-covered structures are a quick way to produce shade. When choosing vines to use in your garden, match the eventual size of the plant to the space available. Also consider the weight of the vine when fully grown. The mature mass of some species is so great that they should only be sited on durable structures. Delicate climbers are suited for smaller spaces and require less-robust supports. They provide good foliage quality, and often cover themselves with flowers. All vines form strong backdrops in the garden, enhancing the vertical plane.

There are other, rampantly invasive vines not described in this book that can be a major destructive force in shaded ecosystems. Examples include Chinese wisteria, bittersweet, five-leaved akebia, mile-a-minute vine, porcelain berry, silver lace vine, and kudzu. Responsible gardeners should remove these plants as soon as possible; if they escape from gardens, they will overwhelm and destroy natural areas. For gardeners in North America, the skin-irritating oils of poison ivy and poison oak vines may be a major headache, but they are actually native plants. Regardless, you may want to carefully remove them, especially in gardens used by children or pets.

Flowering vines, like *Clematis* 'Comtesse de Bouchaud', can be grown through shrubs or up a wall with supports.

## Aristolochia macrophylla

Dutchman's pipe

Bright or part shade | Moist, well-drained soil
Zones 5–8 | 20–30 ft. tall, 6–10 ft. wide

*Aristolochia macrophylla* is a southeast North American native woody vine with very large, heart-shaped leaves. It is effective at providing shade when grown over an arbor or trellis. Its unusual flowers are pipe-shaped and mottled brown with a distinct odor. This plant can be attractive in a large container with a support. There are tropical *Aristolochia* species that have showier flowers.

## Clematis 'Betty Corning'

clematis 'Betty Corning'

Bright or part shade | Moist, well-drained soil
Zones 4–9 | 5–10 ft. tall, 3–6 ft. wide

*Clematis* is a genus of beautiful flowering garden plants that will grow in bright or partial shade. These plants take up little space because they grow up and through other plants and structures. Plant clematis with their crowns slightly below the soil and add a stone on top to keep the roots cool. This procedure will allow the plants to grow strongly and resist clematis wilt.

My favorite small-flowering cultivar is 'Betty Corning', which has light purple flowers that dangle from the vine. I like to grow this cultivar scrambling over a partly shaded fence. This and other clematis can be planted at the base of a tree or shrub and encouraged to grow up through the branches. Some other worthwhile species and cultivars are *C. glaucophylla*, *C. paniculata*, *C. viorna*, *C.* 'Comtesse de Bouchaud', *C.* 'Jackmanii', *C.* 'Nelly Moser', *C.* 'Rooguchi', and *C.* 'Silver Moon'.

*Aristolochia macrophylla* at Bartram's Garden in Philadelphia, Pennsylvania.

*Clematis* 'Betty Corning'

*Euonymus fortunei* 'Emerald Gaiety'

*Hedera helix* flowers and leaves.

## Euonymus fortunei
wintercreeper

Bright to full shade | Medium soil | Zones 5–9
2 ft. tall and indefinitely wide as a groundcover;
15 ft. or more tall as a climbing vine

*Euonymus fortunei* cultivars are tough and will grow in almost any shady conditions. They cling to surfaces, creeping along the ground and growing up trees and over walls. Their vigorous growth is welcome where little else will survive. In favorable conditions, however, their growth will be too aggressive, so check their invasive status in your region before you plant them. I have seen wintercreeper in urban plazas performing well under stressful conditions. This is an appropriate situation for these plants.

*Euonymus fortunei* 'Emerald Gaiety' has white-margined leaves that can take on a pink cast in cold weather. 'Silver Queen' is a related cultivar, but its growth habit is shrubbier. They are both used in shade gardens where their variegated leaves brighten up deep shade.

## Hedera helix
common ivy, English ivy

Bright to full shade | Medium soil | Zones 4–9
15–80 ft. or more tall and wide

*Hedera helix* is a vigorous, sometimes invasive vine grown for its shiny, evergreen leaves. It will grow along the soil as a dense, smothering groundcover, and climb trees and walls by clinging to them. Only plant this species where a tough plant is required, and be prepared to control its growth.

There are hundreds of cultivars with different leaf shapes and variegations that are less aggressive than the straight species, but beware that they may revert. Some of these are useful as potted plants for a shaded terrace. In their adult form, they are shrub-like and are sold as shrub ivy. In its native Europe, it is a great wildlife plant, but use caution if you garden in other areas of the world.

## Hydrangea anomala subsp. petiolaris | climbing hydrangea

Bright or part shade | Moist, well-drained soil | Zones 4–7 | 36–80 ft. tall

Most hydrangeas are shrubs, but this species is a deciduous clinging woody vine. The climbing hydrangea is used in the shade garden to grow up tree trunks or to cover sturdy structures such as stone walls. It grows upward by clinging with aerial roots and can become quite tall. However, it can also be trimmed to suit a smaller garden. It has attractive, broad, green leaves and white summer flowers. The stem has exfoliating bark that gives winter interest. The climbing hydrangea grows best in afternoon shade in acidic to neutral soil that is well drained but moist.

The climbing hydrangea can be easily confused with the similar-looking Japanese hydrangea vine, *Schizophragma hydrangeoides*. It grows in the same way as the climbing hydrangea, and may be substituted for it in the shade garden. There are numerous cultivars of both, some with variegated leaves and others with larger and more dramatic flowers.

## Lonicera sempervirens | trumpet honeysuckle

Bright or part shade | Moist, well-drained soil | Zones 4–9
8–15 ft. tall, 3–6 ft. wide

Plants in the genus *Lonicera* have tubular flowers that are great for pollinators such as bees or hummingbirds. Some species proliferate too readily and may be invasive, so choose plants that are native to your area.

*Lonicera sempervirens* is native to central and eastern North America. Its nonfragrant red or yellow flowers are produced over a long season, with the best flush in spring. I grow them over an arch as this vine does need the support of a fence or other garden structure. Prune it after it flowers to maintain its size. Suggested cultivars include the yellow-flowered 'John Clayton' and the striking red 'Major Wheeler' and 'Alabama Crimson'.

The flowers of *L. periclymenum* have the classic honeysuckle scent. Different cultivars bloom in a range of colors including pinks, reds, whites, and yellows. This plant is native to Europe.

*Lonicera sempervirens* 'Alabama Crimson'

## Parthenocissus quinquefolia
### Virginia creeper

Bright to full shade | Average soil | Zones 4–9 | 30–50 ft. tall or more

*Parthenocissus quinquefolia* is a deciduous woody climber that grows by tendrils and sticks to walls using adhesive pads. It is grown for its leafy coverage and brilliant fall color. This vigorous vine will climb up into trees, over pergolas, fences, stumps, and rocks. It is a great choice to cover unsightly structures for summer. In autumn, its palmately divided leaves turn bright red and are very decorative. It is native to eastern North America. A closely related species, *P. tricuspidata*, known as Japanese creeper or Boston ivy, has three-lobed leaves. Both plants have cultivars that are varied in color and leaf size.

*Parthenocissus quinquefolia*

## *Passiflora caerulea*
blue passionflower

Bright or part shade
Medium to well-drained soil
Zones 6–9 | 10–25 ft. tall or more

*Passiflora caerulea* is grown for its distinctive summer flowers. This vine looks great growing through a loose shrub or a garden structure where it can clamber up using its curling tendrils. It does best in warm climates, but will regrow from its roots if the top growth is killed by cold winter weather. *Passiflora incarnata*, the maypop, has a similar flower and is native to eastern North America. There are many tropical passionflowers with a similar flower structure but different coloration, such as the purple *P. ×violacea* and the brilliant red *P. racemosa*.

*Passiflora caerulea*

# FERNS

Ferns are naturally adapted to wooded areas and are perfect understory plants in the shade garden. They are a staple of shaded spaces around the world and look at home in most garden styles. Their attractive leaflike fronds are often dissected and feathery in texture, and look fresh throughout the growing season. Delicately textured ferns are often planted in combination with the undivided leaves of other herbaceous plants for contrast.

Ferns have no flowers or seeds; they reproduce from spores. Most ferns carry their spores on the back of their fronds in structures called sori, but a few hold their spores in separate fertile fronds. The sori and the fertile fronds are often ornamental features. Ferns may also spread by underground rhizomes to make new plants.

Some species are reliably evergreen, but many of them die down for the winter and grow new fronds in spring that emerge as fiddleheads. The fiddleheads are a true early season delight as they unfurl.

When choosing ferns for your garden, look at their shade requirements and also the amount of soil moisture that they need. Most ferns thrive in moist to wet conditions, but there are some that will grow in dry shade once they are established.

Some ferns, such as *Polypodium interjectum*, intermediate polypody, have noteworthy sori.

## Adiantum | maidenhair fern

The delicate-looking green fronds of maidenhair ferns are attached to wiry black stalks known as stipes. These plants make lacy, elegant mounds that contrast well with larger-leaved plants.

### ▶ *Adiantum capillus-veneris*
southern maidenhair fern

Bright or part shade
Medium to moist | Zones 7–11
8–18 in. tall and wide

In the wild, this species may be found in cracks in limestone, so give it slightly alkaline soil in the garden. Soft, divided fronds make a graceful patch outdoors where it is warm. Elsewhere, grow it as a houseplant and take it outside to the shady garden in summer.

### ▶ *Adiantum pedatum*
northern maidenhair fern,
five-fingered fern

Bright or part shade
Medium to moist soil | Zones 3–8
12–20 in. tall, 12–18 in. wide

The upright, wiry black stipes of the northern maidenhair fern carry flat, horseshoe-shaped tops. The bright green fronds radiate outward and have a fine texture that pairs well with larger and bolder foliage such as that of *Mukdenia* or *Rodgersia*. Plant it densely in humus-rich, slightly acidic soil for a beautiful groundcover.

*Adiantum pedatum*

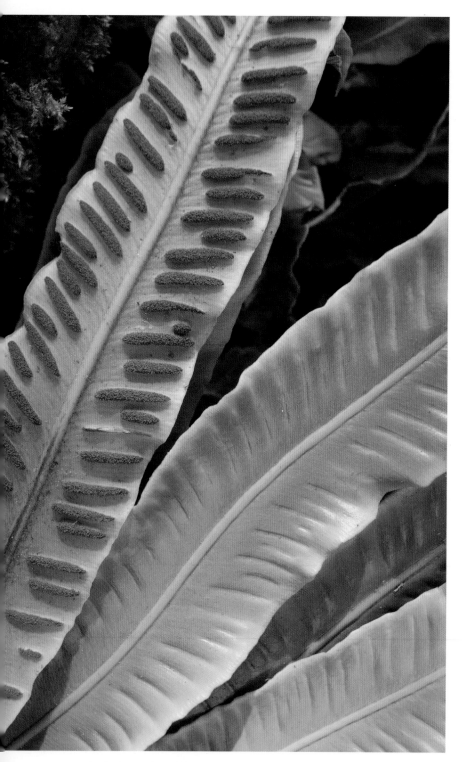

Asplenium scolopendrium

## *Asplenium scolopendrium*
### hart's tongue fern

Part to full shade
Moist, well-drained soil   |   Zones 6–8
12–24 in. tall, 24 in. wide

Unlike other ferns, a frond of *Asplenium scolopendrium* is not divided but, true to its common name, resembles a pointed tongue. The spores are in lines on the backs of the bright green fronds. Hart's tongue fern was my favorite fern when I was growing up in England, where it grew in the hedgerows on shaded banks. Grow it in neutral to alkaline soil on a slope and add some primroses and bluebells for a perfect vignette. For a different look, choose cultivars with ruffled edges such as *A. scolopendrium* 'Angustatum'. *Asplenium nidus*, bird's-nest fern, is a popular tender houseplant that can be brought outside in summer.

## *Athyrium* | athyrium

The genus *Athyrium* consists of a wide variety of cold-hardy, deciduous ferns. They grow well in moist, acidic to neutral garden soil with very little care. The initial plant spreads slowly to make a low rounded clump and gently jumps around the shade garden when conditions are suitable. Site these ferns away from path edges, as their fronds snap easily.

### ▶ *Athyrium filix-femina*
lady fern

Part to full shade | Moist soil
Zones 3–8 | 24–36 in. tall, 24 in. wide

*Athyrium filix-femina* appears delicate, but is a tough garden plant that thrives with some moisture and humus in acidic to neutral soil. Throughout the growing season it sends up new fronds so it continues to look fresh. The species is a light green but there is a popular cultivar with reddish stipes known as 'Lady in Red'.

### ▶ *Athyrium niponicum* var. *pictum*
Japanese painted fern

Part to full shade | Moist soil
Zones 4–8 | 12–24 in. tall, 24 wide

Japanese painted fern has an unusual silvery color with threads of red. To retain the best frond color, plant it where it will receive soft morning light. Combine it with plants that pick up the dark mahoganies and burgundies in the frond, such as dark-leaved *Heuchera*, hardy *Begonia*, or red-stemmed *Hosta*. Japanese painted fern is one of the parents of the hybrid 'Ghost', which is taller and paler.

*Athyrium niponicum* var. *pictum*

*Cyrtomium falcatum*

*Dennstaedtia punctilobula*

*Dryopteris erythrosora*

## Cyrtomium falcatum | holly fern

Part to full shade | Moist, well-drained soil | Zones 7–10 | 12–24 in. tall, 24–36 in. wide

With their bold plant shape, holly ferns provide a strong texture to the shade garden. Each plant grows in a whorl, and contrasts well with more feathery ferns. The shiny fronds resemble prickly holly leaves and can reach 30 inches long. They are evergreen in warm climates, and they are softer to the touch than they appear. Where *Cyrtomium falcatum* is hardy, it looks great at the base of shrubs such as *Rhododendron* in acidic soil. This is one of the more heat-tolerant ferns and grows well in the southern United States.

## Dennstaedtia punctilobula | hay-scented fern

Bright to full shade | Dry to moist soil | Zones 3–8 | 18–30 in. tall, unlimited spread

Hay-scented fern spreads by long rhizomes to fill a large area, so be careful where you plant it—this eastern North American native is aggressive. If you have a wild area on your property, this might be a good choice of groundcover. The fronds are upright, lance-shaped, and deciduous. *Dennstaedtia punctilobula* is a soft yellowy green and has a sweet hay-like fragrance when crushed.

## Dryopteris | wood fern, buckler fern

This enormous group of temperate ferns grows naturally in rich, acidic woodlands and many of them make admirable garden plants. Over time, individual plants will increase in diameter, so provide them with ample space. They need moisture to get established, but after that they are more adaptable. Emerging *Dryopteris* fronds are highly ornamental and a joy to watch unfurl.

### ▶ Dryopteris affinis
golden shield fern, golden-scaled male fern

Bright to full shade | Moist soil, but can tolerate dry soil once established | Zones 4–8
36–48 in. tall, 24–48 in. wide

Golden shield fern is named for its bronzy scales, particularly lower on the plant. This clump-forming fern is native to Europe, but does well in other parts of the world including humid climates. There are cultivars of this species with crested fronds such as 'Cristata'. This fern pairs well with *Epimedium*.

### ▶ Dryopteris erythrosora | autumn fern

Bright to full shade | Medium to moist soil | Zones 5–9 | 18–30 in. tall, 12–24 in. wide

This is one of my favorite ferns for its unusual rich, bronzy foliage in spring and fall. Its summer frond color is a glossy green. Autumn fern needs a soil rich in organic matter and some watering in the first few years, but it can tolerate heat and drought once established. The cultivar 'Brilliance' has bright copper coloration. Grow it with pinkish-bronze-foliaged *Heuchera* to echo the tones of its emerging fronds.

### ▶ *Dryopteris filix-mas* | male fern

Bright to full shade | Medium soil | Zones 3–8 | 18–36 in. tall and wide

*Dryopteris filix-mas* is widely used in gardens, as it can grow in a variety of conditions and once it is established, you can neglect it. It may be deciduous or evergreen depending on the climate. There are cultivars that can be used as an accent or a focal point, including some with highly unusual fronds, such as 'Parsley' and 'Linearis Polydactyla'.

### ▶ *Dryopteris marginalis* | marginal wood fern

Part to full shade | Dry to medium soil | Zones 3–8 | 18–24 in. tall and wide

This tough, leathery fern can withstand both cold winters and hot, dry summers. Water this fern for the first couple of seasons to get it started in the garden. Marginal wood fern is a fairly slow-growing, clumping fern that is a great companion for early spring bloomers like *Hyacinthoides*. It is often found on slopes in the wild, so mimic this situation in the garden.

## *Matteuccia struthiopteris* | ostrich fern

Bright to full shade | Moist soil | Zones 2–8 | 36–72 in. tall, 36–60 in. wide

This statuesque fern has great presence in a shade garden because of its vertically held fronds that resemble large ostrich plumes. Ostrich fern grows best where summers are cool and is ideal next to a naturalistic water feature. The outer green infertile fronds die down in fall, revealing the central fertile fronds that remain for the winter. This fern spreads enthusiastically by underground rhizomes to colonize a large area, as long as the soil is moist. It is a great pass-along plant because it produces many offsets that can be dug up and shared. The emerging fiddleheads of the ostrich fern are considered a spring delicacy.

## *Onoclea sensibilis* | sensitive fern, bead fern

Bright to full shade | Medium to moist, well-drained soil | Zones 4–9 | 24 in. tall and wide

*Onoclea sensibilis* has distinctive, simple sterile fronds that are a translucent light green color. It also has separate, fertile fronds with spore cases that are bead-like and remain as decorative elements in the winter shade garden. This fern will spread around the garden in shaded areas from a fat brown rhizome. If you want to propagate it yourself, the rhizome is very easy to divide. When I first moved to my property, this was one of the only plants that was holding its own against a mass of invasives.

*Matteuccia struthiopteris*

*Onoclea sensibilis*

*Osmunda regalis*

## *Osmunda* | osmunda

These ferns are ideal garden plants for wet areas. They are large ferns that make a bold statement and can be used as a background plant in a wet border. Some species of *Osmunda* are ancient and have remained the same since the time of the dinosaurs.

### ▶ *Osmunda cinnamomea*
cinnamon fern

Dappled or part shade | Moist soil
Zones 2–10 | 36–60 in. tall, 24–36 in. wide

Cinnamon fern is very tolerant of hot or cold climates, but requires humus-rich, moist, acidic soil. In spring, the fertile fronds emerge from the middle of the fern clump. They later turn a cinnamon brown color, hence the common name. This fern has a vase-shaped profile and looks good rising from low groundcovers. The cinnamon fern may also be called *Osmundastrum cinnamomeum*.

### ▶ *Osmunda regalis* | royal fern

Dappled or bright shade
Moist to wet soil | Zones 3–10
36–72 in. tall, 96–144 in. wide

*Osmunda regalis* earns its name from its regal stature in the landscape. Some of its simply divided fronds have a fertile section at the tip, giving another decorative element to this already statuesque fern. It looks great in a wet or boggy bed with *Rodgersia* and *Astilbe*. Give this large plant plenty of room to grow in wet, acidic soils.

## *Polypodium vulgare*
common polypody

Bright to full shade
Dry to moist, well-drained soil
Zones 5–8　|　6–18 in. tall and wide

*Polypodium vulgare* is a tough fern that will tolerate drought after it has been established. Its simply divided fronds are evergreen, and so make a good addition to a winter garden in combination with *Galanthus*. In summer, its bright yellow or orange sori are an additional decorative feature, and later fade to a chestnut brown. When adding this fern to your garden, throw some additional grit and organic matter into the planting hole. The North American *P. virginianum* is hardier. Both species can grow in walls, rock crevasses, and at the base of trees when grown from spores.

*Polypodium vulgare*

# Polystichum | polystichum

*Polystichum* is a widespread group of evergreen ferns. They are easy to grow in the shade garden in humusy soil. Their divided fronds are a great contrast to rounder-leaved herbaceous plants.

### ▶ *Polystichum acrostichoides* | Christmas fern

Bright to full shade | Dry to moist soil | Zones 3–9 | 15–24 in. tall, 20–24 in. wide

*Polystichum acrostichoides* is one of the easiest evergreen ferns for winter interest. Each little section of the deep green frond looks like a miniature sock or Christmas stocking. The fronds are shiny and the clump has a strong presence. The old fronds can be cut off in early spring for a neater look or left in place in a more naturalistic garden.

### ▶ *Polystichum polyblepharum* | tassel fern, Japanese lace fern

Part to full shade | Moist, well-drained soil | Zones 6–8 | 15–24 in. tall, 20 in. wide

The tassel fern has dark green, glossy fronds that reflect light around the shade garden. The stipe is covered with brown fuzzy scales. This fern should be planted in a well-drained area that remains moist. The new spring growth arrives early in the year and should be protected from late frosts with a layer of leaves.

### ▶ *Polystichum setiferum* | soft shield fern

Part to full shade | Moist soil | Zones 5–8 | 12–36 in. tall, 36 in. wide

The soft, feathery fronds of *Polystichum setiferum* splay out from the central crown. The stipes have a dense covering of russet-colored scales that stand out against the green of the frilly fronds. This fern needs a moist soil that does not stay waterlogged. Soft shield fern is extremely variable and there are many different attractive cultivars. I like *P. setiferum* (Divisilobum Group) 'Herrenhausen'.

*Polystichum acrostichoides*

# HERBACEOUS PERENNIALS

Herbaceous plants make up the ground plane of your shade garden. Leaves, flowers, and seeds are produced during the growing season and then, when autumn arrives, most species retreat belowground to await the new gardening cycle. The majority of herbaceous plants are perennial, meaning they have multiyear life spans.

Select herbaceous perennials by looking for those that would naturally thrive in the shade and soil conditions you have in your garden. For example, if there is a continuously boggy section of your shady space, pick plants that require consistent soil moisture. If you have an area that is rocky and dry, there are perennials perfect for that spot.

Herbaceous plants make up the attractive and varied ground-covering carpet of greenery that is such a key feature of a successful shade garden. Long-lasting leaf effects are easy to achieve by selecting plants for the color, texture, size, and form of their foliage. For visual interest, pick plants with contrasting leaf types; for example, pair simple, bold leaves with feathery or soft strap-like leaves or play with color effects. Include evergreen perennials to prolong the display.

Herbaceous plants provide the additional attraction of flowers and seedheads from spring to summer, into fall and through winter. These beauties enliven the understory layer with an ever-changing series of floral combinations. If you use your garden year-round, pick groups of plants that flower in every season. Choose bulbs, spring ephemerals, and other blossoms for spring, and boldly blooming plants for summer. For fall, select perennials that flower late in the season, and for winter, species that have persistent seedheads or berries, and bulbs that bloom in late winter.

There are herbaceous plants for any shade garden situation and size. Large gardens need bigger swaths of perennials grouped together to suit the scale of the landscape. A very small space can be enlivened by an exquisite collection of your favorite perennials.

A shaded bed filled with an assortment of herbaceous perennials, including *Dodecatheon*, *Asarum*, *Phlox*, *Mertensia*, *Hosta*, *Galanthus*, and *Polygonatum*, has a long season of interest, but looks especially good in spring.

Aconitum carmichaelii

## Aconitum carmichaelii
monkshood

Part shade | Moist soil | Zones 3–8
48–60 in. tall, 12–18 in. wide

*Aconitum carmichaelii* is a great fall-blooming perennial that makes a vertical accent in the landscape. It is grown for its striking indigo-blue hooded flowers that open when the deciduous trees change their colors. *Aconitum* is an unexpected pleasure in the late season shade garden. It is best grown in cool, moist conditions and appreciates afternoon shade. There are other monkshood species and cultivars worth looking for, such as *A. napellus* and *A. carmichaelii* (Arendsii Group) 'Arendsii'. Wear gloves when handling these plants because they are toxic.

## *Actaea* | baneberry, bugbane

*Actaea* is a genus of tall flowering rhizomatous perennials native to Northern temperate woodlands. These are decorative plants that provide excellent foliage, flowers, and fruit. This genus now contains members of the old genus *Cimicifuga*.

### ▶ *Actaea pachypoda*
doll's eyes, white baneberry

Part to full shade
Moist, well-drained soil | Zones 3–8
18–36 in. tall, 24–36 in. wide

Grow *Actaea pachypoda* for its racemes of white flowers in late spring that are followed by unusual-looking berries. The fruit have been likened to the eyes of a doll, as they have a small black dot in the center of each white berry. Keep their roots evenly moist for best growth. With sufficient moisture, its foliage looks great all season.

### ▶ *Actaea simplex*
autumn bugbane

Bright to full shade | Moist soil
Zones 3–8 | 48–84 in. tall, 24 in. wide

*Actaea simplex* is an autumn-flowering plant that produces tapering, bottlebrush-like white flowers that rise above the surrounding green foliage and catch the eye in the shade. The elegant flowers are particularly striking when backlit by the setting sun. For a different look, try *A. simplex* cultivars with dark mahogany foliage, like (Atropurpurea Group) 'Brunette'. Plant autumn bugbane and the related *A. racemosa* in your garden to extend the season of bloom as *A. simplex* blooms later than *A. racemosa*.

*Actaea pachypoda*

*Agastache foeniculum*

*Ajuga reptans* 'Chocolate Chip'

*Alchemilla mollis*

*Allium thunbergii* 'Ozawa'

## *Agastache foeniculum* | anise hyssop

Edge or part shade | Dry to medium, well-drained soil | Zones 4–9 | 36–48 in. tall, 12–24 in. wide

*Agastache foeniculum* is an appealing perennial with purple flowers that is resistant to deer and rabbit browsing due to the characteristic licorice smell of its foliage. It is very attractive to butterflies, hummingbirds, and other pollinators. I grow it as a self-sowing plant that fills in areas of bright, dry shade next to large hollies. Its vertical form stands out behind mounding *Hemerocallis*. To establish my original plants, I watered them in during their first season and after that they have grown well on their own.

## *Ajuga reptans* | bugleweed

Part to full shade | Well-drained soil | Zones 3–9 | 4–12 in. tall, 24 in. or more wide

*Ajuga reptans* is a spreading low groundcover that is grown for its lustrous leaves and vigorous growth habit. It flowers with purple to blue blooms on upright stems in spring. It expands out from a central crown via stolons and is considered invasive in some areas. The cultivars that are available, including 'Burgundy Glow' and 'Variegata', have interestingly colored leaves.

## *Alchemilla mollis* | lady's mantle

Part shade | Medium soil | Zones 4–8 | 20–24 in. tall, 24 in. wide

Lady's mantle has small chartreuse-yellow sprays of flowers in late spring. The pleated circular leaves repel water and make collected raindrops look like liquid silver. It is a very popular plant that has been grown in gardens for hundreds of years. Lady's mantle is drought tolerant once established. *Alchemilla mollis* is a generous self-seeder; some gardeners say that it seeds in too much. If you do not want the plant to spread around, deadhead the flowers. It grows in low clumps that make a great border along a path.

## *Allium thunbergii* | Japanese onion

Edge or part shade | Well-drained soil | Zones 5–8 | 8–14 in. tall, 10 in. wide

*Allium thunbergii* is a late season bloomer, sending up clusters of purple nodding flowers that attract butterflies. This is a useful plant in fall combinations but make sure you give it good drainage by adding grit to the planting hole. The following *Allium* species are also shade-tolerant and all bloom in spring: *A. moly*, *A. ursinum*, and *A. zebdanense*. All of these alliums will seed in if you leave the seedheads on the plant. Their strong onion odor when crushed makes them particularly herbivore-resistant.

*Anemone ×hybrida* 'Andrea Atkinson'

## Anemone | windflower, anemone

There are a wide variety of shade-tolerant plants in the genus *Anemone*, ranging from small spring flowers to tall autumn bloomers. They all have flowers with a central cluster of yellow stamens and showy petals.

### ▶ *Anemone blanda* | Grecian windflower

Dappled or bright shade | Moist, well-drained soil | Zones 4–8 | 6–8 in. tall, 6 in. wide

In spring, the small, delicate flowers of *Anemone blanda* bloom in shades of white, blue, or pink. They make a sweet combination with other spring bulbs such as *Narcissus* 'Hawera', and then go dormant in summer. This plant is grown from autumn-planted tubers that should not be allowed to dry out. In the colder end of its hardiness zones it needs a drier soil and winter protection.

### ▶ *Anemone canadensis*  |  meadow anemone, American meadow anemone

Part shade  |  Moist soil  |  Zones 3–8  |  12–24 in. tall, 24–30 in. wide

*Anemone canadensis* is a vigorous spreader if planted in moist soil and part shade. It is an attractive plant for filling a large space. In spring, its white flowers are held above green divided foliage. Meadow anemone is native to eastern North America.

### ▶ *Anemone ×hybrida*  |  Japanese anemone, hybrid anemone

Part shade  |  Well-drained soil  |  Zones 4–8  |  30–48 in. tall, spreading 24 in. wide or more

When in bloom, hybrid anemones are tall perennials that are among the stars of the autumn shade garden. Use them as a backdrop to lower-growing shade perennials or in the middle of a bed or border as see-through plants. My favorite *Anemone ×hybrida* cultivar is 'Honorine Jobert', which has pure white petals and a yellow ring of stamens, followed by fluffy seedheads. Ironically, while Japanese anemones can be overly vigorous when in the right conditions, they can be hard to establish in some gardens. In colder climates, plant them in spring. If planted later in the season, Japanese anemones may not get their roots growing before winter and often die.

### ▶ *Anemone nemorosa*  |  wood anemone

Dappled or part shade  |  Medium soil  |  Zones 4–8  |  3–14 in. tall, 12 in. wide

Wood anemone is a favorite for slightly acidic to neutral soils in woodlands where its delicate white flowers appear in early spring. Many cultivars are available; try the pale lavender–flowering 'Robinsoniana'. Site hostas or other late-emerging plants near *Anemone nemorosa* to hide its summer-dormant foliage.

## *Anemonella thalictroides*  |  rue-anemone

Part to full shade  |  Moist soil  |  Zones 4–9  |  8–10 in. tall, 10 in. wide

*Anemonella thalictroides* is native to woodlands in eastern North America. It has delicate-looking white or light pink flowers in spring. The leaves of this small beauty look similar to those of *Thalictrum*, but on a smaller scale, and it may be listed as *Thalictrum thalictroides*. It is an excellent plant at the front of a bed or in a border next to low-growing *Epimedium* or other precious spring flowers. Unlike many other early spring bloomers in my garden, the foliage lasts through the summer.

*Anemonella thalictroides*

*Aquilegia canadensis*

## *Aquilegia* | columbine

*Aquilegia* is a fabulous group of garden plants with lovely spring into early summer flowers. In gardens where many species and cultivars are grown, the flowers will easily cross with each other to produce hybrids. They seed around the garden but are such a light and airy plant that they fit well in any planting. Shake the dried brown seedheads around the garden to encourage seeding. I have not found one columbine that I dislike, so it is hard to pick favorites, but I cannot resist the double pink and white flowers of *A. vulgaris* var. *stellata* 'Nora Barlow'.

Columbines can be prone to leaf miner damage. If you see their characteristic, whitish, mazelike tunnels under the surface of leaves, pick off the infected foliage and throw it away. This will reduce your population of these insects.

### ▶ *Aquilegia canadensis*
Canadian columbine

Bright or part shade | Moist soil | Zones 3–8
12–36 in. tall, 12 in. wide

*Aquilegia canadensis* is a woodland gem with nodding red and yellow flowers in late spring that are a magnet for hummingbirds. It is most effective planted in a group, as each individual flower is small. If conditions are favorable, it will multiply in your garden. They are less susceptible to leaf miner damage than hybrids.

### ▶ *Aquilegia* ×*hybrida*
hybrid columbine

Bright or part shade | Moist to dry soil
Zones 3–9 | 12–36 in. tall, 12 in. wide

Hybrid columbines are available in a wide range of flower forms and colors, and are the result of crossing several species. They grow from a basal clump of foliage and produce nodding spring flowers in a variety of pastel and jewellike colors. Hybrid columbines grow larger in rich, moist, well-drained soil but will seed into a gravel path and grow perfectly well there, too.

## Arisaema triphyllum
jack-in-the-pulpit

Part shade | Moist soil | Zones 4–8
12–30 in. tall, 20–24 in. wide

*Arisaema triphyllum* blooms in spring with an upright, green or green-and-purple tubular flowering structure. Its architectural form captivates gardeners who like to grow something unusual. In late summer, it produces clusters of bright red berries that extend its season of interest. Its three-parted foliage goes dormant in summer, so combine it with hostas or ferns that leaf out and fill in the space.

Most plants in the genus *Arisaema* prefer cool, moist soil in shade. Try *A. dracontium* and *A. sikokianum*, related species that both have deeply lobed leaves and similar hooded flowers. They grow from tubers and prefer to be left undisturbed. Use gloves when handling them, as all of these plants are toxic. Incidentally, their toxicity reduces browsing by herbivores.

## Arum italicum subsp. italicum 'Marmoratum'
Italian arum 'Marmoratum'

Part shade | Moist soil | Zones 5–9
12–20 in. tall, 18 in. wide

This Italian arum is widely grown for its patterned leaves. They are a glossy dark green color with veins of light green to cream. Additional garden interest comes from hooded flowers early in the year followed by decorative red-orange seedheads that persist into fall. In some climates, this plant may be too aggressive, but in my garden it is well behaved and looks good with *Galanthus*. All parts of this plant are poisonous, so handle it with gloves.

*Arisaema triphyllum* growing among ferns.

*Arum italicum* subsp. *italicum* 'Marmoratum'

## Aruncus dioicus | goat's beard

Dappled or part shade
Moist to wet soil | Zones 3–8
48–72 in. tall, 24–72 in. wide

Goat's beard is named for its fluffy inflorescences of small, creamy white flowers in late spring or early summer. Mass plants of *Aruncus dioicus* in partly shaded areas with plenty of moisture for the best effect. They are a dramatic addition to a shade garden because of their height and showy flowers. A related dwarf species, *A. aethusifolius*, is an excellent choice for a smaller shade garden. In drier conditions or hot afternoon sun, the leaves of all *Aruncus* will brown at the edges.

*Aruncus dioicus*

## *Asarum* | hardy ginger, wild ginger

Hardy gingers are valued garden plants for their carpet of leaves that are perfect for the front of a shady border. Grow them in slightly acidic soil for best growth. *Asarum* does not have anything to do with the ginger that we eat; it is called hardy ginger because its underground rhizomes smell like the spice.

### ▶ *Asarum canadense*
American wild ginger, Canadian ginger

Part to full shade | Moist, well-drained soil
Zones 3–8 | 4–10 in. tall, 12 in. wide

*Asarum canadense* is a ground-covering perennial that is native to eastern North America. It has rounded to kidney-shaped soft green leaves that die to the ground in winter. In spring, look under the leaves to find strange, brown triangular flowers that are pollinated by ground beetles. *Asarum shuttleworthii*, also native to eastern North America, has patterned evergreen leaves. *Asarum caudatum* is native to northwestern North America, and is a better choice as a groundcover for this region.

### ▶ *Asarum europaeum*
European wild ginger

Part to full shade | Moist, well-drained soil
Zones 4–8 | 6–8 in. tall, 10 in. wide

European wild ginger is grown as an evergreen groundcover. Flowers of *Asarum europaeum* are insignificant and hidden under the glossy dark green leaves. The plant spreads out nicely to make a patch that can easily be dug up and divided after a couple of years. This ginger's lustrous leaves combine well with *Tiarella* and *Anemonella*.

*Asarum europaeum*

### *Astilbe* species | false spiraea

Part to full shade | Moist soil | Zones 4–8, but may vary | 18–24 in. tall and wide; varies by cultivar

*Astilbe* is a genus of moisture-loving shade perennials that are some of the best plants for summer color. Their long-lasting, spiked flowers come in colors ranging from white, to pink, purple, and dark crimson red. Inflorescences may range from half a foot to two feet in length, depending on the species or cultivar. Grow *Astilbe* in masses of one type for best effect. A planting site near ponds or streams is best since it requires consistently damp soil. Add some compost or leaf mold to the soil to help keep the roots moist.

There are a wide variety of species and cultivars available, so choose them by their height and the color of their plume-like blooms. Some of the most popular cultivars are white-flowered 'Deutschland' (*A. japonica* hybrid), and red-flowered 'Fanal' (*A. ×arendsii*). 'Rheinland' (another *A. japonica* hybrid) has fluffy pink flowers carried above dark green foliage. *Astilbe chinensis* cultivars and hybrids can take slightly drier soils but still perform best with consistent moisture. Try 'Vision in Pink'.

### *Astilboides tabularis* | common astilboides

Part shade | Medium to moist, well-drained soil | Zones 5–8 | 36–48 in. tall, 24–36 in. wide

*Astilboides tabularis*, formerly known as *Rodgersia tabularis*, is a large plant that is grown for its bold foliage and plumes of creamy white flowers in summer. Its big, rounded, lobed leaves are excellent grown with plants like *Aruncus* or *Carex*. Cool climates combined with humus-rich, moist soil will produce optimum growth.

### *Astrantia major* | great masterwort

Part shade | Medium to wet soil | Zones 5–7 | 24–36 in. tall, 12–18 in. wide

*Astrantia major* is a clump-forming perennial that grows best where the soil is cool, moist, and humus-rich. Greenish white, pink, or red flowers are held above the numerous basal lobed leaves and have a straw-like texture. They are produced in late spring to midsummer. Great masterwort grows best with cool night temperatures and consistent soil moisture. Suggested cultivars include 'Alba', with white flowers, and 'Hadspen Blood', with dark red blooms.

*Begonia grandis*

*Bergenia cordifolia*

## *Begonia grandis* | hardy begonia

Part to full shade | Moist soil | Zones 6–9 | 15–20 in. tall, 18 in. wide

*Begonia grandis* is the hardiest begonia that grows in temperate gardens. This plant does not emerge from the ground until late spring, so it makes a perfect companion for spring ephemerals such as *Mertensia*. The leaves are quite large in size and have an interesting coloration of green with red veins. Dangling pink flowers start in summer and continue until frost. Even after the petals drop, they remain ornamental due to their developing fruit. Site this begonia on a bank to see the flowers more easily. There is a white-flowered variety available.

## *Bergenia cordifolia* | pigsqueak

Part shade | Medium to moist soil | Zones 4–8 | 24 in. tall and wide

*Bergenia cordifolia* is grown in gardens for its evergreen, glossy foliage and late winter flower stalks. The large, waxy leaves make a squeaking sound when rubbed, hence the common name. The green basal leaf rosettes turn purple-bronze or red in cold weather. The pinkish-purple flowers emerge in the late winter or early spring on stems that rise above the leaves.

Plants in the genus *Bergenia* grow best in moist, partly shaded areas. In hot climates, they require afternoon shade. In the landscape, they have a coarse, bold look that can be paired with the smaller, softer foliage of evergreen ferns, such as *Polystichum acrostichoides*. There are many species and cultivars to choose from and most can be used to form an evergreen edging. They grow best where the winter weather is moderate as they suffer under snow or in severe frost.

## *Bletilla striata* | Chinese hardy orchid

Part shade | Medium to moist, well-drained soil | Zones 5–8
10–18 in. tall, 6–8 in. wide

For most gardeners, the idea of growing an orchid outside is irresistible. *Bletilla striata* is one of the easiest hardy species to try. It does well in soil that is moist, well-drained, and humus-rich. The tantalizing orchid flowers are pinkish purple and produced at the tops of slender spikes in late spring. The lance-like, pleated leaves look good intermixed with low groundcovers like *Sedum ternatum*, *Heuchera*, or hardy *Geranium*. There is a lovely white form of *Bletilla*, and a number of cultivars with variegated foliage. Apply mulch in colder zones to insulate the underground pseudobulbs from heat and cold.

## *Brunnera macrophylla*

heartleaf brunnera, Siberian bugloss, perennial forget-me-not

Edge to full shade | Medium to moist soil | Zones 3–8
12–18 in. tall, 24 in. wide

Perennial forget-me-not has large, heart-shaped leaves and blue spring flowers. They are valuable shade garden plants as they retain good leaf quality throughout the growing season. The most desirable cultivars have strong silver markings such as 'Alexander's Great' and 'Silver Heart'.

   *Brunnera macrophylla* self-sows in the right conditions and will seed itself into areas of dry shade, even next to tree trunks. *Brunnera* plants are deer resistant because their leaves and stems have bristle-like hairs. Plants, like *Hosta*, that are eaten by deer may be protected if interplanted with *Brunnera* to camouflage them. Wear gloves when handling the bristly foliage.

*Bletilla striata*

*Brunnera macrophylla* 'Silver Heart'

## *Camassia leichtlinii* | large camas

Edge or bright shade | Medium to moist soil | Zones 3–8 | 18–30 in. tall, 18 in. wide

*Camassia leichtlinii* has sky blue flowers arising on tall stalks among strap-like foliage. It looks good intermixed with *Alchemilla mollis* in a bed or in an orchard with *Fritillaria meleagris* and *Leucojum aestivum*. Plant it in generous groups for best display. Different cultivars are available that have darker blue or white flowers. This late spring-blooming bulb is native to northwestern North America.

## *Carex* | sedge

Sedges are grass-like plants that grow from tufted clumps and spread out as groundcovers. In general, they are low-maintenance, useful plants for the shade garden. Due to the shape of their thin, elongated leaves, they look good in combination with broad-leaved perennials. There are many different types of sedges with varying heights, colors, and textures. *Carex pensylvanica* has fine, dark green leaves and is great for full shade and dry soil. *Carex plantaginea* is a tough plant with wider, bright green, seersucker-textured leaves.

### ▶ *Carex flacca* 'Ice Dance' | sedge 'Ice Dance'

Bright or part shade | Moist, well-drained soil | Zones 5–8 | 12–18 in. tall, 6–12 in. wide

*Carex flacca* 'Ice Dance' has cream and green variegated strap-shaped leaves and looks great in a container. Place it near perennials that have bold foliage such as *Rohdea*, or against a backdrop of *Hydrangea arborescens*.

Another *C. flacca* cultivar, 'Blue Zinger', has a gray-blue, glaucous coloration that I like to pair with dark-colored *Ophiopogon planiscapus* 'Nigrescens'. The combination of the two has formed a striking groundcover in my garden. They took a few years to get established, but now tolerate the dry conditions under a tree.

## *Chasmanthium latifolium* | quaking oat grass, North America wild oats

Part to full shade | Moist, well-drained soil | Zones 3–8 | 18–40 in. tall, 12 in. wide

*Chasmanthium latifolium* has grassy leaves with oat-like flower stalks that arch over with the weight of its flattened seedheads. The leaves and seeds are green and then fade to a tawny brown in autumn. Like all grasses, quaking oat grass produces large volumes of viable seed that can spread to new places in the garden. This grass, when happy, will cover a large area, so beware if you have a small garden.

*Camassia leichtlinii*

**bottom left** *Carex* growing next to a stone-lined pond.

**bottom right** *Chasmanthium latifolium*

*Chelone lyonii*

## Chelone lyonii | pink turtlehead

Edge or part shade | Moist soil | Zones 4–8
24–30 in. tall, 18 in. wide

*Chelone lyonii* has pink, late summer flowers that resemble the head of a snapping turtle with the upper petal hanging out over the lower one. Pinch back the top of the stems in spring to encourage fuller growth. *Chelone glabra* is similar but has white flowers. Both are native to eastern North America.

Turtleheads are perfect for a shady space with moist soil. Their glossy green leaves held on vertical stalks have good foliage quality during the growing season and the blooms provide late summer interest.

## Chionodoxa sardensis
glory-of-the-snow

Dappled or part shade | Well-drained soil
Zones 4–8 | 4–6 in. tall, 2–3 in. wide

Dappled deciduous woodlands provide perfect conditions for *Chionodoxa* to carpet the ground before tree leaves emerge. It is excellent anywhere, particularly at the front of a border. In autumn, plant bulbs of glory-of-the-snow in the gaps between tree roots. Cluster them to get maximum impact from the small blue flowers that have white eyes. Leave them in place and they will slowly spread by seed to make a larger patch. Cultivars come in pinks and whites as well as blue. *Chionodoxa sardensis* is similar in stature and garden use to *C. forbesii* and *C. luciliae*. If you like the look of these little spring bloomers, also try bulbs in the genera *Puschkinia* and *Scilla*.

A patch of *Chionodoxa sardensis* in early spring.

## Chrysogonum virginianum
green and gold

Bright to full shade | Medium to moist soil
Zones 5–8 | 4–6 in. tall, 12 in. wide

*Chrysogonum virginianum* is a cheerful addition to the shade garden. This low-growing plant has fuzzy green leaves and bright yellow-gold daisy-like flowers that bloom in spring. It is native to eastern North America, where it is found in shady woods. *Chrysogonum* is wonderful as a rhizomatous groundcover that gently spreads out from the initial planting site. It can grow in moderately dry soil and is deer tolerant. I grow mine as an underplanting to taller *Hosta*. It is easy to divide and propagate a section from the parent plant after flowering.

## *Claytonia virginica* | spring beauty

Dappled or part shade
Moist, well-drained, slightly acidic soil | Zones 4–8
4–10 in. tall, 4–8 in. wide

Spring beauty truly lives up to its common name with starry white flowers that have hints of pink. They are easily grown among other low groundcovers in well-aerated soil. If you grow *Claytonia virginica* in a lawn, enjoy the bloom, and then allow the plant four weeks to set seed before mowing. This is not often found for sale but beg a clump from a gardening friend and you will look forward to its emergence each spring.

*Chrysogonum virginianum*

*Claytonia virginica*

*Colchicum cilicicum*

*Conoclinium coelestinum*

## Colchicum cilicicum | colchicum

Edge or bright shade | Medium, very well-drained soil | Zones 5–8
4–6 in. tall, 6 in. wide

*Colchicum cilicicum* has many purple-pink flowers per corm, and blooms in fall. Slugs may attack the flowers, so take precautions. Good drainage is the key to success. My colchicums are grown in a raised bed among ferns. Try it on a bank where you can easily admire the blooms.

The leaves of all colchicums emerge from underground corms in spring and then die down, so disguise them by interplanting with perennials that have good summer foliage. The flowering stalks come up in late summer or fall in colors of light pink, lilac, or white. All species are poisonous and are thus resistant to deer and vole damage. I grow *C. speciosum* 'Album' combined with white-spotted *Pulmonaria*. Plant *Colchicum* corms as soon as they are available in late summer.

## Conoclinium coelestinum | blue mistflower

Edge or part shade | Medium to moist, well-drained soil
Zones 5–9 | 24–36 in. tall and wide

*Conoclinium coelestinum*, which used to be called *Eupatorium coelestinum*, is a great plant for the late season shade garden, blooming from late summer into fall. The fluffy periwinkle blue flowers are an unusual color and resemble *Ageratum*. They spread by rhizomes as well as by seed, so they may become overabundant. Blue mistflower is a good choice for flower arranging.

## Convallaria majalis | lily-of-the-valley

Bright to full shade | Moist soil | Zones 2–8 | 6–12 in. tall, 8 in. wide

Lily-of-the-valley has green leaves that shelter white, bell-shaped spring-blooming flowers. The iconic fragrance can be best enjoyed when planted near a walkway, or when picked and put in a vase. It will grow in a wide range of shade conditions and in any garden soil. In cooler climates, lily-of-the-valley may spread too rapidly once established. In any climate, it is best planted on its own to form a clump. Top-dress with leaf mold in autumn. There are lovely pink-flowered varieties such as *Convallaria majalis* var. *rosea*. Additionally, cultivars with variegated leaves are available.

## Corydalis lutea | yellow corydalis

Edge or part shade | Medium to moist soil | Zones 5–8
12–18 in. tall and wide

*Corydalis lutea* forms a mound of divided, soft green foliage that is topped with numerous yellow flowers in spring through summer. It is excellent in a shaded rock garden, or along a path. It will grow in a wide range of conditions, including neutral to slightly alkaline soil. It is an opportunistic grower that will seed itself into wall cracks or crevices where you could not have planted anything. It is not usually a nuisance because seedlings can be easily removed. I like to grow it with *Helleborus* and with a similar-looking species that has white flowers, *C. ochroleuca*.

*Convallaria majalis* var. *rosea*

*Corydalis lutea*

### *Crocus tommasinianus* | tommies

Edge or part shade | Medium, well-drained soil | Zones 3–8 | 4 in. tall, 2 in. wide

Early spring-blooming *Crocus tommasinianus* grow from small fall-planted corms. Their lavender, purple, or lilac chalice-shaped flowers are attractive to pollinators when little else is in bloom. I love them planted in drifts, especially under deciduous trees where they will naturalize by self-sown seed. They also grow beautifully in lightly shaded lawns, especially if you wait to mow the grass until after the foliage has died down late in spring.

Tommies seem to be eaten less often than other *Crocus* species. I grow the cultivars 'Roseus', 'Barr's Purple', 'Lilac Wonder', and 'Ruby Giant'. There are many other species of *Crocus* that are great additions to the early spring landscape in well-drained soil, but most will not proliferate as well as *C. tommasinianus*.

### *Cyclamen coum* | hardy cyclamen

Part to full shade | Well-drained soil | Zones 5–9 | 4–6 in. tall and wide

*Cyclamen* is a genus of low-growing plants known for their mottled foliage as well as spring- or autumn-blooming flowers. They are grown from corms that resemble little brown plates that should be barely covered with soil. Each year, the corms will increase in size and more flowers will arise from the base. They need great drainage and too much water on top of the corms causes them to rot. Try growing them among greedy tree roots or on a shady bank. Be careful not to mulch over their leaves.

*Cyclamen coum* has lightly fragrant pink, purple, or white flowers that are a treat in late winter to early spring. I have a lovely patch of these cyclamen growing in a raised area under a Japanese maple. Early spring–blooming *C. coum* and the related fall-blooming *C. hederifolium* are on either side of the same tree. *Cyclamen hederfolium*, the ivy-leaved cyclamen, has, as the name would suggest, leaves that resemble those of English ivy.

### *Dicentra eximia* | fringed bleeding heart

Part to full shade | Medium to moist soil | Zones 4–8 | 10–18 in. tall, 12–18 in. wide

The charming flowers of *Dicentra eximia* may be pink or white and are carried on arching stems. It may self-sow around the garden and its soft, ferny texture combines well with *Aquilegia* and *Epimedium*. It blooms most profusely in spring, and then continues to flower sporadically throughout the growing season. *Dicentra eximia* is native to the eastern United States, and the similar *D. formosa* is native to western North America.

Other species in the genus to try are *D. canadensis* and *D. cucullaria*, both of which are spring ephemerals that have primarily white flowers and go dormant by summer. The genus *Dicentra* no longer includes the larger old-fashioned bleeding heart, which is now in the genus *Lamprocapnos*.

*Crocus tommasinianus*

**bottom left**  A carpet of *Cyclamen coum* in bloom showing diversity of leaf form and color.

**bottom right**  *Dicentra eximia*

## Digitalis purpurea | common foxglove

Part shade | Medium to moist soil | Zones 4–8
48–60 in. tall, 24 in. wide

Plants in the genus *Digitalis* have spikes of bell-shaped flowers in a range of colors: white, pink, purple, yellow, and rusty tones. All are great punctuation marks in the shady garden where their spires rise above the mounding foliage of hostas and other low growers.

*Digitalis purpurea* is the common woodland foxglove. Flowers are borne on tall stems and are pinkish purple or white in spring. This is a biennial, so sprinkle seed for two years to get your permanent population started, and then allow plants to self-sow. One of my favorite English gardeners, Gertrude Jekyll, selected for the pure white foxglove with no spots inside the flower tube. Follow her example and use white-flowered forms, as they show up well in low light. *Digitalis lutea*, straw foxglove, grows in moist soil in bright or part shade. It has small, yellow summer flowers and is slender in profile.

## Diphylleia cymosa | umbrella leaf

Part to full shade | Moist soil | Zones 5–8
24–36 in. tall, 12–24 in. wide

*Diphylleia cymosa* is native to the southern Appalachian Mountains in the United States and requires cool nights and consistent moisture to thrive. It spreads slowly by rhizomes and often grows near streams in the wild. It has white flowers in late spring or early summer, which are followed by blue berries on red stalks held above its large-lobed green leaves. It is an unusual plant, but well worth adding to your garden.

*Digitalis purpurea*

*Diphylleia cymosa*

## *Disporopsis pernyi*

dwarf Solomon's seal, evergreen Solomon's seal

Part to full shade  |  Moist, well-drained soil  |  Zones 6–9
10–16 in. tall, 12–18 in. wide

*Disporopsis pernyi* produces white and green fragrant flowers in early summer. The glossy deep green leaves stay attractive all season long on arching stems. The plant will eventually spread by rhizomes to form a good groundcover. It combines well with other plants at the front of a shady border, and I have mine planted in a small bed with *Primula*. It is very similar in appearance and is closely related to *Polygonatum*.

## *Dodecatheon meadia*  |  shooting star

Dappled or part shade  |  Medium to moist soil  |  Zones 4–8
8–18 in. tall, 8–12 in. wide

*Dodecatheon meadia* is a spring-blooming plant that can be a beautiful addition to a shaded garden. Early in the year, the lettuce-like leaves emerge in a rosette. The flowering stalk arises from the center of the leaves and spreads out with whorls of tiny starlike flowers. Swept back white or purple petals surround the downward pointing tip.

Delicate and exquisite, shooting stars are best at the front of a bed so that you can observe their tiny details. Grow them next to a later-blooming plant such as *Tricyrtis* that will cover its foliage as it dies down in summer. If conditions are suitable, with good woodsy soil, *D. meadia* will self-sow. These beautiful woodland ephemerals are native to the United States. Although the straight species is magenta-pink, I love the white-flowered f. *album* because it shows up well in shady places. I pair them with *Polemonium reptans* and *Iris cristata*.

*Disporopsis pernyi*

*Dodecatheon meadia*

*Epimedium ×versicolor* 'Sulphureum'

## *Epimedium ×versicolor* 'Sulphureum'

bishop's hat 'Sulphureum'

Part shade   |   Medium soil   |   Zones 4–8
6–15 in. tall and wide

Plants in the genus *Epimedium*, commonly known as bishop's hat or barrenwort, are great garden groundcovers for the shade. Some of them will tolerate dry shade around the base of trees. However, their growth is most lush in part shade, rich soil, and with sufficient moisture, but no standing water.

*Epimedium ×versicolor* 'Sulphureum' was one of the first epimediums that I grew and is the best increaser that I have, making it a great pass-along plant. It is a clump-forming perennial with attractive heart-shaped foliage throughout the growing season and delicate hanging yellow flowers in spring. Cut back last season's foliage in late winter to see the new growth emerge.

*Epimedium ×youngianum* 'Jenny Wren', with long-spurred purple and white flowers, is another one of my favorite cultivars. I also love *E. ×youngianum* 'Niveum', which has fresh green leaves and very white small flowers. All plants in this genus are easy to care for and are great shade garden additions. They provide a long season of interest as their fall colors can be subtly attractive and some are evergreen.

## *Eranthis hyemalis* | winter aconite

Part shade | Medium soil | Zones 4–8
2–4 in. tall, 2–3 in. wide

*Eranthis hyemalis* has buttercup-like golden yellow flowers with a green ruff of leaves and is one of the first flowers to emerge in late winter. Although this diminutive plant only rises a couple of inches above the surface of the frozen soil, its bright color stands out and gives hope for the arrival of spring. The best way to establish this plant is to get a scoop of them from a gardening friend. The tiny brown tubers are sold in autumn, but are often too desiccated to grow. Once you have them established, you too will be giving them away. They look best under the canopy of a tree and once they seed themselves in, they will grow right next to the tree trunks. Winter aconite thrives in neutral to alkaline soil.

## *Erythronium* 'Pagoda'

erythronium 'Pagoda'

Dappled or part shade | Medium to moist soil
Zones 4–8 | 10–16 in. tall, 6–8 in. wide

Plants in the genus *Erythronium* are found in damp, deciduous woodlands, and are commonly called trout lilies or fawn lilies. These bulbs bloom in spring to early summer and many have blotched foliage. Erythroniums will spread out from their initial planting, but not aggressively.

'Pagoda' is a good garden-worthy cultivar. It is a vigorous hybrid that bears yellow flowers with slightly reflexed petals in spring. Its lightly patterned green leaves die down later in summer, so plant them next to hardy *Geranium* or other, season-long groundcovers. It looks great in combination with *Tulipa sylvestris*, which shares similar coloring. I also grow *E.* 'White Beauty' and admire *E. americanum* and *E. dens-canis*. Most species need moisture and good drainage. Burrowing animals and deer may eat *Erythronium*, so site it in a protected area.

*Eranthis hyemalis*

A carpet of *Erythronium* 'Pagoda'.

## *Euphorbia amygdaloides* var. *robbiae*
Mrs. Robb's bonnet, wood spurge

Part shade | Dry to moist soil | Zones 6–8 | 20–24 in. tall, 12 in. wide

*Euphorbia amygdaloides* var. *robbiae* is a tough spurge that can grow in dry shade. Chartreuse bracts that look like little flying saucers surround the late spring flowers. Its stacked whorls of dark green foliage make an effective backdrop to its bright flower heads. As with all euphorbias, its white sap is irritating, so wear gloves to handle this plant. However, because of the sap, animals do not browse it. Plant it *en masse* for an evergreen groundcover.

## *Eurybia divaricata* | white wood aster

Edge or part shade | Medium soil | Zones 3–8 | 24–36 in. tall and wide

*Eurybia divaricata*, formerly called *Aster divaricatus*, blooms in late summer or early autumn with clusters of airy white flowers on blackish-purple stems. It tolerates heavy shade and some soil dryness, although it will be less floriferous in these conditions. When in bloom, its airy texture mingles well with the larger leaves and white flowers of *Anemone ×hybrida* 'Honorine Jobert'. This plant is native to eastern North America.

## *Farfugium japonicum* | farfugium

Part shade | Moist, well-drained soil | Zones 7–8 | 24 in. tall and wide

*Farfugium japonicum* looks best growing in groups either in the ground or in a pot. Its unusually shaped leaves may be green, or variegated with white margins or yellow spots, depending on the cultivar. It grows naturally next to streams, and makes a wonderful addition to a shady water's edge. In areas where it is borderline hardy, mulch it in winter. It may be invasive in some areas.

## *Filipendula rubra* | queen-of-the-prairie

Edge or part shade | Medium to wet soil | Zones 3–9 | 48–84 in. tall, 36–48 in. wide

*Filipendula rubra* is a tall plant that would be a good addition to a large, partly shaded rain garden. It readily spreads in moist soil to produce impressively large stands. It blooms in summer with fluffy pink flower heads that are held above the lobed green foliage. Queen-of-the-prairie is native to the central and eastern United States. Try the cultivar 'Venusta', which makes a good border plant in damp soil.

*Euphorbia amygdaloides* var. *robbiae*

*Eurybia divaricata*

*Farfugium japonicum*

*Filipendula rubra* 'Venusta'

## Fritillaria meleagris | guinea hen fritillary, checkered lily

Bright shade | Moist, well-drained soil | Zones 4–8 | 12–15 in. tall, 2–3 in. wide

Plants in the genus *Fritillaria* have bell-shaped flowers that come in a variety of colors and sizes, and many can grow in some shade. *Fritillaria meleagris* is a spring-blooming bulb with unusual checkerboard flower markings that give rise to its common names. Most *F. meleagris* flowers are a mix of lighter and darker purple, but there is also a lovely white form. In the wild, it grows along river floodplains, so place it in moist soil in your garden. It is tolerant of alkaline soils and prefers cool, damp summers. I like to plant this with *Camassia*. *Fritillaria michailovskyi* is another species that will grow in dappled shade. I have it combined with *Ophiopogon japonicus* 'Gyoku-ryu'.

## Galanthus nivalis | common snowdrop

Edge or part shade | Medium to moist, well-drained soil | Zones 3–8 | 4–8 in. tall, 4–6 in. wide

Plants in the genus *Galanthus*, called snowdrops, have small, white, dangling flowers that bloom during the cold months of the year. Place these autumn-planted bulbs in large drifts for best impact. However, even a small patch emerging from the snow is a treat. I am a galanthophile, a person that loves snowdrops. The pleasure I find in watching my snowdrops emerge in the shade garden sustains me through the wintertime—beware that once you start collecting snowdrops, you too might become hooked!

*Galanthus nivalis* is one of the first bulbs to bloom in the shade garden in late winter. The pure white, bell-shaped flowers are marked with green on the inner petals. These markings allow identification of different cultivars, of which there are hundreds. This snowdrop has strap-like, gray-green leaves. The whole plant will survive being frozen, even when in bloom. My very favorite cultivar of this species is 'S. Arnott', because it is a great garden plant with larger flowers and a sweet honey scent. I also love an old double-flowered form that increases readily in my garden, *G. nivalis* f. *peniflorus* 'Flore Pleno'.

Other species worth growing are *G. elwesii*, giant snowdrop, and *G. woronowii*, Woronow's snowdrop. *Galanthus elwesii* has gray-green leaves and stands tall at 8–12 inches. *Galanthus woronowii* has glossy green leaves and multiplies well for me.

## Galium odoratum | sweet woodruff, fragrant bedstraw

Part shade | Medium to moist soil | Zones 4–8 | 8–12 in. tall, indefinitely wide

*Galium odoratum* is a low-growing shade perennial that has small white starry flowers held above its foliage in spring. The green whorls of leaves spread to cover the ground. This plant will grow in dry, dappled shade but performs better with a little more moisture. Sweet woodruff is an herbal plant that was used as a fragrant bedding material for centuries, hence its common name. The best fragrance comes from the cut and dried foliage. Sweet woodruff may be invasive in some areas. It needs more shade in the southern United States.

A clump of *Galanthus nivalis* in late winter.

top left  *Fritillaria meleagris*

left  *Galium odoratum*

*Gentiana andrewsii*

## *Gentiana andrewsii*
bottle gentian

Bright or part shade
Moist, well-drained soil  |  Zones 3–7
18–30 in. tall, 24 in. wide

*Gentiana andrewsii* has blue bottle-shaped flowers that never fully open. They bloom in late summer to early fall and attract pollinators. Watching a bumblebee wiggle inside is quite a sight to behold! The bottle gentian is one of the easiest gentians to grow in a typical garden situation. It is native to North America and may be confused with the very similar *G. clausa*. Another hardy, shade-tolerant gentian, *G. asclepiadea*, willow gentian, commands attention when in bloom. It is a cascading plant with vibrant blue, trumpet-shaped flowers that open in late summer.

## *Geranium*  |  geranium, cranesbill

*Geranium* is a large and varied genus that contains many worthwhile shade garden plants. In addition to the species listed below, I have found *G. ×cantabrigiense* 'Biokovo' to be very shade and dry soil tolerant, growing in my garden under an established magnolia tree. I also would recommend *G. maculatum* 'Espresso' for its dark bronzy-purple foliage and purple-pink flowers.

### ▶ *Geranium macrorrhizum*  |  bigroot geranium, bigroot cranesbill

Bright to full shade  |  Dry to medium soil  |  Zones 3–8  |  12–18 in. tall, 12 in. wide

*Geranium macrorrhizum* has magenta flowers in late spring until midsummer. Once established, it is drought tolerant, and the strong smell of its fuzzy leaves repels deer and rabbits. Over time, it will spread from the initial plant by rhizomes to make a nice patch. Try the old cultivar 'Ingwersen's Variety', which has light pink flowers and darker stems. I grow several cultivars of this species, as it is one of the best groundcovers for dry shade. Combine it with *G. maculatum*, the spotted cranesbill, under shrubs and in partly shaded borders.

## ▶ *Geranium sanguineum*
bloody cranesbill

Edge or part shade   |   Well-drained soil
Zones 3–8   |   8–12 in. tall, 12 in. wide

Bloody cranesbill has spring-blooming pink or magenta flowers on a nice mound of dissected foliage. It is great planted at the front of the border and tolerates hot weather well. *Geranium sanguineum* var. *striatum*, formerly var. *lancastrense*, is my favorite, with its light pink petals veined with a darker pink. I also love the white-flowering 'Album' near white-barked birches.

## *Gillenia trifoliata*
Bowman's root

Bright or part shade   |   Moist soil
Zones 4–8   |   24–48 in. tall, 12–36 in. wide

Bowman's root has delicate white flowers in late spring borne on long, flexible reddish stems, which are good for cutting. The bushy, airy quality of *Gillenia trifoliata* makes it a perfect partner for plants like *Digitalis* or *Geranium*.

I like it in a shaded border or near a seat in the garden where I can observe its details up close. This plant, which was formerly known as *Porteranthus trifoliatus*, has continued interest into autumn as its foliage changes color. It is native to North America, growing best in moist, acidic to neutral soil, where it spreads via rhizomes.

*Geranium sanguineum* 'Album'

*Gillenia trifoliata*

*Hakonechloa macra* 'Aureola'

### *Hakonechloa macra* | Hakone grass, Japanese forest grass

Bright or part shade | Moist, well-drained soil | Zones 5–9 | 12–18 in. tall and wide

*Hakonechloa macra* is one of the most attractive grasses to grow in the shade. Its gently cascading leaves look like flowing water when planted in a drift on a hillside or in a large container. Place this plant where there is adequate soil moisture for best growth. Hakone grass is tolerant of air pollution, so it makes a good choice in the urban landscape.

The straight species is plain green and is useful for subtle textural contrast with any broad-leaved perennials or woody plants. Cultivars are available in a variety of gold or silver variegated forms and they may change color in autumn. Any cultivar looks great edging a path or patio where it can soften the hard edges. The gold-and-green-striped 'Aureola' is the most commonly grown cultivar and is my favorite. It brightens shady areas when paired with *Alchemilla mollis* and any yellow-toned or golden variegated *Hosta*.

## Helleborus | hellebore, winter rose

Hellebores are a perfect shade garden plant. Their nodding flowers have a long season of bloom from late winter through spring and their foliage looks good for the whole growing season. Plant them in a shady border or use in groups in naturalized woodlands. They are easy-care plants that are not typically browsed by herbivores due to their toxic sap and spiny-edged leaves. Most hellebores thrive in neutral to alkaline soils.

*Helleborus* ×*hybridus* 'Gold Finch'

### ▶ *Helleborus foetidus* | stinking hellebore

Bright or part shade | Moist, humus-rich soil
Zones 6–9 | 18–24 in. tall, 12–18 in. wide

Stinking hellebore suffers from having a poor name—it used to be called worse names, including dungwort—but otherwise it is a fabulous garden plant. The fetid smell is not really noticeable unless you crush the foliage. Its glossy, green, divided evergreen leaves and chartreuse green clusters of flowers look great when combined with *Galanthus* and *Eranthis* in early spring. *Helleborus foetidus* will never be the main plant in a grouping, because it is a relatively short-lived perennial, but it will seed into the garden where conditions are right. Seedlings flower in their second year. I received my first specimen as a pass-along plant at a dinner party. It is a good plant to share with friends.

### ▶ *Helleborus* ×*hybridus* | hybrid hellebore, Lenten rose

Bright or part shade | Moist, well-drained soil | Zones 4–9 | 18–24 in. tall and wide

*Helleborus* ×*hybridus* is a must-have plant with some of the longest-blooming flowers in the shade garden. The nodding flowers emerge early in spring in shades of white, pink, purple, green, yellow, maroon, or almost black. The range of cultivars that are available has increased to include both single and double flowers.

Hybrid hellebores are easy to grow in any average garden conditions as long as the soil is not waterlogged during the year, but especially in winter. Substantive, divided evergreen foliage arises anew each spring. Site *Helleborus* ×*hybridus* at the top of a bank to allow you to admire the downward-facing flowers that shed late snows with abandon. This is a long-lived perennial that you will enjoy for years. I love the Brandywine Hybrids because they are diverse in color and form but they all look good together. In late winter, before the new growth emerges, cut off the old leaves at their bases and dispose of them to reduce fungal diseases. Wear gloves when handling the sharp leaves.

## Hemerocallis fulva 'Flore Pleno' | double orange daylily

Bright or part shade
Moist, well-drained soil | Zones 3–9
36 in. tall, 48 in. wide

*Hemerocallis fulva* 'Flore Pleno' is an old-fashioned daylily with double orange-red flowers. It has summer blooms that each only last one day, but are produced continuously over the course of several weeks. I love the "plant it and forget it" nature of daylilies that will survive with little care. There are thousands of other shade-tolerant daylily cultivars and species, and I especially like the yellow-flowered and fragrant *H. lilioasphodelus* and hybrid *H.* 'Hyperion'.

## Hepatica acutiloba

hepatica, liverleaf

Bright to full shade
Medium to moist soil | Zones 3–8
4–8 in. tall, 6–8 in. wide

*Hepatica acutiloba* is an adorable little spring bloomer with flowers that emerge before its three-lobed leaves. The delicate flowers last well in cool spring weather and range in color from white to pale pink or lavender blue. Tuck these plants near a rock to protect their roots and make them easy to locate. Group *Hepatica* plants together for maximum impact. Site them in neutral to alkaline soil and add leaf mold before planting.

In addition to *H. acutiloba*, I recommend the closely related *H. americana*, which has more rounded leaves. These are both native to eastern North America. There are related species and cultivars of *Hepatica* that come from the Asian and European continents. There is taxonomic confusion about the genus *Hepatica*, with some taxonomists putting it in the genus *Anemone*.

*Hemerocallis fulva* 'Flore Pleno'

*Hepatica acutiloba*

## Heuchera | coral bells

The plants in the genus *Heuchera* are chiefly grown in gardens for their patterned or colored foliage. They have flower spikes that are attractive to pollinators. The leaves look very similar to those of *Tiarella*. There is a cross between *Heuchera* and *Tiarella* called ×*Heucherella* that also does well in the shade.

### ▶ *Heuchera villosa*
hairy alumroot

Bright or part shade
Dry to moist, well-drained soil
Zones 5–9 | 18 in. tall, 12 in. wide

*Heuchera villosa* has soft and fuzzy large green leaves that look good all season long. In late summer or early fall, its creamy white spikes of little flowers rise above the foliage. I like to grow them at the front of borders, but they also look good used as a ground-cover. Hairy alumroot is native to North America. The cultivar *H. villosa* 'Autumn Bride' has showier flower heads than the straight species. *Heuchera villosa* 'Palace Purple' has decorative purple-bronze foliage, perfect for contrasting with lighter-colored plants.

### ▶ *Heuchera* hybrids
hybrid heuchera

Edge or part shade | Moist, well-drained soil
Zones 4–9
18 in. tall and wide; size varies by cultivar

*Heuchera* 'Marmalade' and *H.* 'Obsidian'

Heucheras are a staple of many shade gardens. They flower in summer, but most gardeners grow them for their foliage. They are popular plants because they come in a wide range of leaf colors. Select cultivars that are appropriate for your color scheme. *Heuchera* 'Caramel' has sunset-colored leaves and pairs well with the fern *Dryopteris erythrosora* 'Brilliance' because it picks up its warm tones. *Heuchera* 'Citronelle', a bright lime-green cultivar, does best in part shade and is relatively heat tolerant. There can be some slug and snail damage to *Heuchera* hybrid leaves in wetter areas, so try planting them in window boxes or in pots raised off the ground if your region is wet.

*Hosta* cultivars with a mix of glaucous blue-gray and yellow-green coloration.

# *Hosta* | hosta

Dappled or part shade | Moist, well-drained soil | Zones 3–8 | Size varies by cultivar

Hostas are the backbone of many shade gardens. They are grown primarily for their decorative leaves, which range in size from miniature to massive. *Hosta* leaves can be green, blue-green, chartreuse, or variegated with white, cream, or yellow. Their bold, unserrated foliage pairs well with delicate fern fronds in a classic shade garden combination. *Hosta* flowers emerge after the leaves and provide summer interest. Flower colors range from white to purple, and some have a wonderful scent, such as those of *H.* 'Fragrant Bouquet' and *H.* 'Fragrant Dream'.

Many animals, including deer and slugs, eat *Hosta*. To protect your specimens from deer damage, tuck them next to deer-resistant plants like *Helleborus*. To ward off slugs, grow them in terracotta pots, which act as physical barriers, or choose to grow tougher, thick-leaved cultivars such as *H.* 'Liberty' or *H.* 'Blue Mouse Ears'. Miniature hostas, in particular, look great grown in troughs and containers. Some of my favorite hostas are *H.* 'Royal Standard', *H.* 'The Razor's Edge', *H. fortunei* 'Striptease', *H.* 'Pineapple Upsidedown Cake', *H.* 'June', *H.* 'Blue Cadet', *H.* 'Stiletto', *H. sieboldiana* 'Frances Williams', and *H.* 'Ginko Craig'.

## *Hyacinthoides non-scripta*
English bluebell, common bluebell

Bright or part shade
Moist, well-drained soil   |   Zones 5–8
12–18 in. tall, 6–8 in. wide

*Hyacinthoides non-scripta* is prized for its fragrance and charming blue flowers. It is perfect planted in large drifts or carpeting a woodland floor. In a smaller shade garden, clumps of these bluebells are lovely poking through a low groundcover. This is an iconic countryside plant in England, where it naturalizes in open woods, perfuming the late spring air. *Hyacinthoides hispanica*, Spanish bluebell, is similar but has a less delicate look in the garden and may be invasive in some areas. Do not confuse either of these bluebells with *Mertensia*, which is also commonly called bluebells, but is unrelated.

*Hyacinthoides non-scripta*

*Iris cristata*

## *Iris* | iris

*Iris*, a hugely diverse genus with distinctive, three-parted flowers, contains a number of plants that are excellent choices for the shade garden.

### ▶ *Iris cristata*
dwarf crested iris, crested woodland iris

Bright to full shade | Medium to moist soil | Zones 3–9
3–8 in. tall, 15 in. wide

*Iris cristata* is a great plant for the front of the border. A low clump of leaves eventually spreads out from the initial planting to make a good groundcover. In spring, blue or white flowers rise above the foliage. To make more plants, divide it after flowering. This beautiful wildflower is native to eastern North America and looks excellent near other spring bloomers like woodland *Phlox* and *Anemone blanda*.

### ▶ *Iris domestica* | blackberry lily

Edge or part shade | Well-drained soil | Zones 5–10
24–48 in. tall, 8–24 in. wide

*Iris domestica*, formerly called *Belamcanda chinensis*, forms fans of long green foliage. Their clusters of spotted orange or yellow flowers open in succession and retain their color best in afternoon shade. The seedheads that follow are filled with black pearl-like seeds, which look like blackberries when fully ripe, giving rise to its common name. I like to grow *Iris domestica* along a partly shaded gravel path where it seeds itself in randomly.

### ▶ *Iris foetidissima*
stinking iris, stinking Gladwyn

Bright to full shade | Dry to moist, well-drained soil
Zones 7–9 | 18–24 in. tall, 18 in. wide

*Iris foetidissima* is an evergreen iris that has unremarkable flowers in spring that are followed by seedpods containing decorative red-orange seeds. These remain on the plant and add a colorful accent to the winter shade garden. The name, stinking iris, should not stop you from growing this plant because the odor is not noticeable unless the leaves are crushed. It will grow in dry shade, but less vigorously.

## Jeffersonia diphylla | twinleaf

Part to full shade | Moist, well-drained soil
Zones 5–8 | 8–18 in. tall, 6–8 in. wide

*Jeffersonia diphylla* is one of the curiosities of the spring garden, with a divided leaf that is joined in the center, hence its common name, twinleaf. This herbaceous perennial has small white flowers in early spring, and is native to North America. An unusual seed capsule with a hinged top quickly replaces the ephemeral flower. Grow the plant in neutral to slightly alkaline soil, and top dress it with leaf mold every year. The genus *Jeffersonia* is named for Thomas Jefferson, who grew the plant in his garden at Monticello in Charlottesville, Virginia.

A related species, *J. dubia*, is similar but has pale lavender flowers; it is well worth acquiring. Whichever species you grow, it will enchant you.

*Jeffersonia diphylla*

## Kirengeshoma palmata
yellow wax bells

Part to full shade | Medium to moist soil
Zones 5–8 | 36–48 in. tall, 24–48 in. wide

*Kirengeshoma palmata* is not a common plant, but is worth growing for its good foliage quality and late season blooms. The large, maple-shaped leaves lend a bold look to the garden composition. Nodding, yellow, waxy-textured flowers emerge from the end of the stems and never fully open. These dramatic perennials enliven the shade garden in late summer and early fall. Throughout the growing season, the vertical nature of the stems contrasts well with lower growing perennials. Grow *Kirengeshoma* in slightly acidic soil, and pair it with *Epimedium* and *Asarum*.

*Kirengeshoma palmata*

## Lamium maculatum 'Beacon Silver'

spotted dead nettle 'Beacon Silver'

Edge to full shade | Average soil | Zones 3–8
8 in. tall, 18–36 in. wide or more

*Lamium maculatum* 'Beacon Silver' is a fast-growing groundcover for tough conditions, such as the dry soil above tree roots. 'Beacon Silver' is grown for its heart-shaped, silver-centered leaves with pinkish-purple flowers in spring. Spotted dead nettles are useful plants, but are considered a weed in some areas and invasive in others. They aggressively spread by runners to fill a large area, so plant them with care. 'White Nancy' is similar in appearance, but has white flowers.

## Lamprocapnos spectabilis

common bleeding heart

Bright or part shade | Medium to moist soil
Zones 2–9 | 18–36 in. tall, 18–30 in. wide

*Lamprocapnos spectabilis*, formally known as *Dicentra spectabilis*, is a wonderful, old-fashioned perennial that is a stalwart of the spring shade garden. Arching stems bear many dangling, heart-shaped, pink and white flowers along their lengths. The pastel colors of the common bleeding heart pair beautifully with the blues of *Mertensia virginica* and *Myosotis sylvatica*.

In hotter summers, *Lamprocapnos* foliage dies down to the ground, so grow it next to a fern or *Hosta* to cover the resulting space. I grow the straight species in profusion and encourage it to seed itself around my woodland garden. There is an all-white-flowering cultivar, 'Alba', which I like to combine with other white-flowered spring perennials such as *Iris cristata* 'Tennessee White'. Another cultivar, 'Gold Heart', makes an unusual sight with its yellowish foliage and bright pink flowers.

*Lamium maculatum* 'Beacon Silver'

*Lamprocapnos spectabilis*

## *Leucojum aestivum* | summer snowflake

Bright or part shade | Moist, well-drained soil | Zones 4–8
12–18 in. tall, 10 in. wide

*Leucojum aestivum* has multiple, bell-shaped, white flowers with green dots on the petal tips. Despite its common name, summer snowflake blooms in spring. Its unevenly oblong seedheads that dangle and weigh down the stems after flowering are an additional ornamental feature. It has strap-like green leaves that stay fresh into summer and then disappear. Summer snowflake will naturalize itself along streambanks, so in the garden, site it in moist soil for best results. In the southeastern United States, snowflakes are often called snowdrops, which may be confusing.

*Leucojum vernum*, spring snowflake, blooms very early in spring and is shorter than summer snowflake. It blooms at the same time as *Galanthus nivalis* and they both look charming planted next to hybrid *Helleborus*.

*Leucojum aestivum*

## *Lilium martagon* | martagon lily, Turk's-cap lily

Edge or dappled shade | Well-drained soil | Zones 3–8
36–48 in. tall, 18 in. wide

*Lilium martagon* is a tall, delicate-looking plant with many small, purple-red, nodding flowers in early summer. I prefer the white variety, var. *album*, which reads well in the shaded landscape. A perfect position for this lily would be on the edge of a tree-shaded area where the sunlight is not too harsh. Site this long-lived lily in soil with good drainage, and do not disturb the bulbs. I like martagon lilies to grow up through low-growing perennials such as ferns that shelter the underground bulb and keep it cool and moist.

Two related summer-blooming North American lilies, *L. superbum* and *L. canadense*, also grow well in some shade. *Lilium superbum*, American Turk's-cap lily, is a tall plant that blooms with spotted orange flowers. *Lilium canadense*, Canada lily, has yellow, orange, or red flowers.

*Lilium martagon* var. *album*

*Liriope muscari* 'Variegata'

## *Liriope muscari*  |  blue lily turf

Bright or part shade  |  Medium soil  |  Zones 4–10
8–16 in. tall, 12 in. wide

*Liriope muscari* is widely grown in low-maintenance situations where it forms sweeping carpets. It has upright, purple spikes of late summer flowers and it has increased in popularity due to its grasslike leaves that retain their good looks all season. Silver variegated cultivars can be used to brighten up a dark place. These plants are strong growers that can overwhelm other perennials, so do not plant them in mixed beds or borders. *Liriope* is considered invasive in some places, and so is a poor choice for a garden near a wild area.

## *Lobelia*  |  lobelia

The species in the genus *Lobelia* introduce splashes of bright color into the late season shade garden. *Lobelia erinus*, trailing lobelia, has small, bright blue flowers and is used extensively as an annual in container plantings.

### ▶ *Lobelia cardinalis*  |  cardinal flower

Bright or part shade  |  Medium to wet soil  |  Zones 2–9
24–48 in. tall, 12–24 in. wide

Cardinal flower is a short-lived perennial that hops around the garden as it seeds in. It is grown for its vertical spires of brilliant red flowers that attract hummingbirds in summer. *Lobelia cardinalis* is a good choice for the banks of a stream or pond, but will perform well in a garden bed with sufficient moisture. It is native to a wide swath of North America and does well in rain gardens, wildlife gardens, and summer shade plantings.

### ▶ *Lobelia siphilitica*

great blue lobelia, blue cardinal flower

Bright or part shade  |  Medium to wet soil  |  Zones 4–9
24–36 in. tall, 12 in. wide

*Lobelia siphilitica* is prized for its sky blue flowers that attract hummingbirds and butterflies to the partly shaded garden. The stiff flower spikes provide vertical accents and should be used where a splash of blue is needed in the late summer garden. This perennial is naturally found along streams, in low woodlands, and near swamps in eastern North America. It may seed around the garden, and where conditions are ideal, this plant can also spread vigorously from its initial clump. The best way to acquire great blue lobelia is to dig up a plant from a friend's garden in spring.

*Lobelia cardinalis*

## *Luzula nivea* | snowy woodrush

Bright to full shade | Moist soil | Zones 4–9
12–30 in. tall, 18 in. wide

*Luzula nivea* is a moisture-loving plant that gets its common name from its summer tufts of white flowers. During the rest of the year, it remains attractive due to its persistent green, grasslike leaves that are edged with a fringe of white hairs. It looks good as an edging to a path, or massed in a wet area.

Greater woodrush, *L. sylvatica* 'Aurea', is grown for its golden-yellow leaf color that combines well with yellow variegated *Hosta*. It is best planted near ponds, streams, or in other moist situations, but will cope with the competition of tree roots.

## *Lycoris squamigera*
magic lily, surprise lily

Edge or part shade
Medium to moist, well-drained soil | Zones 5–9
18–24 in. tall and wide

*Lycoris squamigera* is grown for its fragrant, blue-tinged pink flowers that erupt from the ground like fireworks in late summer or early autumn. In spring, the bright green, elongated foliage emerges and then dies down. Interplant magic lilies with a ground-cover like hardy *Geranium* to hide their browning foliage in summer. *Lycoris radiata*, red spider lily or red magic lily, has brilliant red fall flowers with exceptionally long stamens.

*Luzula nivea*

*Lycoris squamigera*

*Maianthemum racemosum*

## Maianthemum racemosum
false Solomon's seal

Edge to full shade  |  Moist, well-drained soil
Zones 3–8  |  24–36 in. tall and wide

*Maianthemum racemosum* is a rhizomatous North American native woodland plant. Its terminal clusters of white, late spring to early summer flowers show up from a distance in the shade garden when it is in bloom. They have a pleasant, soft scent. Speckled red berries follow the flowers in late summer and are great food for wildlife. The arching stems of false Solomon's seal look elegant planted with *Trillium* and *Mertensia*. *Maianthemum racemosum*, previously called *Smilacina racemosa*, needs deep, acidic soil, rich in humus.

    *Maianthemum canadense*, Canadian lily of the valley, is a related species with a short stature that has shiny green leaves and small clusters of fragrant, white, starlike flowers in spring. Its speckled late summer berries mature to red.

## Mazus reptans  |  creeping mazus

Bright or part shade  |  Medium to wet soil
Zones 5–8  |  2–4 in. tall, 6–12 in. or more wide

*Mazus reptans* is a very low-growing plant that creeps over the ground and roots as it spreads. It can take light foot traffic and is a lovely choice to grow between stepping stones or bordering a gravel or stone path. It has small, late spring flowers in shades of blue, light purple, or white. During the remainder of the growing season, the miniscule fresh green foliage remains attractive.

*Mazus reptans* used as a groundcover between wooden steps.

## Meconopsis grandis
Himalayan blue poppy

Bright or part shade  |  Moist, well-drained soil
Zones 5–8  |  36–48 in. tall, 24 in. wide

*Meconopsis* species are sought-after, often short-lived poppies that come in bright colors of blue, yellow, and pink. Where these plants can grow, grow them and grow lots of them. *Meconopsis grandis* and other related blue Himalayan poppies inspire an instant desire to grow them once you see them. It is an unusual and eye-catching flower in the shade garden with its translucent blue petals and mass of yellow stamens. Unfortunately, this poppy requires very specific conditions: cool summers, humus-rich neutral to slightly acidic soil, and a location that, in winter, is either sheltered from harsh weather or is consistently insulated with a thick layer of snow.

Welsh poppy, *M. cambrica*, has buttercup-yellow flowers and seeds around where conditions are right.

*Meconopsis grandis*

## Mertensia virginica
Virginia bluebells

Bright or part shade  |  Moist, well-drained soil
Zones 3–9  |  18–24 in. tall, 12–18 in. wide

*Mertensia virginica* is a spring ephemeral that grows before deciduous trees leaf out and then gradually dies down by summer. Its beautiful, bell-shaped flowers are sky blue to light purple in color and look enchanting in large groups. Virginia bluebells can be massed or can be mixed with shade-tolerant *Narcissus*, *Lamprocapnos*, *Brunnera*, and *Stylophorum* for a pastel spring picture. This eastern North American native is a lovely addition to a spring garden and should be paired with summer-interest perennials or ferns to cover the dying foliage.

*Mertensia virginica*

## Mukdenia rossii | mukdenia

Dappled or part shade | Moist, well-drained soil | Zones 4–9 | 8–18 in. tall, 12–24 in. wide

The small, creamy spring flowers of *Mukdenia rossii* are held above its large, maple-like leaves. The color of the leaves provides interest as they change from green in spring to red over the course of the growing season. I grow this mukdenia next to a stone-lined drainage run in my shade garden where it can keep its roots cool in the heat of summer. If you plan to plant this unusual perennial, choose a moist area and add some stones, grit, or gravel to the planting bed. Its bold foliage complements the smaller leaves of plants like *Tricyrtis* and *Chrysogonum*.

## Muscari 'Mount Hood' | grape hyacinth 'Mount Hood'

Bright or part shade | Well-drained soil | Zones 4–8 | 6–8 in. tall, 1–2 in. wide

*Muscari* 'Mount Hood' has clusters of fragrant, spring blooming flowers, blue at the base and white at the top, resembling a snow-capped mountain. Other worthwhile shade-tolerant *Muscari* species are *M. armeniacum*, *M. azureum*, and *M. botryoides*. I like *M. armeniacum* cultivars 'Dark Eyes', 'Peppermint', and 'Valerie Finnis'. Most *Muscari* plants will self-sow into the garden, which I enjoy, but some gardeners do not appreciate. Although low growing, it mixes well with taller *Narcissus*. For best impact, plant *Muscari* in swaths in the garden.

## Myosotis sylvatica | woodland forget-me-not

Edge or bright shade | Moist, well-drained soil | Zones 3–8 | 6–12 in. tall, 6–8 in. wide

Plants in the genus *Myosotis* tend to be short-lived and self-sow freely in moist soils. Woodland forget-me-not is a classic spring plant that weaves among other plants to lend cohesion to a garden picture. Light blue flowers with white and yellow eyes are borne in profusion on low-growing foliage. Leave the plants in the garden until you see the brown seedheads, then pull them up and shake the seeds where you would like future plants to be. It is a perfect plant for a garden under an old apple tree with *Narcissus*, *Tulipa sylvestris*, or *Erythronium* 'Pagoda'.

## Narcissus 'Hawera' | daffodil 'Hawera'

Edge or part shade | Average soil | Zones 4–9 | 8–12 in tall, 2–3 in. wide

Daffodils are autumn-planted bulbs that are a glory in the spring garden. There are many hundreds of cultivars, some of which are perfect in edge and other partially shaded conditions. *Narcissus* 'Hawera' has buttery yellow, nodding, fragrant flower heads borne in clusters of two to six on each stem. Every bulb produces multiple stems, giving a delicate but noticeable presence in the spring garden. I love this daffodil for its ability to mix in the garden and the fact that its slender, reed-like foliage disappears unobtrusively. Pair it with *Fritillaria*, *Anemone blanda*, *Muscari*, or *Ophiopogon*. Other daffodils that do well in some shade include *N.* 'Actaea', *N.* 'Baby Moon', *N.* 'February Gold', *N.* 'Jenny', *N.* 'Silver Chimes', *N.* 'Sun Disc', and *N.* 'Thalia'.

top left  *Mukdenia rossii*

top middle  *Muscari* ˙Mount Hood˙

top right  *Myosotis sylvatica*

left  Pale yellow *Narcissus* ˙Hawera˙ growing with *Muscari*.

## Nectaroscordum siculum | Sicilian honey garlic

Bright or part shade | Medium to moist soil | Zones 6–10
24–30 in. tall, 12 in. wide

*Nectaroscordum siculum* has unusual dangling, bell-shaped, green, cream, and dark pink flowers. Grown from an autumn-planted bulb, it blooms in early to midsummer. Site it in damp situations where you want an element of surprise—the flowering stalks rise high above the strap-like foliage. Additional interest comes form the seedheads that follow the flowers, which point upward in a cluster. They are resistant to herbivore browsing because their foliage smells like garlic. The subspecies *bulgaricum* may be easier to find. This plant is sometimes listed as *Allium siculum*.

## Ophiopogon planiscapus 'Nigrescens'
black mondo grass, black lilyturf

Bright or part shade | Moist soil | Zones 6–10
6–8 in. tall, 12–16 in. wide

*Ophiopogon* is a genus of clumping perennials with grasslike leaves that spread by rhizomes and are used as groundcovers. *Ophiopogon planiscapus* 'Nigrescens' is grown for its dark mahogany-black foliage that makes a good contrasting garden partner to *Galanthus* in early spring and white-flowering *Nicotiana* in summer. It will also enhance brightly colored or variegated forms of *Heuchera*. Evergreen in milder climates, it does get damaged by bad winters and benefits from a consistent cover of snow.

*Ophiopogon japonicus* 'Gyoku-ryu', dwarf Mondo grass, is an effective groundcover or path edging, especially in the southern United States. Its small scale suits it for growing in a trough or other container with miniature *Hosta*.

*Nectaroscordum siculum*

*Ophiopogon planiscapus* 'Nigrescens'

*Pachysandra terminalis*

## *Pachysandra* | pachysandra

Plants in the genus *Pachysandra* are used in the garden as easy-care groundcovers for a wide range of shade conditions.

### ▶ *Pachysandra procumbens* | Allegheny spurge

Bright to full shade | Medium to moist soil | Zones 5–9 | 8–12 in. tall, 12 in. wide

*Pachysandra procumbens*, an eastern North American native, is grown for its green and brown speckled foliage. Its unusually shaped, fragrant spring flowers are cream and blush pink. I grow this spurge in combination with *Polygonatum* and *Uvularia*. This species is slower growing and less aggressive than *P. terminalis*.

### ▶ *Pachysandra terminalis* | Japanese spurge

Part to full shade | Any soil | Zones 4–9 | 8–12 in. tall, indefinitely wide

*Pachysandra terminalis* has glossy, evergreen leaves with a white spike of flowers in late spring. It is a useful plant for covering steep banks and for under the deep shade of coniferous trees. Use caution in good garden conditions, as it can take over large areas to the exclusion of other plants. Overused to the point of boredom in much of the United States, in other areas of the world it is not so common and therefore is considered more favorably.

The colorful seedhead of *Paeonia obovata*.

## *Paeonia obovata* | woodland peony

Bright or part shade | Medium soil | Zones 5–8
24–36 in. tall and wide

The genus *Paeonia* is better known for sun-loving garden perennials, but there are a few woodland species that are suitable for the shady garden. *Paeonia obovata* has two main seasons of interest: in spring, an elegant single white or pink flower is followed by a seedpod. In autumn, the seedpods open to reveal shiny red and dark blue seeds. Plant this slow-growing peony in good woodland soil in part shade. Another woodland peony, *P. japonica*, has similar characteristics and growing requirements. Both species should be left to grow undisturbed with the occasional addition of leaf mold.

## *Penstemon digitalis* 'Husker Red'

penstemon 'Husker Red', beardtongue 'Husker Red'

Dappled or part shade | Dry to moist soil | Zones 4–8
24–30 in. tall, 18–24 in. wide

Penstemons, also known as beardtongues, have tubular flowers in a variety of colors. All are grown for their vertical habit as an accent in the garden or as wildlife plants. There are several species especially suited for the shade garden, including *P. digitalis*, *P. pallidus*, and *P. smallii*.

*Penstemon digitalis* 'Husker Red' has deep burgundy stems and burgundy-flushed dark green leaves. In midsummer, its white to pale purple flowers contrast exceptionally well with its foliage. It is a perfect plant massed in drifts for a wild area, or along the banks of a rain garden. All *P. digitalis* plants will do well in hot summers and cold winters. Another beardtongue, *P. smallii*, has pink to purple flowers with a white center in late spring and requires excellent drainage. *Penstemon pallidus* has white flowers and will grow in dry soil and part shade.

*Penstemon digitalis* 'Husker Red'

## Persicaria virginiana Variegated Group

variegated Virginia tovara

Bright or part shade   |   Moist, well-drained soil
Zones 4–8   |   12–24 in. tall, 24–36 in. wide

*Persicaria virginiana* Variegated Group consists of North American native plants, grown for their variegated green-and-cream leaves that make a splash in the shade garden. They have fuchsia-pink threadlike inflorescences. They can grow too aggressively and spread over large areas of your garden, so plant them in an area where they can be contained or give these perennials less than perfect conditions to restrain their vigor.

I grow mine where it is backed by *Hydrangea* with a woodchip path in front. I have learned to take off the spent flowers after blooming so that there is less seeding onto the path. 'Painter's Palette' is the most widely available cultivar of Virginia tovara and has a V-shaped red mark in the center of the leaf. Related Eurasian species of *Persicaria*, such as *P. bistorta* and *P. amplexicaulis*, grow well in moist to wet soils in part shade and are popular in England.

*Persicaria virginiana* Variegated Group

## Petasites hybridus 'Variegatus'

variegated butterbur

Bright or part shade   |   Moist soil   |   Zones 5–9
24–36 in. tall and wide

Plants in the genus *Petasites* are rhizomatous perennials grown for their dramatic kidney- or heart-shaped leaves. They have wonderful large leaves that can be used to add bold texture to the shade garden. Some species, such as the popular *P. japonicus*, may be invasive, so plant with caution. The especially large giant butterbur, *P. japonicus* var. *giganteus*, is only suitable for a large garden.

I grow variegated *P. hybridus* 'Variegatus' in an isolated spot by a pond to restrain its growth. It has captivating, round flower heads that emerge in early spring before the appearance of the creamy yellow and green leaves. It is less vigorous than *P. japonicus*.

The early spring flowers of *Petasites hybridus* 'Variegatus'.

*Phlox divaricata* 'Blue Moon'

## *Phlox divaricata*  |  woodland phlox, wild sweet William

Dappled or part shade  |  Moist, well-drained soil  |  Zones 3–9
12–15 in. tall, 12–20 in. wide

Phlox are famous for their showy, five-parted flowers. Woodland phlox are low-growing spring bloomers native to North America. Plant them with plenty of organic matter in the soil. *Phlox divaricata* is grown for its mounds of slightly fragrant spring flowers in hues of blue and white. They look great lining a path as they gently spread to make a good patch. I like 'London Grove Blue' and 'Blue Moon', but any cultivar, grown in large patches, is a spring treat. They pair well with *Iris cristata* and *Anemone blanda*.

The related *P. stolonifera*, creeping phlox, forms a good groundcover all season long. The straight species has clear blue-lavender flowers in spring. Cultivars also come in pink, white, and purple, for example, 'Home Fires', 'Bruce's White', and 'Sherwood Purple', respectively.

## *Podophyllum peltatum*  |  May apple

Part shade  |  Medium to moist soil  |  Zones 4–8
18 in. tall, 8–12 in. wide

*Podophyllum peltatum* is grown for its deeply dissected leaves, which have a vaguely circular outline. Their white flowers emerge only on plants that are old enough to have two leaves with a fork between them. The fruit, for which the may apple is commonly named, hangs down below the foliage and is edible once ripe. The whole plant dies down in summer heat.

Plant May apples in a naturalistic woodland garden in acidic soil on a slight slope for better drainage and visibility of the flowers. I like to combine *Podophyllum* with *Mertensia* and *Sanguinaria* for a perfect spring show. I am careful to also include something, like *Brunnera*, in the group to cover the bare patch left when the spring ephemerals' leaves disappear for the year.

*Podophyllum peltatum*

## Polemonium reptans | creeping Jacob's ladder

Bright or part shade | Moist, well-drained soil | Zones 3–8
6–12 in. tall, 12 in. wide

*Polemonium* is a genus of herbaceous plants that have groups of petite blue flowers. The leaves are arranged in a ladder-like pattern, hence the common name of Jacob's ladder.

I grow the eastern North American native *Polemonium reptans* for its sky blue flowers in spring and fresh green foliage that lasts the growing season. It is a charming small plant that looks good with *Primula veris* and *Disporopsis pernyi*. When planted in good, humus-rich soil, Jacob's ladder will self-sow and make a good-sized patch. *Polemonium caeruleum* has the same lovely blue flowers, but the entire plant is on a larger scale.

## Polygonatum odoratum var. pluriflorum 'Variegatum'

fragrant Solomon's seal, angled Solomon's seal

Part to full shade | Moist, well-drained soil | Zones 3–8
18–24 in. tall, 24 in. wide

Plants in the genus *Polygonatum*, known as Solomon's seal, are rhizomatous perennials grown for their graceful, arching habit as well as their foliage and flowers. All species grow best in fertile, humus-rich soil in part to full shade.

The habit of the fragrant Solomon's seal is one of its most admired features. Its curved, reddish stems have variegated cream and green leaves that shelter dangling teardrop flowers in spring. *Polygonatum odoratum* var. *pluriflorum* 'Variegatum' also pairs well in the garden with plants that have a more vertical habit, such as *Chelone*, *Digitalis*, or *Penstemon*. Other *Polygonatum* worth growing include the North American *P. biflorum*, and the dwarf, green-leaved *P. humile*.

*Polemonium reptans* has self-seeded in my woodland garden to produce plants that vary in height and leaf size.

*Polygonatum odoratum* var. *pluriflorum* 'Variegatum' surrounding the trunk of *Acer griseum*.

*Primula denticulata* 'Ronsdorf'

## *Primula* | primrose

Primroses are spring-blooming woodland and woodland-edge perennials. Flowers arise from a circle of basal leaves and are found in many different colors including yellow, pink, purple, red, or white. Choose primroses to suit your particular growing conditions. Many garden species need moist, humus-rich soil.

### ▶ *Primula denticulata* | drumstick primrose

Edge or part shade | Moist, well-drained soil | Zones 3–8
8–10 in. tall, 12 in. wide.

*Primula denticulata* has balls of lavender or white flowers on strong stems that emerge in early spring. This primrose will only grow well in moist, humus-rich soil, so do not let it dry out, particularly in summer. I grow a selection of cultivars in pink and purple shades and combine them with *Geranium maculatum* and *Erythronium*.

*Primula japonica*, one of the candelabra primroses, needs even more moisture for healthy growth and is best sited directly next to water. Its dramatic whorls of bright pink or white flowers bloom over a period of weeks; it is especially eye-catching when planted in groups.

### ▶ *Primula vulgaris*
primrose, English primrose

Edge or part shade | Medium to moist soil | Zones 4–8
8 in. tall, 14 in. wide

The English primrose is a heartwarming sight in the early spring garden. The pale yellow flowers have a soft scent and look great with *Anemone blanda* and *Narcissus* 'Hawera'. There are many cultivars available in a variety of colors, including some with double flowers. Divide large clumps of *Primula vulgaris* after flowering to multiply your stock.

*Primula veris*, cowslip, is a similar and charming member of this genus that has nodding yellow flowers borne on an upright stem. Plant in drifts and intersperse with *Hyacinthoides non-scripta* and *Myosotis*. Cowslips are enchanting when planted in elevated beds or on banks to allow you to appreciate their precious blooms.

# Pulmonaria saccharata

lungwort, Bethlehem sage

Part to full shade   |   Medium to moist, well-drained soil
Zones 3–8   |   6–10 in. tall, 12–24 in. wide

*Pulmonaria saccharata* has long been a stalwart of shade gardens. Its early spring blooms come in shades of pink and blue, and some cultivars' flowers change from one to the other as they mature. The spotted and speckled leaves give a long season of interest and are a great companion to the plain green leaves of *Helleborus*.

All lungworts are grown for their attractive lance-shaped, hairy, and often patterned leaves. I like to form carpets of *Pulmonaria* that make a pretty pastel picture in spring when they bloom and cover the ground effectively for the rest of the year. Plants will spread slowly by rhizomes to make a nice clump. I grow many cultivars, and favor plants in the *P. saccharata* Argentea Group, as well as *P. longifolia* 'Bertram Anderson' and the hybrid *P.* 'Majesté'.

In hot, dry climates, lungwort may develop powdery mildew in late summer. To minimize this problem, choose hybrids that are more resistant, such as *P.* 'Raspberry Splash' or *P.* 'Trevi Fountain', and add more compost to the soil to keep the roots moist. All *Pulmonaria* plants require good drainage year-round, but especially in the winter, or their crowns may rot. Try them in a raised bed or on a hillside to improve drainage.

A carpet of various *Pulmonaria saccharata* and *P. longifolia* cultivars intermingling with smaller *Hosta* leaves.

## *Rodgersia* species   |   rodgersia

Edge or part shade   |   Moist soil   |   Zones 5–8
36–48 in. tall and wide, varies slightly by species and cultivar

*Rodgersia* is a genus of clump-forming rhizomatous perennials with large leaves that grow in moist woodlands. Tall, fluffy, off-white, white, or pink flower spikes emerge from the center of the plant in summer. They pair well with other moisture-loving plants like *Aruncus*, *Astilbe*, and *Astrantia*. *Rodgersia aesculifolia* is a sizeable, palmately leaved plant that adds drama to a consistently moist or wet area of your shade garden.

There are other garden-worthy rodgersias that grow well in the same conditions, for example *R. pinnata* and *R. podophylla*. Both of these species have the added benefit of bronzy fall coloration. All rodgersias have an imposing presence in borders and beds and are notoriously difficult to differentiate from one another as they hybridize readily.

*Rodgersia* in flower.

## Rohdea japonica | sacred lily

Part to full shade  |  Moist soil  |  Zones 6–9  |  10–15 in. tall and wide

*Rohdea japonica* is a low-maintenance, clump-forming plant that has glossy, dark green leaves for most of the year. Its strange cream flowers are followed by red seedheads that persist into the winter. I grow it with *Carex* and *Chelone lyonii*. There are variegated cultivars available. Although they will tolerate dry shade, grow *Rohdea* in moist, fertile soil for healthy plants; otherwise they are prone to a fungal disease called rust.

## Sanguinaria canadensis | bloodroot

Bright to full shade  |  Medium, well-drained soil  |  Zones 3–9  |  6 in. tall, 8 in. wide

*Sanguinaria canadensis* is one of the earliest spring-blooming North American wildflowers. The peculiar common name of bloodroot is due to the red, blood-like juice that emerges from cut roots and stems. Bloodroot has single or double flowers that are a pristine white. Watch carefully for the emergence of this perennial, because you do not want to miss the flowers, which only last a few days. The variably indented leaves persist into summer. I like this wildflower with almost every other early blooming plant, but particularly with *Scilla siberica* 'Spring Beauty'.

## Saruma henryi | upright wild ginger

Part shade  |  Medium to moist, well-drained soil  |  Zones 4–8  |  18–24 in. tall, 10–18 in. wide

*Saruma* is a genus of unusual shade plants that are naturally found along wooded streams and in valleys. They have heart-shaped, fuzzy leaves, and small yellow flowers in spring. More of a curiosity than a true beauty, *Saruma henryi* is a good filler plant, especially when used to cover the dying foliage of spring ephemerals. This upright wild ginger has a spicy smell when crushed, but it is not a true ginger. I grow it with *Lamprocapnos* and *Helleborus*.

## Saxifraga stolonifera | strawberry saxifrage, creeping saxifrage

Part to full shade  |  Well-drained soil  |  Zones 6–9  |  12–15 in. tall and wide

*Saxifraga stolonifera* has scalloped, kidney-shaped green leaves with white veins and purple-red undersides. In spring, delicate masses of white flowers rise above the foliage. The leaves continue to be attractive until the first hard frost. This easy-to-care-for plant multiplies vegetatively by stolons to form a large patch, even around tree roots.

*Saxifraga* ×*urbium*, known as London pride, has white or pink flowers and rosettes of foliage. It is often used as an edging along paths and has more moisture tolerance than most *Saxifraga* species. I am fond of London pride because I remember seeing it as a child in my grandmother's garden.

*Rohdea japonica*

An established patch of *Sanguinaria canadensis* along a gravel path.

*Saruma henryi*

*Saxifraga stolonifera*

*Scilla siberica* 'Spring Beauty'

*Sedum ternatum*

## *Scilla siberica* | Siberian squill

Bright or part shade | Well-drained soil | Zones 3–8
3–6 in. tall, 3 in. wide

*Scilla siberica* has brilliant blue early spring flowers that look best when planted in a large drift. These bulbs will multiply by seed or you can dig them up after flowering to spread them around. Their rich blue flower color is one of the best indicators that spring is on its way. 'Spring Beauty' is my preferred cultivar.

Most scillas flower in late winter or early spring and combine well with other bulbs such as *Narcissus* and *Eranthis*. I also grow the related and appealing *S. bifolia* under a pink-flowering *Prunus mume*.

## *Sedum ternatum*

whorled stonecrop, woodland stonecrop

Bright or part shade | Well-drained soil | Zones 4–8
2–6 in. tall, 12–18 in. wide

Whorled stonecrop is a valuable plant for a well-drained or rocky area in the shade garden. Starry white flowers rise above the succulent foliage in late spring. It is native to the eastern part of North America. Try the cultivar 'Larinem Park', which forms a nice soft spring picture combined with *Phlox stolonifera* and *Iris cristata* 'Tennessee White'. Wet winter conditions will kill this plant, so place it in a well-drained location and add extra grit to the planting hole.

There are other sedums that could be used in rock gardens, green roofs, or other dry situations in bright or dappled shade, including *S. cauticola*, *S. glaucophyllum*, *S. kamtschaticum* var. *ellacombeanum*, and *S. spurium*.

## Spigelia marilandica

pinkroot, Maryland pinkroot

Bright or part shade | Medium to moist soil | Zones 6–9
24 in. tall, 12–24 in. wide

An unusual, summer-blooming shade plant, *Spigelia marilandica* has tubular flowers of yellow and red. Maryland pinkroot will grow in average to moist garden soil and is nice next to a path, or in a raised bed so that you can observe it up close. It will seed gently around the garden if you are lucky. Native to southeastern North America, this plant attracts migratory hummingbirds, making it a good choice for a wildlife garden.

## Stylophorum diphyllum

wood poppy, celandine poppy

Bright or part shade | Medium to moist soil | Zones 4–8
12–18 in. tall and wide

*Stylophorum diphyllum* is a North American woodland poppy that blooms with yellow, cup-shaped flowers in spring. Their cheerful sunny color mixes well with *Lamprocapnos*, *Mertensia*, and *Myosotis* and is a great way to brighten your garden. Its lobed foliage is retained on the plant through summer as long as the surrounding soil stays sufficiently moist. Wood poppies are generous self-seeders and can become too abundant. Decide where in the garden you want the poppy and ruthlessly remove it from anywhere else that it appears. Be sure to wear gloves when handling *S. diphyllum*, as its yellow-orange sap will stain your hands.

*Spigelia marilandica*

*Stylophorum diphyllum*

## Symphytum grandiflorum
large-flowered comfrey

Part shade | Medium to moist soil | Zones 3–8
12 in. tall, 12–24 in. wide

Plants in the genus *Symphytum* have hairy leaves and spread vigorously to form a midsized groundcover. So long as the soil is adequately moist, the leaf quality remains good through the season. *Symphytum grandiflorum* has clusters of small pendulous white to blue flowers in spring. A superior cultivar, *S.* 'Hidcote Blue', has prolific brighter blue blooms. Comfreys are generally easy-care plants. An extra benefit is that their leaves are rich in nitrogen, so they make a great addition to your compost pile.

## Syneilesis aconitifolia | shredded umbrella plant

Part to full shade | Medium, well-drained soil | Zones 4–8
15–24 in. tall, 10 in. wide

*Syneilesis aconitifolia* emerges out of the ground in spring like a folded umbrella that then unfurls. Its leaves are covered in fine silver hair when they are young, and then become greener by summer. The mature, highly dissected green leaves are held above the ground on upright stems. Although this plant does flower in summer, it is primarily grown for its foliage, which looks especially handsome with delicate ferns such as *Adiantum pedatum* and lower-growing perennials like *Alchemilla* and *Heuchera*.

*Symphytum grandiflorum*

*Syneilesis aconitifolia*

## Thalictrum rochebruneanum
lavender mist meadow rue

Part shade | Moist, well-drained soil | Zones 4–8
48–72 in. tall, 24 in. wide

*Thalictrum rochebruneanum* is a tall perennial that brings height to the summer shade garden when it blooms. Small lavender flowers with a boss of yellow stamens in the center are borne on towering, flexible stems. The light and airy texture of the flowers can make a see-through screen between one area of the garden and the next, or may be the focal point of a bed. Its foliage is delicate and pairs well with bolder-leaved plants like *Kirengeshoma* and *Hydrangea*. Site this plant at the edge of a woodland in moist soil. *Thalictrum aquilegiifolium* is shorter, and can take a little more shade. It blooms in spring and has powder puff–like purple flowers.

## Tiarella cordifolia | Allegheny foamflower

Part to full shade | Medium to moist soil | Zones 3–8
8–18 in. tall and wide

*Tiarella* is a genus of plants grown primarily for their spikes of spring flowers and good-quality foliage that lasts throughout the season. *Tiarella cordifolia* is native to eastern North America and is perfect as a groundcover plant or as an edging for a woodland pathway. Its hairy, heart-shaped, lobed leaves have red to burgundy markings in the center or along the veins, depending on the cultivar. In fall, the color of the leaves becomes darker and redder. The flowers are fluffy white to pink and rise above the foliage in late spring.

Allegheny foamflower spreads by runners and can cover the ground around tree roots to make large patches. Tiarellas are best in moist, humus-rich soil, with sufficient drainage. They grow well in slightly raised beds, which prevents root rot. I grow the cultivars 'Oakleaf', 'Running Tapestry', and any plants in the River Series, such as 'Brandywine' and 'Delaware'. *Tiarella wherryi* is more compact and clumping in habit but is just as desirable in the shade garden.

*Thalictrum rochebruneanum*

*Tiarella cordifolia* 'Running Tapestry'

*Tradescantia virginiana* 'Alba'

## Tradescantia virginiana | Virginia spiderwort

Edge or part shade | Medium to moist, well-drained soil
Zones 4–9 | 18–30 in. tall, 24–30 in. wide

*Tradescantia virginiana* is an easy-care plant for a wilder section of your garden, including the edges of a rain garden. Its linear, folded leaves arch up from the central crown and three-petaled blue-violet flowers emerge one or two at a time on central stalks in late spring to early summer. Virginia spiderwort is a vigorous grower once established, so do not plant it next to small woodland treasures, as it tends to sprawl. Cut the foliage back hard after flowering to remove untidy leaves. There are various cultivars, including 'Alba' with white flowers.

## Tricyrtis formosana 'Samurai'

toad lily 'Samurai'

Part to full shade | Rich, moist, well-drained soil | Zones 4–9
18–30 in. tall, 12–18 in. wide

The fascinating flowers of *Tricyrtis* may be purple, white, or yellow, and are often extravagantly spotted. The blooms are greatly anticipated each fall when they emerge out of leaf axils beginning at the tips of arching stems and progressing downwards. Toad lilies are best grown near a path or sitting area so that their unusual flowers and elegant habit can be seen and admired closely. They are excellent plants for the late season shade garden. They are eaten by some herbivores, so protect your plants if this is a problem in your area.

I love *T. formosana* 'Samurai', which has white flowers liberally flecked with purple, and a yellow-rimmed center. Its leaves have narrow gold edges that add to its appeal throughout the growing season. I also grow *T. formosana* 'Dark Beauty', the hybrid *T.* 'Sinonome', and *T. hirta*, among others. I recommend that you try a wide variety to extend the season of bloom.

*Tricyrtis formosana* 'Samurai'

## Trillium grandiflorum

large-flowered trillium, white wake-robin

Part to full shade | Moist, well-drained soil | Zones 3–8
16–24 in. tall, 24 in. wide

Trilliums are stars of the spring shade garden. Both the flowers and the leaves are in three parts. Their foliage dies down later in summer, so plant them near other perennials that will cover the gap they leave in the bed, like *Actaea*, *Epimedium*, or *Maianthemum*. They benefit from an annual mulching with leaf mold. Part of their allure is that they are slow to grow and difficult to procure. A well-grown patch of trillium elicits awe and envy from other gardeners as it takes some years to grow a significant clump.

*Trillium grandiflorum* has eye-catching flowers that are a brilliant white but fade to a blush pink. Large-flowered trilliums are native to forests in eastern North America and require deep, humus-rich acidic to neutral soil. I cluster this plant with *Dodecatheon meadia* 'Alba' and *Lamprocapnos spectabilis* 'Alba' for a splash of brightness in the shade of *Cercis canadensis*.

Try other wakerobins, such as *T. luteum*, with yellow flowers and mottled leaves, and *T. erectum*, with nodding burgundy flowers held above the foliage. Trilliums have historically been dug from the wild and have been depleted in their natural habitats, so always be sure to buy them from a reputable nursery.

## Tulipa sylvestris | woodland tulip

Edge or part shade | Well-drained soil | Zones 3–8
12–14 in. tall, 2 in. wide

*Tulipa sylvestris* has slender, pointed, fragrant flowers. The green-flushed yellow petals curve outward as they age. Woodland tulips die down in summer, so underplant them with a groundcover such as *Geranium macrorrhizum*. To echo the color of the flowers, pair *T. sylvestris* with *Erythronium* 'Pagoda'.

Try other, smaller species tulips in part shade and good drainage, such as *T. biflora*, *T. clusiana*, *T. orphanidea* Whittallii Group, or *T. turkestanica*. While many of these are described elsewhere as needing full sun, in my garden they grow underneath arches, arbors, and in the shade of small shrubs. All tulip bulbs are fall planted and are eaten by herbivores, so grow them in protected areas.

*Trillium grandiflorum* surrounded by the blue flowers of *Brunnera macrophylla*.

*Tulipa sylvestris*

*Uvularia grandiflora*

The creased foliage of *Veratrum nigrum*.

## Uvularia grandiflora | large-flowered bellwort, merrybells

Part to full shade | Moist, well-drained soil | Zones 3–8
12–24 in. tall, 12–18 in. wide

*Uvularia grandiflora* has rich yellow flowers that dangle below arching foliage in spring. It is best planted in a group, as it is quite delicate in appearance. Plant it in humusy soil in a woodland garden or wildflower border. Large-flowered bellwort looks good near *Trillium luteum* and *Mertensia virginica*. There are only a few species of *Uvularia*, and all are woodland flowers that bloom in shades of yellow and are native to North America.

## Veratrum nigrum | black false hellebore

Part shade | Moist, well-drained soil | Zones 4–7
36–60 in. tall, 24 in. wide

*Veratrum nigrum* is grown for its large clump of bright green, pleated basal leaves and its striking flowers. It produces many individual star-shaped dark maroon flowers that are arranged on a tall stem that rises above the foliage in summer. Black false hellebore is an unusual and dramatic addition for a moist shade garden and pairs well with *Rodgersia* and *Hosta*. *Veratrum viride*, the green false hellebore, has taller spikes bearing green flowers, and is native to North America, where it is found in swamps and boggy woods. Both species are toxic, so use caution when handling them.

## *Vinca minor* | common periwinkle

Part to full shade | Medium soil | Zones 4–9
2–6 in. tall, indefinitely wide

*Vinca minor* is a love-it-or-hate-it plant. Some people adore it because it can cover large shady areas with its glossy foliage and spring-blooming, star-shaped, periwinkle-colored flowers. Others find its spreading habit too aggressive because it can out-compete more delicate shady beauties. *Vinca* grows from a central crown and roots where its stems touch the ground. I find it a useful workhorse plant where I do not want bare soil. If I have too much of it, I rip it out or use shears to cut it off just above the crown. There are several cultivars with different flower colors and variegated leaf forms to brighten up the shade.

## *Viola labradorica*

Labrador violet, American dog violet

Part shade | Moist, well-drained soil | Zones 2–8
2–6 in. tall, 12 in. wide

*Viola labradorica* has small lavender flowers and new spring leaf growth that is purple. As the growing season progresses, the foliage turns greener, although the undersides of the leaves remain a rich color. The Labrador violet is native to North America and is very hardy. Combine this violet in a bed with the similarly scaled *Tiarella* and *Asarum shuttleworthii* for a petite garden vignette.

There are many other hardy *Viola* species that are perfect for a shaded situation. Their flowers can be all one color or can have a distinct "eye" of another color. Others have speckled or splotched petals. *Viola sororia* 'Freckles' is a favorite of mine. Try *V. biflora*, *V. pedata*, or *V. striata*. If perennial violets spread too much, it is easy to pull them out, but they will probably be back, as they spread by seed as well as by underground tubers.

*Vinca minor*

*Viola labradorica*

The addition of brightly colored tropical plants like *Solenostemon scutellariodes* 'Mt. Washington' add pizzazz to garden compositions.

# TROPICALS AND ANNUALS

The plants listed in this section are those that grow well where the temperatures are warm year-round. They often require plentiful soil moisture for optimum growth. In warmer regions, many of these tropical plants are hardy outside, but in cooler climates they are only enjoyed in the garden during the warmer months of the year.

The plants listed here are mostly perennials, because they will grow for several years outside in tropical climates. However, because low temperatures kill them, gardeners in temperate regions commonly treat them as annuals, buying them anew each spring. In order to reuse them, in areas with cold winters, bring these plants inside and store them before the first frost.

Tropical plants are not the mainstay of most cool-weather shade gardens. They are frequently planted as accents in pots, window boxes, or other containers. Some gardeners use pots planted with tropicals or annuals to fill empty spaces in their borders. Their lush foliage, often in vivid colors, adds an element of surprise and excitement to the summer garden. Their bold form and structure stands out against the primarily green foliage of hardy perennials.

True annuals serve the same function as tropicals in the garden. However, they complete their life cycle in one growing season and then die, so they need to be bought or propagated from seed each year. Use tropical perennials and true annuals to add unusual beauty to your shaded scene.

Many of these plants benefit from being "pinched back." This entails removing small lengths from the growing tips, just above a leaf node. Pinching back produces a full, less leggy plant.

## *Alocasia sanderiana* | Kris plant

Part shade | Moist, well-drained soil | Zones 10–14
36–72 in. tall and wide

*Alocasia sanderiana* is grown for its large, arrowhead-shaped, vein-patterned leaves that add a bold accent to borders and containers. The leaves hang down from flexible stems twisting and twirling in the wind, providing movement in the garden. Flowers are small spathes and are followed by clusters of inedible reddish fruit. Keep this plant well watered and fertilized to allow the leaves to grow to their full size.

## *Angelonia angustifolia* | angelonia

Edge or part shade | Moist, well-drained soil | Zones 9–11
12–18 in. tall, 12 in. wide

*Angelonia angustifolia* has small, snapdragon-like flowers clustered on upright spikes. The blooms can be white, purple, pink, or bicolor and flower color lasts best with afternoon shade. Grown as a bedding or container annual, this plant is heat tolerant and blooms in flushes throughout the growing season. Deadhead the flowering spikes for best bloom. I choose white or pink cultivars, and combine them with *Euphorbia* 'Diamond Frost'.

*Aspidistra elatior*

## *Aspidistra elatior*
cast iron plant

Part to full shade  |  Well-drained soil
Zones 8–10  |  24–36 in. tall, 12–24 in. wide

*Aspidistra* has shiny, leathery green foliage and grows well in full shade. Its common name comes from its toughness; this is a plant that can survive neglect. It can grow with little water, even when planted next to tree trunks. In warm areas, it is used as a groundcover and it is most impressive when grown in large groups. In cooler climates, it is a container plant valued for its long, solid green leaves. The cultivar 'Variegata' has white-striped foliage.

## Begonia | begonia

This massive genus has many excellent shade plants, some of which are grown for their flowers, others for their patterned foliage.

### ▶ Begonia rex | rex begonia

Part to full shade | Moist, well-drained soil
Zones 10–11 | 12–24 in. tall, 12–18 in. wide

Rex begonias are grown for their large, attractive, patterned leaves that have a silvery sheen in lower light levels. Foliage colors can be green, red, and silver in distinctive patterns according to the cultivar. They are immensely popular, both as houseplants and as annual outdoor shade plants, and there are many cultivars from which to choose. Do not let these plants sit in water, as their rhizomes will rot.

### ▶ Begonia Semperflorens Cultorum Group
wax begonia

Bright or part shade | Moist, well-drained soil
Zones 10–11 | 6–18 in. tall, 6–12 in. wide

Wax begonias are colorful plants that are generally used as bedding annuals, as path edging, or in pots. In colder climates, these plants are planted out after the last frost in spring. Their flowers bloom all growing season in shades of pink, white, orange, or red. Leaves are green, dark red, or bronze with a shiny surface. A particularly hardy member is 'Kaylen', which will overwinter with protective mulching in zone 7. There are many different cultivars, including the popular Cocktail Series with bronzy leaves.

### ▶ Begonia ×tuberhybrida | hybrid tuberous begonia

Part to full shade | Moist, well-drained soil | Zones 9–11 | 6–18 in. tall, 6–12 in. wide

Begonia ×tuberhybrida is grown for its large, sometimes double flowers in an assortment of bright colors including pink, red, orange, yellow, or white, some with contrasting edges. The leaves emerge in early spring from flat tubers. Plant hybrid tuberous begonias in friable, well-drained soil in a container or hanging basket anywhere you want a strong splash of color. I prefer the look of one or two cultivars grouped together to that of a wild, multicolored mix. They perform best in cooler summer temperatures, as they dislike hot and humid weather.

Begonia 'Kaylen' (Semperflorens Cultorum Group)

## Browallia speciosa | bush violet

Edge or part shade | Medium soil | Zones 9–11 | 12–18 in. tall and wide

*Browallia* is a genus of annuals and perennials from shady, damp, tropical woodlands. *Browallia speciosa* can be added to borders or grown as a container annual, and looks especially good in hanging baskets. It has green, pointed leaves and profuse, flat-faced, purple-blue or white flowers. Keep plants well watered during the growing season. I like bush violets combined with *Catharanthus* and *Angelonia*.

## Caladium species | elephant ear, angel wings

Dappled to full shade | Moist, well-drained soil | Zones 9–11 | 12–18 in. tall and wide

*Caladium* is a genus of tuberous perennials with large leaves that come from woodland margins. Plants in this genus are grown for their colored leaves in combinations of white, green, pink, or red. Elephant ears can be used as container plants, in the ground as border plants, or as the focal point in a bed. The white-leaved cultivars are especially eye-catching in full shade. Caladium 'Candidum' is one of the best white-leaved cultivars, with dark green veins. For leaves with red coloration, look for the cultivars 'Blaze' or 'Brandywine'. The green and white 'Aaron' is more petite and suitable for small containers. The tubers may be dug up and stored in a frost-free area to overwinter.

## Catharanthus roseus | Madagascar periwinkle

Bright or part shade | Moist, well-drained soil | Zones 9–12 | 8–16 in. tall, 8–12 in. wide

The Madagascar periwinkle is grown as an annual bedding or container plant. Its five-petaled flowers can be pink, red, purple, or white, and are produced more heavily if its roots are kept evenly moist. I grow *Catharanthus roseus* at the front of beds and in window boxes. It is an indispensible filler plant for display containers, as it blooms all season long and its glossy green leaves have good substance.

## Colocasia esculenta 'Black Magic' | taro 'Black Magic'

Bright or part shade | Medium to wet soil | Zones 8–11 | 36–72 in. tall and wide

Plants in the genus *Colocasia* have dramatic, large, arrow-shaped leaves that bring a distinctly tropical look to the shade garden. Slow to establish at the beginning of the season, by midsummer when the temperature warms up, they become an impressive accent in the garden.

*Colocasia esculenta* 'Black Magic' has an iridescent sheen to its purple-black leaves that is brought out by pairing it with purple-flowered plants. Add plenty of organic matter to the planting holes and keep the soil moist or wet throughout summer. If you garden beyond its hardiness zones, dig up the tuberous roots and store them in a frost-free basement for the winter.

*Browallia speciosa*

*Caladium* 'Candidum'

*Catharanthus roseus*

*Colocasia esculenta* 'Black Magic' underplanted with purple *Angelonia* and *Plectranthus*.

*Cordyline fruticosa* 'Auntie Lou'

## *Cordyline* species | cordyline, cabbage tree

Part to full shade | Medium to moist soil
Zones 9–12, varies by species
8–20 ft. tall, 36–72 in. wide; varies by species

*Cordyline fruticosa*, the ti tree, has broad leaves and is widely used in tropical regions of the world, where it is grown both ornamentally and as a food crop. The decorative leaves of the cultivars may be solid or variegated green, white, pink, or dark, bronzy purple. This bold plant may be used as the dramatic focal point of a shaded tropical planting.

A related species, *C. australis*, has a distinctive, upright form with spiky, strap-like leaves. Young plants are often used as the centerpieces in container plantings and reach a modest size of 24–36 inches tall. If planted in the ground where it is hardy, it will mature into a palmlike tree. *Cordyline australis* will tolerate the sea spray of coastal sites. 'Torbay Dazzler' is a white variegated form.

## *Dichondra argentea* 'Silver Falls' | dichondra

Edge or bright shade | Dry to medium soil | Zones 10–12
3 in. tall, 36–48 in. wide

*Dichondra argentea* 'Silver Falls' is a small-leaved prostrate plant used to trail over the edge of containers or as a groundcover in warm areas. These creeping plants grow across the soil surface by rooting at their nodes. The soft, silver foliage is unusual for a shade plant, and so is great in pots, serving as a contrast to darker-foliaged, more upright plants such as *Plectranthus* 'Mona Lavender' or *Strobilanthes dyeriana*.

*Dichondra argentea* 'Silver Falls' drapes over a decorative column.

## *Euphorbia* 'Diamond Frost'

euphorbia 'Diamond Frost'

Part shade | Dry to medium soil | Zones 10–12
12–18 in. tall and wide

*Euphorbia* 'Diamond Frost' is a perfect mixing plant in a container or at the front of a shady border. It is delicate in texture and grows among other plants to give a cohesive look. Tiny white bracts that look like petals surround the true flowers that are borne on wiry-looking stems. Its airy habit makes it particularly attractive in window boxes.

As with all plants in the massive genus of *Euphorbia*, handle it while wearing gloves, because its milky sap is an irritant. *Euphorbia pulcherrima*, known commonly as poinsettia, will grow in part shade, and is used as hedging in sufficiently warm climates (zones 9–11).

## *Fuchsia* hybrids | fuchsia hybrids

Dappled or bright shade | Moist, well-drained soil
Zones 8–11, may vary by cultivar | Size varies by cultivar

Prolific flowers are the hallmark of *Fuchsia* hybrids, particularly where summers are cool. Their dangling flowers have two sections: the outer portion and the inner tube. Blooms come in a vast array of sizes and color combinations, consisting mainly of pinks, purples, corals, reds, and whites. In North America, the flowers attract hummingbirds.

The cascading cultivars are perfect for a hanging basket or dangling over the side of a pot. Some are shrub-like and look good in a large container or in the ground, and can be trained as standards or pyramids. 'Mrs Popple' is a popular cultivar for growing in the ground. 'Gartenmeister Bonstedt' is a more upright, rounded shrub, perfect for growing as a specimen in pots or in combination with other plants. *Fuchsia magellanica* is one of the hardiest species, surviving outdoors in zones 6–9.

*Euphorbia* 'Diamond Frost'

*Fuchsia* 'Gartenmeister Bonstedt'

*Hedychium densiflorum* 'Assam Orange'

## Hedychium densiflorum | ginger lily

Part shade | Moist, well-drained soil | Zones 8–11
5–10 ft. tall, 4–6 ft. wide

Flowering in late summer with a vertical spike of orange, white, red, or yellow blooms held above long, green, ovular leaves, *Hedychium densiflorum* adds a tropical look to the shade garden. Its flowers may be fragrant and are held in bottlebrush-like inflorescences. This rhizomatous, shrub-sized perennial is hardy in the ground in warmer climates, but can be grown in a pot and taken indoors for the winter in the rest of the world. Try 'Stephen' or 'Assam Orange'. Ginger lily is considered invasive in New Zealand.

## Hypoestes phyllostachya | polka-dot plant

Part shade | Medium to moist soil | Zones 10–11
6–24 in. tall and wide

Polka-dot plant is grown for its colorful speckled foliage in shades of cream, green, pink, or red. It thrives in the heat of summer. *Hypoestes* is best grown in a container in combination with other plants that pick up some of its foliage colors. Pinch the growing tips back to keep the plant compact. Look for the Splash Series and the Confetti Series. I grow 'Confetti White' in a pot with *Athyrium niponicum* var. *pictum* and *Caladium* 'Candidum'.

*Hypoestes phyllostachya* 'Pink Splash'

## Impatiens | impatiens, balsam

Impatiens typically grow in damp woodlands in warm areas of the world. Garden plants in the genus have fleshy stems and brightly colored flowers.

### ▶ Impatiens hawkeri
New Guinea impatiens

Part shade | Moist, well-drained soil
Zones 9–12 | 12–14 in. tall and wide

New Guinea impatiens are grown for their colorful flowers that are produced all summer and their glossy leaves that remain healthy until the frost. They are best sited in afternoon shade in humus-rich soil. Flower colors can be white, pink, purple, red, or salmon. New Guinea impatiens are often used in containers, hanging baskets, or as bedding plants. I think they look best if planted together in masses of one cultivar or in combination with other plants that pick up their flower color. They are more rabbit tolerant than other plants in the genus.

### ▶ Impatiens walleriana
busy Lizzie, impatiens

Part to full shade | Moist, well-drained soil
Zones 10–11 | 6–18 in. tall and wide

*Impatiens walleriana* is a low-growing shade plant that is a gardening favorite for its wide range of flower colors and its ability to bloom all summer. Flowers are white, pink, salmon, orange, or purple and may be single or double, depending on the cultivar you choose. This plant is equally valuable in containers as it is in beds or borders. In some areas, there is a devastating problem with a fungus called downy mildew that kills *I. walleriana*, so buy your plants from a reliable source or choose a cultivar that is disease resistant.

*Impatiens hawkeri*

*Nicotiana alata*

## *Nicotiana* | tobacco plant

Plants in the genus *Nicotiana* are grown for their tubular flowers. All species have large, tobacco-like leaves.

### ▶ *Nicotiana alata* | flowering tobacco

Edge or part shade | Moist, well-drained soil | Zones 10–11 | 24–48 in. tall, 12 in. wide

*Nicotiana alata* is a tender perennial, which is grown as a self-sowing annual in most climates. Leaves form at the base and then a flowering stalk emerges in summer. The tubular flowers flare out at the ends into starlike shapes in colors of white, lime green, burgundy, pink, or purple. The blooms are fragrant in the evening, so these are a good choice planted near a doorway or along a walkway. Attractive to pollinators, *Nicotiana* plants may cross with each other, producing surprising new seedlings in the following growing season. These easy-care plants are a cheerful addition to a shady summer border.

### ▶ *Nicotiana sylvestris* | woodland tobacco, flowering tobacco

Edge or part shade | Moist, well-drained soil | Zones 10–11 | 60 in. tall, 24 in. wide

Woodland tobacco has green, slightly sticky large leaves, in a rosette and on its tall stem. Its trumpet-shaped white flowers are sweetly fragrant, primarily at night, making them good plants for a patio. When they bloom in late summer, their white flowers are especially striking in a dark area of your shade garden. This statuesque plant produces thousands of seeds, so deadhead it if you do not want them to spread prolifically. I love *Nicotiana sylvestris*, and allow it to seed freely around my garden.

## Philodendron xanadu | xanadu philodendron

Part shade | Moist, well-drained soil | Zones 10–11
24–36 in. tall, 36–48 in. wide

Plants in the genus *Philodendron* are well known for their large, glossy leaves. Often grown as houseplants, they are perfect in a shady garden where you need some bold texture. They look good as specimen plants in large containers on a shaded terrace. In hotter climates, they will need full shade.

*Philodendron xanadu* has highly divided, deep green leaves with a polished sheen. Grow these plants in humus-rich soil with good moisture in summer and drier soil in winter. Their fine texture and shrub-like stature suits them to the home landscape. In zones where they are hardy, they are perfect grown under palm trees or as a foundation planting. In colder climates, *P. xanadu* can be grown in containers, which will restrict its overall size.

## Plectranthus | plectranthus

*Plectranthus* is a genus of fleshy-foliaged plants, which may be aromatic when touched.

### ▶ *Plectranthus forsteri* 'Marginatus'
variegated Swedish ivy

Part shade | Dry to medium soil | Zones 10–11
8–12 in. tall, 12–36 in. wide

*Plectranthus forsteri* 'Marginatus' is grown in containers as a trailing plant. Its fuzzy leaves are green with a creamy white margin and have a slight scent, which discourages browsing by herbivores. It combines well with *Impatiens* or *Catharanthus*, and can also be used to camouflage plants prone to deer browsing. This sprawling plant is easy to propagate from cuttings and is a low-maintenance choice for the shade garden.

### ▶ *Plectranthus* 'Mona Lavender'
plectranthus 'Mona Lavender'

Part shade | Medium soil | Zones 10–11 | 12–24 in. tall and wide

*Plectranthus* 'Mona Lavender' is used as an annual in container plantings for its green leaves that have purple undersides. Lavender-colored flower spikes are produced over a long period and are especially attractive late in the season. Keep this plant pinched back to encourage more flowering and sturdier growth. Combine it with *Viola* and *Angelonia*.

*Philodendron xanadu*

*Plectranthus* 'Mona Lavender'

## Sabal minor | dwarf palmetto

Edge or part shade | Moist, well-drained soil | Zones 7–10
36–72 in. tall and wide

The leaves of *Sabal minor* are large, upright, pleated, and fan shaped. The palmlike leaves are a great contrast to other, more delicate shade foliage plants such as ferns, and are evergreen where the plant is hardy. Use dwarf palmetto as a focal point in the garden, or massed as a screen. This plant will grow in shade and will also shade smaller plants beneath it. *Sabal minor* is native to southeastern North America.

## Sansevieria zeylanica
snake plant

Part to full shade | Well-drained soil | Zones 10–12
18–30 in. or more tall, 18 in. wide

Plants in the genus *Sansevieria* have stiff, vertical, often variegated and pointed leaves, and are used as accents in the shade garden. In areas where they are not hardy, they make good houseplants that can be taken outside for the growing season. Whether you grow them in the ground or in pots, make sure they have gritty, well-drained soil with moisture in the summer months. They are easy-care plants, thriving on neglect, and can increase rapidly.

*Sansevieria zeylanica* has silver and green variegated leaves in an attractive, irregularly banded pattern. Another species, *S. trifasciata*, often has yellow-gold margins, and a range of variegation depending on the cultivar you choose.

*Sabal minor*

*Sansevieria zeylanica* grown in an elevated pot with *Solenostemon*.

## *Solenostemon scutellarioides* | coleus

Bright or part shade | Moist, well-drained soil
Zones 10–11 | 12–48 in. tall, 12–36 in. wide; size varies by cultivar

Plants in the genus *Solenostemon* are some of the best plants to grow in the shade for vivid leaf colors. Their foliage may be lime green, red, cream, dark mahogany, yellow, or pink, or may be any combination of these colors. They are suitable for planting in a shady bed or border and perfect in a container. Pinch the growing tips back above pairs of leaves to encourage fuller, shrubby growth, or train them as standards. Either way, remove the insignificant flowering stalks for a neater look. They are easy to care for and can be brought inside in winter as houseplants.

There are hundreds of cultivars available, but some of my favorites are 'Winter Sun' and plants in the Wizard Series. I like to use 'Inky Fingers' with *Colocasia esculenta* 'Black Magic'. The range of leaf sizes and colors is extensive, so look for combinations that suit your planting schemes when you are selecting cultivars.

*Solenostemon scutellarioides* 'Kong Lime Sprite'

## *Strobilanthes dyeriana* | Persian shield

Part shade | Moist, well-drained soil | Zones 10–12
12–36 in. tall and wide

Persian shield is grown for its purple and green foliage, which has a silvery sheen. The attractive leaves retain their color best in part shade. It is excellent in containers or grown as an annual in beds. *Strobilanthes dyeriana* grows well in fertile, free-draining soil and should be pinched to maintain bushiness. I have grown it with *Euphorbia* 'Diamond Frost' and purple *Angelonia*. This plant may also be listed as *Strobilanthes dyerianus*.

*Strobilanthes dyeriana*

*Sutera cordata* 'Snowflake'

## *Sutera cordata* | ornamental bacopa

Edge or part shade | Moist, well-drained soil
Zones 9–11 | 3–6 in. tall, 18 in. wide

Ornamental bacopa mingles well in window boxes or hanging baskets with other part shade plants. The small, profuse flowers are produced over a long period of time and may be white, pink, muted blue, or purple. They are alternately called *Bacopa* or *Chaenostoma*. Cultivar 'Snowflake' has bright white flowers with a yellow eye and combines well with *Hypoestes phyllostachya* 'White Splash' and white *Catharanthus*.

## *Torenia fournieri* | wishbone flower

Bright or part shade | Moist soil
Zones 11–12 | 6–18 in. tall, 6–12 in. wide

*Torenia fournieri* has trumpet-shaped flowers that are attractive to hummingbirds and other pollinators in colors of purple, blue, pink, white, or yellow. Used at the front of the border or in containers and hanging baskets, wishbone flowers add color to the summer shade garden. I like them on their own in urns or in combination with white or purple *Sutera*. Pinch back tips to encourage branching for a fuller plant. There are many cultivars from which to choose; I recommend the Summer Wave Series or the Clown Series.

*Torenia fournieri*

## *Viola* | violet, pansy

Violas are grown for their cheery little flowers that are borne on short plants. They are one of the most popular and versatile of the small flowering shade plants and are available in a wide range of colors to suit your preference—blue, yellow, purple, white, bronze, pink, or red. In some areas, they can be short-lived perennials, but they are mostly grown as annuals. They are indispensable in containers and are also useful as bedding plants. Continue to deadhead violas to keep their flowers blooming and trim back the tips to keep the plants compact. Violas are cool-season plants, so they thrive in spring and autumn in hot climates. They will last through summer where the climate is cooler.

### ▶ *Viola tricolor*
Johnny-jump-up, heartsease

Dappled or part shade | Moist, well-drained soil
Zones 3–9 | 6 in. tall, 6–8 in. wide

Johnny-jump-ups have small flowers in shades of purple, violet, pink, white, and yellow. Primarily grown in containers for maximum impact, they can also be used at the front of a bed, in an herb garden, or lining a path. Use them in spring containers with small bulbs, or in fall groupings with *Heuchera*. I love to see their cheery faces peeking out wherever they seed themselves in.

### ▶ *Viola* ×*wittrockiana* | pansy

Dappled or part shade | Moist, well-drained soil
Zones 6–10 | 6–8 in. tall, 6–12 in. wide

Pansies are grown for their colorful flowers that add a splash of brightness to the shade garden in the cool seasons of the year. I like them best grown in pots, each planted with one cultivar but grouped together for maximum impact. They are a great addition to window boxes. There has been extensive breeding of pansies, and so there are a multitude of cultivars from which to choose. Site your pansies where you will see them every day, as they are very cheerful flowers. Many pansies have a soft, sweet scent that can be enjoyed if you pick yourself a small nosegay.

*Viola* ×*wittrockiana*

# METRIC CONVERSIONS AND HARDINESS ZONES

| INCHES | CM |
|--------|-----|
| ½ | 1.3 |
| 1 | 2.5 |
| 2 | 5.1 |
| 3 | 7.6 |
| 4 | 10 |
| 5 | 13 |
| 6 | 15 |
| 7 | 18 |
| 8 | 20 |
| 9 | 23 |
| 10 | 25 |

| FEET | M |
|------|-----|
| 1 | 0.3 |
| 2 | 0.6 |
| 3 | 0.9 |
| 4 | 1.2 |
| 5 | 1.5 |
| 6 | 1.8 |
| 7 | 2.1 |
| 8 | 2.4 |
| 9 | 2.7 |
| 10 | 3 |
| 20 | 6 |
| 30 | 9 |
| 40 | 12 |
| 50 | 15 |
| 100 | 30 |
| 1000 | 300 |

## TEMPERATURES

$$°C = 5/9 \times (°F - 32)$$

## PLANT HARDINESS ZONES

### Average Annual Minimum Temperature

| Zone | Temperature (deg. F) | Temperature (deg. C) |
|------|----------------------|----------------------|
| 1 | Below –50 | Below –46 |
| 2 | –50 to –40 | –46 to –40 |
| 3 | –40 to –30 | –40 to –34 |
| 4 | –30 to –20 | –34 to –29 |
| 5 | –20 to –10 | –29 to –23 |
| 6 | –10 to 0 | –23 to –18 |
| 7 | 0 to 10 | –18 to –12 |
| 8 | 10 to 20 | –12 to –7 |
| 9 | 20 to 30 | –7 to –1 |
| 10 | 30 to 40 | –1 to 4 |
| 11 | 40 to 50 | 4 to 10 |
| 12 | 50 to 60 | 10 to 16 |
| 13 | 60 to 70 | 16 to 21 |

# SUGGESTED READING

## GENERAL SHADE GARDENING

Armitage, Allan M. 2008. *Herbaceous Perennial Plants: A Treatise on Their Identification, Culture, and Garden Attributes.* 3rd ed. Champaign, Illinois: Stipes Publishing.

Chatto, Beth, and Erica Hunningher. 2002. *Beth Chatto's Woodland Garden: Shade-loving Plants for Year-round Interest.* London: Cassell Illustrated.

Cullina, William. 2002. *Native Trees, Shrubs & Vines: A Guide to Using, Growing, and Propagating North American Woody Plants.* Boston: Houghton Mifflin.

Culp, David L., with Adam Levine. 2012. *The Layered Garden: Design Lessons for Year-round Beauty from Brandywine Cottage.* Portland, Oregon: Timber Press.

Darke, Rick, and Douglas W. Tallamy. 2014. *The Living Landscape: Designing for Beauty and Biodiversity in the Home Garden.* Portland: Timber Press.

Dirr, Michael A. 2009. *Manual of Woody Landscape Plants: Their Identification, Ornamental Characteristics, Culture, Propagation and Uses.* 6th ed. Champaign, Illinois: Stipes Publishing.

Dirr, Michael A. 2011. *Dirr's Encyclopedia of Trees and Shrubs.* Portland, Oregon: Timber Press.

Jekyll, Gertrude. 1899. *Wood and Garden: Notes and Thoughts, Practical and Critical, of a Working Amateur.* London, England: Longmans, Green, and Co.

Robinson, William, and Rick Darke. 2009. *The Wild Garden: Expanded Edition.* Portland: Timber Press.

Schmid, Wolfram George. 2002. *An Encyclopedia of Shade Perennials.* Portland, Oregon: Timber Press.

Wiley, Keith. 2006. *Shade: Planting Solutions for Shady Gardens.* Portland, Oregon: Timber Press.

## MISCELLANEOUS GENERA

Bennett, Masha. 2003. *Pulmonarias and the Borage Family.* Portland, Oregon: Timber Press.

Burrell, C. Colston, and Judith Knott Tyler. 2006. *Hellebores: A Comprehensive Guide.* Portland, Oregon: Timber Press.

Case, Frederick W., Jr., and Roberta B. Case. 1997. *Trilliums.* Portland, Oregon: Timber Press.

Lane, Chris. 2005. *Witch Hazels.* Portland, Oregon: Timber Press.

Martin, Annie. 2015. *The Magical World of Moss Gardening.* Portland, Oregon: Timber Press.

Nold, Robert. 2003. *Columbines: Aquilegia, Paraquilegia, and Semiaquilegia.* Portland, Oregon: Timber Press.

Rogers, Ray. 2008. *Coleus: Rainbow Foliage for Containers and Gardens.* Portland, Oregon: Timber Press.

Tebbitt, Mark, Magnus Lidén, and Henrik Zetterlund. 2008. *Bleeding Hearts, Corydalis, and Their Relatives.* Portland, Oregon: Timber Press.

## FERNS

Olsen, Sue. 2007. *Encyclopedia of Garden Ferns.* Portland, Oregon: Timber Press.

Steffen, Richie, and Sue Olsen. 2015. *The Plant Lover's Guide to Ferns.* Portland, Oregon: Timber Press.

## GERANIUMS

Parer, Robin. 2016. *The Plant Lover's Guide to Hardy Geraniums.* Portland, Oregon: Timber Press.

Yeo, Peter. 2002. *Hardy Geraniums.* Portland, Oregon: Timber Press.

## HEUCHERAS

Heims, Dan, and Grahame Ware. 2005. *Heucheras and Heucherellas: Coral Bells and Foamy Bells.* Portland, Oregon: Timber Press.

Oliver, Charles G., and Martha Oliver. 2006. *Heuchera, Tiarella and Heucherella: A Gardener's Guide.* London: Batsford.

## HOLLIES

Bailes, Christopher. 2006. *Hollies for Gardeners.* Portland, Oregon: Timber Press.

Galle, Fred C. 1997. *Hollies: The Genus Ilex.* Portland, Oregon: Timber Press.

## HOSTAS

Grenfell, Diana, and Michael Shadrack. 2009. *The New Encyclopedia of Hostas.* Portland, Oregon: Timber Press.

Shadrack, Kathy Guest, and Michael Shadrack. 2010. *The Book of Little Hostas: 200 Small, Very Small, and Mini Varieties.* Portland, Oregon: Timber Press.

## HYDRANGEAS

Dirr, Michael. 2004. *Hydrangeas for American Gardens.* Portland, Oregon: Timber Press.

Van Gelderen, C. J., and D. M. van Gelderen. 2004. *Encyclopedia of Hydrangeas.* Portland, Oregon: Timber Press.

## PRIMULAS

Mitchell, Jodie, and Lynne Lawson. 2016. *The Plant Lover's Guide to Primulas.* Portland, Oregon: Timber Press.

Richards, John. 2003. *Primula.* Portland, Oregon: Timber Press.

# GARDEN AND PHOTOGRAPHY CREDITS

## GARDEN CREDITS

Tony, Madge, and Glenn Ashton garden, Trevose, Pennsylvania

Asticou Azalea Garden, Northeast Harbor, Maine,

Ambler Arboretum, Temple University, Ambler, Pennsylvania

The Andalusia Foundation, Andalusia, Pennsylvania

Badminton Estate, Badminton, Gloucestershire, UK

Bartram's Garden, Philadelphia, Pennsylvania,

Bateman's, East Sussex, England, National Trust

Biddulph Grange Garden, Staffordshire, England, National Trust

Bonny Hall Plantation, Yemassee, South Carolina

Carol and Richard Bushell garden, Upway, Oxfordshire, UK

Jenny Rose and Gus Carey garden, Northview, Ambler, Pennsylvania

Cato Ranch, Wayland and Marion Cato, Sheridan, Wyoming

Chanticleer, Wayne, Pennsylvania

Chicago Botanic Garden, Glencoe, Illinois

Coastal Maine Botanical Gardens, Boothbay, Maine

Diane and Rob Cole garden, Meadow Farm, Feckenham, Worcestershire, UK

Charles Cresson garden, Hedgleigh Spring, Swarthmore, Pennsylvania

Docton Mill Gardens, Hartland, Devon, UK

Alex and John Dodge, Ashton Under Hill, Worcestershire, UK

Fuller Gardens, North Hampton, New Hampshire

New England Wildflower Society's Garden in the Woods, Framingham, Massachusetts

Heyward-Washington House, Courtesy of The Charleston Museum, Charleston, South Carolina

Holehird Gardens, The Lakeland Horticultural Society, Windermere, Cumbria, UK

Jenkins Arboretum & Gardens, Devon, Pennsylvania

Ladew Topiary Gardens, Monkton, Maryland

Lady Bird Johnson Wildflower Center, Austin, Texas

Adam Levine garden, Media, Pennsylvania

Penny Marshall garden, Biddeford Pool, Maine

Meadowbrook Farm, Pennsylvania Horticultural Society, Jenkintown, Pennsylvania

Middleton Place, Charleston, South Carolina

Mt. Cuba Center, Hockessin, Delaware

Myriad Botanical Gardens, Oklahoma City, Oklahoma

Olbrich Botanical Gardens, Madison, Wisconsin

Real Alcázar de Sevilla, Spain

Royal Horticultural Society Garden Rosemoor, Devon, UK

Rousham House & Garden, Charles Cottrell-Dormer, Oxfordshire, UK

Sezincote, near Moreton-in-Marsh, Gloucestershire, UK

Shofuso Japanese House and Garden, Philadelphia, Pennsylvania

Sissinghurst Castle Garden, Kent, England, National Trust

Barbara and Robert Tiffany garden, Mill Fleurs, Point Pleasant, Pennsylvania

Winterthur Museum, Garden & Library, Wilmington, Delaware

Royal Horticultural Society Garden Wisley, Surrey, UK

Marion and Brian Wright garden, Lady Hall, Cumbria, UK

Wyck House and Garden, Philadelphia, Pennsylvania

## PHOTOGRAPHY CREDITS

*All photographs by the author, except for the following:*

Rob Cardillo, pages 236 and 299 (top left)

Hanna von Schlegell, pages 39 (top), 93 (bottom right), 152 (left and right), 182, 195 (bottom left), 251 (bottom), 269 (top)

# ACKNOWLEDGMENTS

Producing a book is a collaborative process. I would like to offer thanks to the following people for their help and contributions:

To the team at Timber Press for making this book possible, especially Juree Sondker and Michael Dempsey.

To two very knowledgeable horticulturists and professors, Eva Monheim and Sue Mrugal, for their many helpful suggestions and plant knowledge.

To everyone who opened their garden gates and let me loose with a camera, I appreciate your willingness to share your shaded spaces with me. To the members of garden clubs across the country who invited me to speak and generously shared their fabulous gardens, which has allowed me to enjoy and explore a wide variety of personal shade garden interpretations.

To the many public gardens and arboreta around the world that educate and lead by example. To their staffs, for showing me around their landscapes and for sharing their experiences. Special thanks to the faculty and staff at Temple University and the Ambler Arboretum, who were always so supportive of me and shared in my enthusiasm. I would also like to acknowledge the talented staff at the Pennsylvania Horticultural Society, especially those at Meadowbrook Farm. Thank you so much for offering encouragement, for answering all my questions, and for allowing me to be the "Garden Paparazzi."

To my professors and garden mentors who have taught me so much and helped push me along the path toward plant addiction. I would particularly like to thank my inspirational gardening neighbors Ted and Marian Elkins for all that they have shared with me in their beautiful garden.

I appreciate all those who have helped me in the gardens at Northview over the years—you know who you are, and I thank you. To Joe Giampa Jr., who is waiting until this book is published to write his own tell-all about Northview, for his help and support over the years in keeping the grounds looking so wonderful.

To my parents and grandparents in England, who instilled in me an early love of gardening, particularly my dad, John Dodge, who taught me to name plants in Latin and to observe the natural world. To the rest of my family, including my sisters, Katy, Rosie, and Lizzie, my nieces, and my stepmother, Alex, who tolerate my passion for gardening and who visit gardens with me on both sides of the Atlantic.

To my head gardener and right-hand lady, Hanna von Schlegell, who kept everything in order and moving along, from editing plants in the garden at Northview to editing this book. It was hard work, but it was fun.

Finally, I would like to acknowledge my long-suffering and loving husband, Gus, who knows more about gardening than he ever lets on, and my intrepid daughters, Meade, Janet, and Emily, who have accompanied me on so many garden visits that they have lost count.

So many people have helped me in the process of writing this book, but any mistakes are my own.

# INDEX

## A

*Abelia ×grandiflora*, 171
*Acer*, 25, 50, 64, 92, 114, 171
*Acer griseum*, 57, 58, 171
*Acer palmatum*, 50, 54, 59, 67, 171
   'Hogyoku', 171
   'Sango-kaku', 171
   'Waterfall', 171
*Acer saccharum*, 168
acidic soils, 67, 108
acidity, 68
*Aconitum*, 50
*Aconitum carmichaelii*, 54, 67, 102, 228
   (Arendsii Group) 'Arendsii', 228
*Aconitum napellus*, 228
*Actaea*, 43, 229, 291
*Actaea pachypoda*, 229
*Actaea racemosa*, 48, 229
*Actaea simplex*, 229
   (Atropurpurea Group) 'Brunette', 229
*Adiantum*, 123, 215
*Adiantum capillus-veneris*, 67, 120, 215
*Adiantum pedatum*, 67, 215, 288
*Adonis amurensis*, 155, 159
*Aechmea*, 118
*Aesculus*, 172
*Aesculus parviflora*, 102, 172
*Aesculus pavia*, 48, 53, 153, 172
afternoon shade, 21, 25
*Agastache foeniculum*, 48, 153, 164, 230, 231
*Agave havardiana*, 117
*Ageratum*, 246
*Ajuga*, 83
*Ajuga reptans*
   'Burgundy Glow', 231
   'Chocolate Chip', 230
   'Variegata', 231
*Alchemilla*, 144, 288
*Alchemilla mollis*, 164, 230, 231, 242, 260
alkaline soil, 67, 126
Allegheny foamflower, 289
Allegheny serviceberry, 153
Allegheny spurge, 83, 277
allelopathy, 75
*Allium*, 231
*Allium moly*, 231
*Allium siculum*, 276
*Allium thunbergii*, 54, 231
   'Ozawa', 230
*Allium ursinum*, 231
*Allium zebdanense*, 231
*Alocasia*, 47
*Alocasia sanderiana*, 118, 295
Ambler Arboretum, 40
*Amelanchier*, 173
*Amelanchier laevis*, 153, 173

*Amelanchier lamarckii*, 173
America mountain laurel, 194
American beech, 168
American dog violet, 293
American elm, 11
American holly, 153, 192
American hornbeam, 54, 179
American meadow anemone, 233
American Turk's-cap lily, 269
American wild ginger, 237
American witchhazel, 189
American yellowwood, 168
Amur adonis, 155, 157, 159
anemone, 232
*Anemone*, 262
*Anemone blanda*, 232, 266, 274, 280, 282
*Anemone canadensis*, 232
*Anemone ×hybrida*, 50, 54, 67, 233
   'Andrea Atkinson', 232
   'Honorine Jobert', 158, 233, 254
*Anemonella*, 237
*Anemonella thalictroides*, 233
*Anemone nemorosa*, 135, 233
   'Robinsoniana', 233
angelonia, 295
*Angelonia*, 298, 299, 307
*Angelonia angustifolia*, 295
angel wings, 298
angled Solomon's seal, 281
animals, 38, 144
anise hyssop, 48, 153, 164, 231
annuals, 294–309
*Anthriscus sylvestris*, 128
apple, 128
*Aquilegia*, 22, 38, 155, 234
*Aquilegia canadensis*, 42, 102, 153, 234
*Aquilegia ×hybrida*, 234
*Aquilegia vulgaris* var. *stellata* 'Nora Barlow', 234
arbors, 32
*Arisaema*, 235
*Arisaema triphyllum*, 235
*Aristolochia*, 209
*Aristolochia macrophylla*, 209
*Aronia*, 50
*Aronia arbutifolia*, 153, 175
*Arum*, 155
*Arum italicum* subsp. *italicum* 'Marmoratum', 235
*Aruncus*, 123, 236, 238, 283
*Aruncus aethusifolius*, 236
*Aruncus dioicus*, 236
*Asarum*, 43, 50, 53, 83, 154, 227, 237, 267
*Asarum canadense*, 155, 237
*Asarum caudatum*, 237
*Asarum europaeum*, 155, 237

*Asarum shuttleworthii*, 293
asexual reproduction, 17
*Asimina*, 175
*Asimina triloba*, 153, 175
*Aspidistra*, 296
*Aspidistra elatior*, 164, 296
   'Variegata', 296
*Asplenium*, 144
*Asplenium nidus*, 216
*Asplenium scolopendrium*, 67, 216
   'Angustatum', 216
*Aster divaricatus*, 254
Asticou Azalea Garden, 110
*Astilbe*, 92, 123, 164, 222, 238, 283
*Astilbe ×arendsii* 'Fanal', 238
*Astilbe chinensis*, 238
   'Vision in Pink', 238, 239
*Astilbe japonica*
   'Deutschland', 238
   'Rheinland', 238
*Astilboides*, 123, 155
*Astilboides tabularis*, 164, 238, 239
*Astrantia*, 283
*Astrantia major*, 238, 239
   'Hadspen Blood', 238
athyrium, 217
*Athyrium*, 16, 217
*Athyrium filix-femina*, 217
*Athyrium niponicum* var. *pictum*, 157, 217, 302
   'Ghost', 217
*Aucuba*, 175
*Aucuba japonica*, 164, 175
autumn, 29, 49–54
autumn bugbane, 229
autumn fern, 50, 54, 219
azalea, 43, 67, 112, 201
*Azalea*, 30

## B

*Bacopa*, 308
bacteria, 62
Badminton Estate, 32
bald cypress, 70, 168
balsam, 303
baneberry, 229
Bateman's, 128
bead fern, 220
beardtongue, 153, 278
beetles, 62, 103
begonia, 297
*Begonia*, 16, 47, 157, 158, 217
   Cocktail Series, 297
   'Kaylen', 297
   Semperflorens Cultorum Group, 297
*Begonia grandis*, 50, 54, 157, 240
*Begonia rex*, 297

*Begonia* ×*tuberhybrida*, 297
*Belamcanda chinensis*, 266
*Bergenia*, 35, 155, 240
*Bergenia cordifolia*, 67, 240
Bethlehem sage, 283
*Betula*, 22, 35, 176
*Betula lenta*, 176
*Betula nigra*, 137, 168, 176
   'Heritage', 176
   'Little King', 176
*Betula papyrifera*, 160, 176
*Betula pendula*, 176
*Betula utilis* var. *jacquemontii*, 176
Biddulph Grange, 111, 135
bigleaf hydrangea, 48, 191
bigroot cranesbill, 258
bigroot geranium, 48, 67, 164, 258
birch, 176
birdbaths, 35
birds, 38, 50, 102–103, 144–146
bird's-nest fern, 216
bishop's hat 'Sulphureum', 83, 164, 252
blackberry lily, 54, 164, 266
black false hellebore, 48, 292
black lilyturf, 276
black mondo grass, 276
black snakeroot, 48
black tupelo, 168
black walnut, 75
*Bletilla*, 241
*Bletilla striata*, 241
bloodroot, 284
bloody cranesbill, 259
bluebells, 265
blue cardinal flower, 270
blue lily turf, 270
blue mistflower, 246
blue passionflower, 213
Boston ivy, 212
bottlebrush buckeye, 102, 172
bottle gentian, 48, 258
Bowman's root, 259
box, 177
box holly, 205
boxwood, 105, 177
branch collar, 79
bright shade, 21
*Browallia*, 158, 298
*Browallia speciosa*, 298, 299
*Brunnera*, 43, 101, 144, 154, 155, 157, 241, 273, 280
*Brunnera macrophylla*, 67, 83, 102, 164, 241
   'Alexander's Great', 241
   'Silver Heart', 155, 241
buckeye, 172
buckler fern, 219
bugbane, 229
bugleweed, 231
bulbs, 11, 38, 41–43, 47, 58–59, 75, 83, 95, 98, 113, 128, 150, 181, 201, 227
bumblebees, 38

burgundy foliage, 157
bush violet, 298
busy Lizzie, 303
butcher's broom, 58, 205
buttonbush, 153, 164, 179
*Buxus*, 177
*Buxus microphylla* var. *japonica* 'Winter Gem', 177
*Buxus sempervirens*, 67, 102, 177
   'Vardar Valley', 177
   'Variegata', 177
*Buxus sinica* var. *insularis* 'Justin Brouwers', 177

**C**

cabbage tree, 300
*Caladium*, 47, 53, 118, 298
   'Blaze', 298
   'Brandywine', 298
   'Candidum', 299, 302
*Calycanthus*, 177
*Calycanthus floridus*, 159, 177
   'Athens', 177
   'Hartlage Wine', 177
*Camassia*, 128, 256
*Camassia leichtlinii*, 242, 243
*Camellia*, 30, 59
*Camellia japonica*, 58, 67, 179
   'Debutante', 178
camellias, 112, 179
Canada lily, 269
Canadian columbine, 42, 102, 153, 234
Canadian ginger, 237
Canadian lily of the valley, 272
candelabra primrose, 113, 164, 282
canopy, 18, 38, 43, 150
cardinal flower, 270
*Carex*, 50, 83, 85, 137, 153, 154, 160, 238, 242, 243, 284
*Carex flacca*
   'Blue Zinger', 157, 242
   'Ice Dance', 242
*Carex pensylvanica*, 242
*Carex plantaginea*, 242
Carolina allspice, 159, 177
*Carpinus*, 179
*Carpinus betulus*, 179
*Carpinus caroliniana*, 54, 178, 179
*Carya*, 168
*Carya ovata*, 168
cast iron plant, 164, 296
*Catharanthus*, 298, 305, 308
*Catharanthus roseus*, 298, 299
celandine poppy, 287
*Cephalanthus*, 137
*Cephalanthus occidentalis*, 153, 164, 178, 179
*Cephalotaxus*, 181
*Cephalotaxus harringtonia*, 102
   'Fastigiata', 180, 181
   'Nana', 181
   'Prostrata', 181

*Cercis*, 38, 128, 181
*Cercis canadensis*, 30, 42, 158, 181, 291
   'Appalachian Red', 180
   'Hearts of Gold', 106
*Cercis siliquastrum*, 181
*Chaenomeles*, 103
*Chaenostoma*, 308
*Chasmanthium*, 50
*Chasmanthium latifolium*, 164, 242, 243
checkered lily, 256
*Chelone*, 164, 281
*Chelone glabra*, 244
*Chelone lyonii*, 244, 284
chemical amendments, 68
chemical fertilizers, 95–97
cherry birch, 176
cherry laurel, 201
cherry trees, 112
Chicago Botanic Garden, 138
children, 140–141
Chinese gardens, 110–112
Chinese hardy orchid, 241
Chinese sweetbox, 58
*Chionanthus*, 41, 181
*Chionanthus retusus*, 181
*Chionanthus virginicus*, 158, 159, 180, 181
*Chionodoxa*, 38, 83, 181, 244
*Chionodoxa forbesii*, 244
*Chionodoxa luciliae*, 244
*Chionodoxa sardensis*, 58, 244
Christmas fern, 225
*Chrysogonum*, 53, 245, 274
*Chrysogonum virginianum*, 83, 245
*Cimicifuga*, 229
cinnamon fern, 222
*Cladrastis kentukea*, 168
clay soil, 63
*Claytonia virginica*, 42, 245
*Clematis*, 21
   'Betty Corning', 209
   'Comtesse de Bouchaud', 208, 209
   'Jackmanii', 209
   'Nelly Moser', 209
   'Rooguchi', 209
   'Silver Moon', 209
*Clematis glaucophylla*, 209
*Clematis paniculata*, 209
*Clematis viorna*, 209
*Clethra*, 43, 137, 182
*Clethra alnifolia*, 67, 153, 159, 182
   'Hummingbird', 182
   'Ruby Spice', 182
climbing hydrangea, 211
Coastal Maine Botanical Gardens, 22, 108, 134
colchicum, 54, 246
*Colchicum*, 50, 246
*Colchicum cilicicum*, 54, 246
*Colchicum speciosum* 'Album', 246
cold-tolerant plants, 41
coleus, 307

*Colocasia*, 47, 53, 118, 298
*Colocasia esculenta* 'Black Magic', 157, 298, 299, 307
columbine, 234
    hybrid, 234
comfrey, 288
common astilboides, 164, 238
common beech, 187
common bleeding heart, 42, 102, 268
common bluebell, 265
common box, 67, 102
common camellia, 58, 67, 179
common foxglove, 42, 102, 250
common ivy, 210
common periwinkle, 293
common polypody, 223
common snowdrop, 67, 102, 164, 256
    'S. Arnott', 58
common winterberry, 153, 193
compacting, 72
compost, 41, 63–64, 89
*Conoclinium coelestinum*, 246
container gardens, 126–127
container plants, 47
*Convallaria*, 158
*Convallaria majalis*, 83, 159, 247
    var. *rosea*, 247
coral bells, 263
cordyline, 300
*Cordyline*, 300
*Cordyline australis*, 300
    'Torbay Dazzler', 300
*Cordyline fruticosa*, 300
corkscrew hazel, 91
cornel, 182
Cornelian cherry, 183
*Cornus*, 50, 67, 128, 182–183
*Cornus alba* 'Sibirica', 183
*Cornus alternifolia*, 154, 157, 182
    'Golden Shadows', 157, 182
*Cornus florida*, 38, 42, 48, 50, 54, 153, 158, 183
*Cornus kousa*, 183
*Cornus mas*, 38, 183
    'Golden Glory', 183
*Cornus sanguinea* 'Midwinter Fire', 183
*Cornus sericea*, 164, 183
*Corydalis lutea*, 247
*Corydalis ochroleuca*, 247
*Corylopsis spicata*, 184
    'Aurea', 184
*Corylus avellana* 'Contorta', 91
courtyard gardens, 124–125
cow parsley, 128
cowslip, 40, 282
cranesbill, 258
cranesbill 'Biokovo', 83
creeping Jacob's ladder, 281
creeping mazus, 272
creeping phlox, 83, 280
creeping saxifrage, 284

crested woodland iris, 266
*Crocus*, 38, 83, 248
*Crocus tommasinianus*, 58, 248
    'Barr's Purple', 248
    'Lilac Wonder', 248
    'Roseus', 248
    'Ruby Giant', 248
custard apple, 175
cyclamen, 248
*Cyclamen*, 83
*Cyclamen coum*, 58, 164, 248, 249
*Cyclamen hederifolium*, 54, 164, 248
*Cyrtomium falcatum*, 67, 218, 219

## D

daffodil, 102
    'Hawera', 274
    'Thalia', 42
daphne, 67, 159, 185
*Daphne*, 159, 185
*Daphne bholua* 'Jacqueline Postill', 185
*Daphne* ×*burkwoodii*, 67, 185
    'Carol Mackie', 185
*Daphne* ×*transatlantica*, 185
    'Jim's Pride', 185
dappled shade, 21
day length, 26
deadheading, 47
decomposers, 62, 152
deer, 101–102
deer-resistant plants, 102
*Dennstaedtia punctilobula*, 83, 218, 219
*Deutzia*, 41
*Deutzia gracilis* 'Nikko', 154, 186
*Dicentra*, 39, 248
*Dicentra canadensis*, 248
*Dicentra cucullaria*, 248
*Dicentra eximia*, 48, 248, 249
*Dicentra spectabilis*, 268
*Dichondra*, 118
*Dichondra argentea* 'Silver Falls', 300
*Dicksonia*, 160
digging, 72, 82
*Digitalis*, 22, 43, 99, 128, 153, 250, 259, 281
*Digitalis lutea*, 48, 250
*Digitalis purpurea*, 42, 102, 250
*Diospyros virginiana*, 55
*Diphylleia cymosa*, 250
diseases, 98, 103
*Disporopsis pernyi*, 83, 251, 281
Docton Mill Gardens, 92, 120
*Dodecatheon*, 38, 126, 227
*Dodecatheon meadia*, 42, 251
    'Alba', 291
    f. *album*, 251
dogwood, 67, 182
doll's eyes, 229
dormancy, 29
doublefile viburnum, 207
double orange daylily, 262

*Dracaena*, 118
dragonflies, 144
drip line, 94
drooping leucothoe, 194
drought-tolerant plants, 21, 115
drumstick primrose, 282
*Dryopteris*, 67, 219
*Dryopteris affinis*, 219
    'Cristata', 219
*Dryopteris erythrosora*, 50, 54, 157, 218, 219
    'Brilliance', 263
*Dryopteris filix-mas*, 220
    'Linearis Polydactyla', 220
    'Parsley', 220
*Dryopteris marginalis*, 220
dungwort, 261
Dutchman's pipe, 209
dwarf buckeye, 172
dwarf crested iris, 83, 266
dwarf fothergilla, 188
dwarf Mondo grass, 276
dwarf palmetto, 164, 306
dwarf Solomon's seal, 83, 251
dwarf sweetbox, 159, 205

## E

earthworms, 62
eastern redbud, 42, 181
edge shade, 21
elephant ear, 298
English bluebell, 42, 265
English holly, 58, 192
English ivy, 210
English primrose, 282
*Enkianthus*, 50, 68, 187
*Enkianthus campanulatus*, 67, 186, 187
*Epimedium*, 38, 41, 50, 157, 233, 267, 291
    'Amber Queen', 42
*Epimedium* ×*versicolor* 'Sulphureum', 83, 164, 252
*Epimedium* ×*youngianum*
    'Jenny Wren', 252
    'Niveum', 42, 252
*Eranthis*, 59, 286
*Eranthis hyemalis*, 58, 67, 166, 253
*Erythronium*, 282
    'Pagoda', 253, 274, 291
    'White Beauty', 253
*Erythronium americanum*, 253
*Erythronium dens-canis*, 253
*Euonymus fortunei*, 210
    'Emerald Gaiety', 210
    'Silver Queen', 210
    var. *radicans*, 83
*Eupatorium coelestinum*, 246
*Euphorbia*, 157
    'Diamond Frost', 301, 307
*Euphorbia amygdaloides* var. *robbiae*, 254, 255
*Euphorbia pulcherrima*, 301
European beech, 168, 187

European wild ginger, 237
*Eurybia*, 128, 160
*Eurybia divaricata*, 254, 255
evergreen plants, 26
evergreen Solomon's seal, 251

**F**

*Fagus*, 187
*Fagus grandifolia*, 168
*Fagus sylvatica*, 168, 187
fall-blooming hardy cyclamen, 54
false Solomon's seal, 54, 67, 272
false spiraea, 238
farfugium, 254
*Farfugium japonicum*, 254, 255
×*Fatshedera*, 118
fences, 32–33, 59
ferns, 41, 43, 71, 75, 92, 94, 101, 102, 137, 160,
     214–225, 306
fertilizing, 95–97
*Filipendula rubra*, 164, 254
     'Venusta', 254, 255
five-fingered fern, 215
flowering dogwood, 42, 54, 153, 183
flowering tobacco, 304
flowers, 158
foamflower, 83
foliage color, 155–157
forget-me-not, 40, 241
fothergilla, 188
*Fothergilla*, 38, 50
*Fothergilla gardenii*, 188
     'Blue Mist', 157, 188
*Fothergilla major*, 188
     'Blue Shadow', 188
fragrant bedstraw, 256
fragrant shade plants, 159
fragrant Solomon's seal, 281
fragrant sumac, 164
     'Gro-Low', 203
fringed bleeding heart, 48, 248
fringe tree, 159, 181
*Fritillaria*, 256, 274
*Fritillaria meleagris*, 42, 242, 256, 257
*Fritillaria michailovskyi*, 256
*Fuchsia*, 118, 158
     'Gartenmeister Bonstedt', 301
     hybrids, 301
     'Mrs Popple', 301
Fuller Gardens, 134
full shade, 17, 18
fungal diseases, 103
fungi, 62

**G**

*Galanthus*, 38, 41, 59, 83, 128, 181, 223, 227, 235, 256
*Galanthus elwesii*, 58, 256
*Galanthus* ×*hybridus* 'Robin Hood', 166
*Galanthus nivalis*, 67, 102, 158, 164, 256, 257
     f. *pleniflorus* 'Flore Pleno', 256

'S. Arnott', 58, 159, 256
     'Viridapice', 59
*Galanthus woronowii*, 256
*Galium odoratum*, 256, 257
Garden in the Woods, 64, 114
garden structures, 32–33
gentian, 258
*Gentiana, Begonia*, 16
*Gentiana andrewsii*, 48, 258
*Gentiana asclepiadea*, 258
*Gentiana clausa*, 258
geranium, 258
*Geranium*, 41, 241, 253, 258, 259, 271
*Geranium* ×*cantabrigiense* 'Biokovo', 83, 258
*Geranium macrorrhizum*, 48, 67, 102, 164, 258, 291
     'Ingwersen's Variety', 258
*Geranium maculatum*, 258, 282
*Geranium sanguineum*, 259
     var. *lancastrense*, 259
     var. *striatum*, 259
giant snowdrop, 58, 256
*Gillenia*, 41
*Gillenia trifoliata*, 259
ginger lily, 302
*Gingko*, 64
*Glaucidium palmatum*, 99
*Gleditsia*, 168
*Gleditsia triacanthos* f. *inermis*, 168
glory-of-the-snow, 58, 244
glossy abelia, 171
goat's beard, 236
golden-scaled male fern, 219
golden shield fern, 219
grape-holly, 197
grape hyacinth, 274
great blue lobelia, 164, 270
great masterwort, 238
Grecian windflower, 232
green and gold, 83, 245
green foliage, 155–157
green frogs, 101
groundcovers, 83, 112
groundhogs, 102
guinea hen fritillary, 42, 256
*Gymnocladus*, 168
*Gymnocladus dioica*, 168

**H**

haircap moss, 108
hairy alumroot, 54, 83, 263
*Hakonechloa*, 50, 91, 154
*Hakonechloa macra*, 260
     'Aureola', 260
*Hakonechloa macra* 'Aureola', 155
Hakone grass, 260
*Hamamelis*, 50, 59, 158, 189
*Hamamelis* ×*intermedia*, 57, 58, 189
     'Aurora', 189
     'Diane', 189
     'Jelena', 189

'Rochester', 159, 189
*Hamamelis vernalis*, 189
*Hamamelis virginiana*, 189
hardiness, 161
hardy begonia, 54, 240
hardy cyclamen, 58, 164, 248
hardy ginger, 83, 237
Harry Lauder's walking stick, 91
hart's tongue fern, 67, 216
Havard's century plant, 117
hay-scented fern, 219
heartleaf brunnera, 67, 83, 102, 164, 241
heartleaf philodendron, 118
heartsease, 309
*Hedera helix*, 83, 210
*Hedychium densiflorum*, 302
     'Assam Orange', 302
     'Stephen', 302
hellebore, 261
hellebore hybrids, 58
*Helleborus*, 41, 43, 75, 91, 144, 157, 160, 247, 261,
     264, 284
*Helleborus foetidus*, 58, 67, 102, 261
*Helleborus* ×*hybridus*, 58, 261
*Hemerocallis*, 48, 231
     'Hyperion', 262
*Hemerocallis fulva* 'Flore Pleno', 262
*Hemerocallis lilioasphodelus*, 262
hepatica, 262
*Hepatica*, 262
*Hepatica acutiloba*, 262
*Hepatica americana*, 262
herbaceous plants, 69, 78, 83, 98, 99, 137, 158, 162,
     214, 227–293
herbicides, 78–82
herbivorous mammals, 100–101, 152
*Heuchera*, 100, 126, 154, 202, 217, 219, 241, 263,
     288, 309
     'Citronelle', 263
     hybrids, 263
     'Marmalade', 263
     'Obsidian', 263
*Heuchera villosa*, 54, 83, 263
     'Autumn Bride', 263
     'Palace Purple', 157, 263
×*Heucherella*, 263
Heyward-Washington House, 105
Himalayan blue poppy, 273
Himalayan sarcococca, 205
Hinoki cypress, 112
Holehird Gardens, 159
holly, 192
holly fern, 67, 219
honeybees, 38
hosta, 147, 264
*Hosta*, 41, 43, 44, 75, 88, 91, 96, 100, 101, 108, 126,
     154, 155, 157, 159, 217, 227, 233, 241, 260, 264,
     276, 292
     'Blue Cadet', 157, 264
     'Blue Mouse Ears', 157, 264

'Ginko Craig', 264
'Golden Tiara', 157, 182
'Halcyon', 157
'June', 264
'Liberty', 264
miniature, 264
'Pineapple Upsidedown Cake', 157, 264
'The Razor's Edge', 264
'Royal Standard', 48, 158, 159, 264
'Stiletto', 264
'Sum and Substance', 155
'Twilight', 182
*Hosta fortunei* 'Striptease', 264
*Hosta sieboldiana* 'Frances Williams', 264
*Hügelkultur* (hill culture), 137
humus, 64
*Hyacinthoides*, 75, 106, 128, 220
*Hyacinthoides hispanica*, 265
*Hyacinthoides non-scripta*, 42, 265
hybrid anemone, 233
*Hydrangea*, 47, 48, 144, 159, 190–191, 279, 289
*Hydrangea anomala* subsp. *petiolaris*, 211
*Hydrangea arborescens*, 190, 242
  'Annabelle', 190
*Hydrangea macrophylla*, 46, 48, 79, 158, 191
  'Endless Summer', 191
  Hortensia hybrids, 191
  Teller Series, 191
  'Tokyo Delight', 191
*Hydrangea paniculata*, 191
  'Limelight', 191
  'Tardiva', 191
*Hydrangea quercifolia*, 54, 190, 191
  'Little Honey', 157
  'Snowflake', 191
  'Snow Queen', 191
*Hypoestes*, 47, 118
*Hypoestes phyllostachya*, 118, 302
  Confetti Series, 302
  'Confetti White', 302
  Splash Series, 302
  'White Splash', 308

**I**

*Ilex*, 50, 59, 68, 192
*Ilex aquifolium*, 58, 192
  'Ferox Argentea', 192
*Ilex glabra*, 164, 192
*Ilex opaca*, 55, 153, 192
*Ilex verticillata*, 137, 153, 192, 193
  'Jim Dandy', 193
  'Red Sprite', 193
  'Southern Gentleman', 193
  'Winter Gold', 193
  'Winter Red', 193
impatiens, 303
*Impatiens*, 46, 47, 158, 303, 305
*Impatiens hawkeri*, 303
*Impatiens walleriana*, 303
Indian bowstring hemp, 306

inkberry, 164, 192
inorganic mulch, 99
insecticides, 103
insects, 38, 102–103, 144
invasive plants, 78, 79, 82
iris, 266
*Iris*, 154, 266
*Iris cristata*, 38, 83, 251, 266, 280
  'Tennessee White', 268, 286
*Iris domestica*, 54, 164, 266
*Iris foetidissima*, 266
ironwood, 179
Italian arum 'Marmoratum', 235
*Itea*, 43, 137
*Itea virginica*, 159, 193
  'Henry's Garnet', 193
  'Little Henry', 193

**J**

jack-in-the-pulpit, 235
Japanese anemone, 54, 67, 233
Japanese creeper, 212
Japanese flowering apricot, 159, 201
Japanese forest grass, 260
Japanese gardens, 110–112
Japanese hydrangea vine, 211
Japanese kerria, 194
Japanese lace fern, 225
Japanese laurel, 175
Japanese maple, 54, 67, 112, 171
Japanese onion, 54, 231
Japanese painted fern, 217
Japanese pieris, 67, 200
Japanese plum yew, 102, 181
Japanese spurge, 277
Japanese wood poppy, 99
*Jeffersonia diphylla*, 42, 67, 99, 152, 267
*Jeffersonia dubia*, 267
Johnny-jump-up, 309
Judas tree, 181
*Juglans nigra*, 74, 75
juglone, 75
juneberry, 173

**K**

*Kalmia*, 41, 68, 200
*Kalmia latifolia*, 67, 194
  f. *myrtifolia* 'Elf', 195
Kentucky coffee tree, 168
*Kerria japonica*, 194
  'Pleniflora', 194, 195
*Kirengeshoma*, 289
*Kirengeshoma palmata*, 48, 267
Kousa dogwood, 183
Kris plant, 295

**L**

Labrador violet, 293
lacecaps, 191
Ladew Topiary Gardens, 130, 142

Lady Bird Johnson Wildflower Center, 115, 144
lady fern, 217
lady's mantle, 164, 231
Lakeland Horticultural Society, 159
*Lamium*, 83
*Lamium maculatum*
  'Beacon Silver', 268
  'White Nancy', 268
*Lamprocapnos*, 38, 155, 248, 273, 284, 287
*Lamprocapnos spectabilis*, 42, 102
  'Alba', 291
  'Gold Heart', 157
*Lamprocapnos spectabilis,*, 268
  'Alba', 268
  'Gold Heart', 268
large camas, 242
large-flowered bellwort, 292
large-flowered comfrey, 288
large-flowered trillium, 42, 291
laurustinus, 207
lavender mist meadow rue, 48, 289
leaf mold, 63
leaf shape, 154
leaf size, 30, 154–155
leaf surface, 155
leaf texture, 154
leatherleaf mahonia, 197
leatherleaf viburnum, 67, 207
leaves, 62–63, 96, 154–155
Lenten rose, 261
leopard slug, 101
*Leucojum*, 38, 41
*Leucojum aestivum*, 164, 242, 269
leucothoe, 67
*Leucothoe*, 67, 194
*Leucothoe axillaris*, 194
*Leucothoe fontanesiana*, 194, 195
*Leucothoe racemosa*, 194
*Lilium*, 128
*Lilium canadense*, 269
*Lilium martagon*, 48, 269
*Lilium superbum*, 269
lily-of-the-valley, 83, 159, 247
limbing-up, 35
*Lindera benzoin*, 102, 153, 194, 195
*Liriodendron*, 166
*Liriodendron tulipifera*, 168
*Liriope muscari*, 270
littleleaf linden, 168
live oak, 168
liverleaf, 262
lobelia, 270
*Lobelia*, 137, 270
*Lobelia erinus*, 270
*Lobelia siphilitica*, 164, 270
London pride, 284
*Lonicera*, 21, 212
*Lonicera sempervirens*, 212
lungwort, 83, 102, 283
*Luzula nivea*, 271

*Lycoris radiata*, 271
*Lycoris squamigera*, 48, 271

## M

Madagascar periwinkle, 298
magic lily, 271
magnolia, 196
   'Leonard Messel', 197
*Magnolia*, 13, 21, 25, 196
*Magnolia kobus*, 197
*Magnolia ×loebneri* 'Leonard Messel', 159,
   196, 197
*Magnolia macrophylla* subsp. *ashei*, 48
magnolias, 30
*Magnolia stellata*, 38, 197
*Magnolia virginiana*, 50, 137, 153, 164, 197
mahonia, 197
*Mahonia*, 59, 71, 197
*Mahonia aquifolium*, 164, 197
*Mahonia bealei*, 197
*Maianthemum*, 291
*Maianthemum canadense*, 272
*Maianthemum racemosum*, 54, 67, 272
maidenhair fern, 215
maintenance
   autumn tasks, 50–54
   fertilizing, 95–97
   mulching, 97–100
   spring tasks, 41–43
   summer tasks, 47
   watering, 47, 92–95
   winter tasks, 59
male fern, 220
*Malus*
   'Donald Wyman', 57
   'Prairifire', 128
maple, 171
marginal wood fern, 220
martagon lily, 48, 269
Maryland pinkroot, 287
*Matteuccia struthiopteris*, 164, 221
May apple, 67, 153, 280
*Mazus reptans*, 272
meadow anemone, 233
*Meconopsis*, 273
*Meconopsis cambrica*, 273
*Meconopsis grandis*, 273
Mediterranean-inspired walled/courtyard
   gardens, 124–125
merrybells, 292
*Mertensia*, 38, 75, 106, 227, 240, 265, 272, 280, 287
*Mertensia virginica*, 42, 268, 273, 292
Mexican feather grass, 117
*Microbiota*, 198
*Microbiota decussata*, 198
microclimates, 94
Middleton Place, 35, 178
Mill Fleurs, 44, 85
mini-microclimates, 94

mockorange, 199
mondo grass, 83
monkshood, 54, 67, 102, 228
mopheads, 191
morning shade, 21
moss, 64, 69, 108, 112
moss gardens, 108–109
mountain laurel, 67, 194
Mrs. Robb's bonnet, 254
Mt. Cuba Center, 152
mukdenia, 274
*Mukdenia*, 215
*Mukdenia rossii*, 274, 275
mulching, 47, 53–54, 95, 97–100
*Muscari*, 53, 274
   'Mount Hood', 274, 275
*Muscari armeniacum*, 274
   'Dark Eyes', 274
   'Peppermint', 274
   'Valerie Finnis', 274
*Muscari azureum*, 274
*Muscari botryoides*, 274
musclewood, 179
mycorrhizae, 70, 71
*Myosotis*, 40, 274, 282, 287
*Myosotis sylvatica*, 268, 275
Myriad Botanical Gardens, 133, 203

## N

*Narcissus*, 38, 41, 53, 102, 128, 183, 273, 274, 286
   'Actaea', 274
   'Baby Moon', 274
   'February Gold', 274
   'Hawera', 232, 274, 275, 282
   'Jenny', 274
   'Lemon Drops', 106
   'Silver Chimes', 274
   Sun Disc', 274
   'Thalia', 42, 274
*Nassella tenuissima*, 117
native plants, 153
*Nectaroscordum siculum*, 48, 276
neutral soils, 67
New England Wild Flower Society, 64, 114
New Guinea impatiens, 303
*Nicotiana*, 47, 158, 304
*Nicotiana alata*, 304
*Nicotiana sylvestris*, 159, 304
nitrogen (N), 95
North America wild oats, 242
northern maidenhair fern, 67, 215
*Nyssa sylvatica*, 168

## O

oak, 70, 85, 153
oakleaf hydrangea, 54, 191
Olbrich Botanical Gardens, 160
*Onoclea sensibilis*, 220, 221
*Ophiopogon*, 83, 274, 276

*Ophiopogon japonicus* 'Gyoku-ryu', 256, 276
*Ophiopogon planiscapus* 'Nigrescens', 158, 242,
   276
orchard gardens, 128–129
Oregon grape-holly, 164, 197
organic matter, 61, 62–64
ornamental bacopa, 308
*Osmanthus fragrans*, 198
*Osmanthus heterophyllus*, 198
   'Goshiki', 157, 198
   'Gulftide', 198
osmunda, 67, 222
*Osmunda*, 67, 222
*Osmunda cinnamomea*, 153, 222
*Osmunda regalis*, 164, 222
*Osmundastrum cinnamomeum*, 222
ostrich fern, 164, 220
outbuildings, 130
Ozark witchhazel, 189

## P

pachysandra, 277
*Pachysandra*, 277
*Pachysandra procumbens*, 83, 277
*Pachysandra terminalis*, 83, 277
*Paeonia*, 278
*Paeonia obovata*, 278
pagoda dogwood, 182
panicle hydrangea, 191
pansy, 309
paperbark maple, 58, 171
parterre, 105
*Parthenocissus quinquefolia*, 212
*Parthenocissus tricuspidata*, 212
part shade, 17–21
*Passiflora caerulea*, 213
*Passiflora racemosa*, 213
*Passiflora ×violacea*, 213
pathways, 132–135
pawpaw, 153, 175
penstemon, 278
*Penstemon*, 128, 153, 278, 281
*Penstemon digitalis* 'Husker Red', 278
*Penstemon pallidus*, 278
*Penstemon smallii*, 278
pergolas, 32, 59
Persian shield, 307
*Persicaria*, 279
*Persicaria amplexicaulis*, 279
*Persicaria bistorta*, 279
*Persicaria virginiana* Variegated Group, 279
   'Painter's Palette', 279
pesticides, 100
pests, 98, 100–103, 152
*Petasites*, 123, 155, 279
*Petasites hybridus* 'Variegatus', 279
*Philadelphus*, 43, 158
*Philadelphus coronarius*, 67, 159, 199
*Philadelphus ×virginalis*, 199

'Minnesota Snowflake', 199
*Philodendron*, 47, 155, 305
*Philodendron hederaceum*, 118
*Philodendron xanadu*, 118, 305
*Phlox*, 38, 96, 106, 155, 227, 266
*Phlox divaricata*, 91, 280
   'Blue Moon', 280
   'London Grove Blue', 280
*Phlox stolonifera*, 83, 280, 286
   'Bruce's White', 280
   'Home Fires', 280
   'Sherwood Purple', 280
phosphorus (P), 95
photosynthesis, 152
*Phytophthora*, 103
*Pieris floribunda*, 200
*Pieris japonica*, 67, 68, 157, 200
   'Dorothy Wyckoff', 200
   'Mountain Fire', 200
pigsqueak, 67, 240
pinkroot, 287
pink turtlehead, 244
pinxterbloom azalea, 202
plant choice factors, 29
plant form, 153–154
planting hole, 89–91
planting techniques
   dividing plants, 88
   preparing, placing, and planting, 89–91
   small root balls, 86–89
   trees, 91
   working in an open area, 82–86
   working next to buildings, 86
   working under trees, 82
plant layers, 150
plant selection
   annuals, 294–309
   ferns, 214–225
   fragrant shade plants, 159
   herbaceous plants, 227–293
   illuminating combinations, 153–160
   native plants, 153
   plant layers, 150
   plant palette, 161–166
   plants for moist to wet soil, 164
   plants for well-drained soil, 164
   powering shade garden, 152
   trees and shrubs, 168–207
   tropical plants, 294–309
   understanding and supporting natural
      processes, 150
   vines, 208–213
plectranthus, 102
*Plectranthus*, 102, 299
   'Mona Lavender', 157, 300, 305
*Plectranthus forsteri* 'Marginatus', 305
plum trees, 112
pneumatophores, 70
*Podophyllum*, 280

*Podophyllum peltatum*, 67, 96, 153, 280
poison ivy, 79
*Polemonium*, 39, 155, 281
*Polemonium caeruleum*, 281
*Polemonium reptans*, 251, 281
polka-dot plant, 302
*Polygonatum*, 39, 160, 227, 251, 277, 281
*Polygonatum biflorum*, 281
*Polygonatum humile*, 281
*Polygonatum odoratum* var. *pluriflorum*
   'Variegatum', 281
*Polypodium interjectum*, 214
*Polypodium virginianum*, 223
*Polypodium vulgare*, 223
polystichum, 225
*Polystichum acrostichoides*, 225, 240
*Polystichum polyblepharum*, 225
*Polystichum setiferum*, 225
   (Divisilobum Group) 'Herrenhausen', 225
*Polytrichum*, 108
ponds, 35
*Populus tremuloides*, 79
*Porteranthus trifoliatus*, 259
potassium (K), 97
potting soil, 89
powdery mildew, 103
primrose, 42, 282
*Primula*, 38, 99, 123, 183, 251, 282
*Primula denticulata*, 282
*Primula japonica*, 113, 164, 282
*Primula veris*, 40, 281, 282
*Primula vulgaris*, 42, 282
propagation, 88
pruning, 47, 79
prunus, 200
*Prunus*, 128, 200
*Prunus laurocerasus*, 201
*Prunus mume*, 38, 159, 201
   'Fragrant Snow', 201
   'Kobai', 201
*Prunus serrula*, 128
*Pulmonaria*, 38, 43, 83, 102, 144, 155, 157, 246
   'Majesté', 283
*Pulmonaria longifolia* 'Bertram Anderson', 283
*Pulmonaria saccharata*, 283
   Argentea Group, 283
purple foliage, 157
*Puschkinia*, 38, 244

**Q**

quaking aspens, 79
quaking oat grass, 164, 242
queen-of-the-prairie, 164, 254
*Quercus*, 43, 64, 70, 153, 168
*Quercus alba*, 168
*Quercus phellos*, 168
*Quercus ruber*, 74
*Quercus virginiana*, 168

**R**

rabbits, 102
rain gardens, 137
rain shadows, 94
raised beds, 135–137
Real Alcázar de Sevilla, 16, 123
red buckeye, 48, 153, 172
redbud, 181
red chokeberry, 153, 175
red foliage, 157
red magic lily, 271
red oak, 74
red-osier dogwood, 183
red spider lily, 271
red-twig dogwood, 164, 183
redvein enkianthus, 187
reflected light, 33
reflecting pools, 35
repetition, 158–160
rex begonia, 297
rhododendron, 67, 201
*Rhododendron*, 21, 38, 66, 67, 68, 126, 158, 200, 201
*Rhododendron atlanticum*, 202
*Rhododendron catawbiense*, 201
*Rhododendron luteum*, 201
*Rhododendron maximum*, 202
*Rhododendron mucronulatum*, 40, 184, 201
*Rhododendron periclymenoides*, 202
*Rhododendron vaseyi*, 202
*Rhododendron viscosum*, 158, 159, 164, 202
*Rhododendron yakushimanum*, 201
*Rhus*, 203
*Rhus aromatica*, 164
   'Gro-Low', 203
*Rhus typhina* 'Tiger Eyes', 203
river birch, 168, 176
rock gardens, 113–114
rodgersia, 164, 283
*Rodgersia*, 41, 101, 123, 164, 215, 222, 283, 292
*Rodgersia pinnata*, 283
*Rodgersia podophylla*, 283
*Rodgersia tabularis*, 238
*Rohdea*, 155, 242
*Rohdea japonica*, 284, 285
root balls, 86–91
root rot, 103
roots
   absorption of water and nutrients, 71
   anchoring, 71
   compacting, 72
   digging, 72
   herbaceous plants around tree roots, 83
   mycorrhizae, 70
   obtaining oxygen, 71
   smothering, 75
   storage, 71
   tree roots, 72–75
rosebay rhododendron, 202
Rousham House and Garden, 123

royal fern, 164, 222
Royal Horticultural Society
  Garden Rosemoor, 16, 120, 138
  Garden Wisley, 66, 187
rue-anemone, 233
*Ruscus aculeatus*, 58, 204, 205
Russian arborvitae, 198
rust, 284

**S**

*Sabal minor*, 164, 306
sacred lily, 284
*Sanguinaria*, 39, 280
*Sanguinaria canadensis*, 88, 284, 285
*Sansevieria*, 306
*Sansevieria trifasciata*, 306
*Sansevieria zeylanica*, 306
*Sarcococca*, 59, 158, 205
*Sarcococca confusa*, 205
*Sarcococca hookeriana* var. *humilis*, 159, 204, 205
*Sarcococca orientalis*, 58, 205
*Sarcococca ruscifolia*, 205
*Saruma*, 155
*Saruma henryi*, 284, 285
*Saxifraga stolonifera*, 284, 285
*Saxifraga ×urbium*, 284
*Schizophragma hydrangeoides*, 211
*Scilla*, 38, 39, 83, 181, 201, 244
*Scilla bifolia*, 286
*Scilla siberica*, 58, 286
  'Spring Beauty', 284, 286
sedge, 83, 242
  'Ice Dance', 242
*Sedum*, 164
*Sedum cauticola*, 286
*Sedum glaucophyllum*, 286
*Sedum kamtschaticum* var. *ellacombeanum*, 286
*Sedum spurium*, 286
*Sedum ternatum*, 241
  'Larinem Park', 286
sensitive fern, 220
Sezincote House and Garden, 123
shade
  garden structures and, 32–33
  reducing, 33–35
  seasonal factors, 26–29
  trees and, 30–32
  types of, 17–21
shade garden
  addition of organic matter to soil, 61
  changing shade levels in, 30–35
  developing in, 16
  maintenance tasks, 41–43, 47, 50–54, 59, 92–100
  microclimates, 94
  powering, 152
  seasonal changes in, 37–59

spring plants, 42
  summer plants, 48
shade garden design
  areas for children, 140–141
  attracting wildlife, 144–146
  container gardens, 126–127
  design plans, 130–146
  Japanese/Chinese gardens, 110–112
  Mediterranean-inspired walled/courtyard gardens, 124–125
  moss gardens, 108
  orchard gardens, 128–129
  pathways, 132–135
  rock gardens, 113–114
  seating area, 138–139
  stumperies, 147
  tropical gardens, 118
  water features, 142–143
  water gardens, 120–123
  woodland gardens, 106
  xeric gardens, 115–117
shagbark hickory, 168
shelf fungus, 63, 103
Shofuso Japanese House and Garden, 112
shooting star, 42, 251
shredded mulch, 98
shredded umbrella plant, 288
shrubs, 168–207
Siberian bugloss, 241
Siberian squill, 58, 286
Sicilian honey garlic, 48, 276
Sissinghurst Castle Garden, 13
slender deutzia 'Nikko', 186
slugs, 100–101
slug traps, 100
*Smilacina racemosa*, 272
smooth hydrangea, 190
smooth witherod, 207
smothering, 75
snails, 100–101
snake plant, 306
snowy mespilus, 173
snowy woodrush, 271
soft shield fern, 225
soil
  addition of organic matter to, 61
  improving, 62–64
  modifying soil pH to increase acidity, 68
  plants for acidic soils, 67
  plants for neutral to alkaline soils, 67
  soil pH, 66
*Solenostemon*, 47, 118, 157, 307
  'Pineapple', 46
*Solenostemon scutellarioides*, 307
  'Inky Fingers', 307
  'Mt. Washington', 294
  'Winter Sun', 307
  Wizard Series, 307
Solomon's seal, 281

southern maidenhair fern, 67, 215
Spain, 16
Spanish bluebell, 265
spicebush, 102, 153, 194
*Spigelia marilandica*, 287
spike winterhazel, 184
split-leaf maples, 171
spotted cranesbill, 258
spotted dead nettle, 268
spotted laurel, 164, 175
spring, 26, 38–43
spring beauty, 42, 245
staghorn sumac 'Tiger Eyes', 203
stepping stones, 112, 136
stinking Gladwyn, 266
stinking hellebore, 58, 67, 102, 261
stinking iris, 266
stolons, 17
stonecrop, 164
stone lanterns, 110
strawberry saxifrage, 284
straw foxglove, 48
*Strobilanthes*, 47
*Strobilanthes dyeriana*, 300, 307
*Strobilanthes dyerianus*, 307
stumperies, 147
*Stylophorum*, 38, 39, 273
*Stylophorum diphyllum*, 287
suckers, 79
sugar maple, 168
sumac, 203
summer, 26, 43–48
summer snowflake, 164, 269
summersweet, 67, 153, 159, 182
sun height, 26
sunlight intensity, 26
surprise lily, 48, 271
*Sutera*, 158, 308
*Sutera cordata*, 308
  'Snowflake', 308
swamp azalea, 159, 164
swamp magnolia, 197
sweetbay magnolia, 153, 164, 197
sweet birch, 176
sweet mockorange, 67, 159, 199
sweet pepperbush, 182
sweet woodruff, 256
*Symphytum*, 288
  'Hidcote Blue', 288
*Symphytum grandiflorum*, 288
*Syneilesis aconitifolia*, 288

**T**

taro 'Black Magic', 298
tassel fern, 225
*Taxodium*, 70
*Taxodium distichum*, 168
*Taxus*, 181
*Taxus ×media*, 204, 205

'Hicksii', 205
tent caterpillars, 103
*Thalictrum*, 43, 128, 155, 233
*Thalictrum aquilegiifolium*, 289
*Thalictrum rochebruneanum*, 48, 289
*Thalictrum thalictroides*, 233
thornless honey locust, 168
"three Ds" (dead, diseased, or damaged), 78
*Tiarella*, 41, 83, 92, 137, 202, 237, 263, 289, 293
*Tiarella cordifolia*, 289
    'Brandywine', 289
    'Delaware', 289
    'Oakleaf', 289
    River Series, 289
    'Running Tapestry', 289
*Tiarella wherryi*, 289
Tibetan cherry, 128
*Tilia cordata*, 168
toad lily, 54
toad lily 'Samurai', 290
tobacco plant, 304
tommies, 58, 248
*Torenia*, 47, 118, 158
*Torenia fournieri*, 308
    Clown Series, 308
    Summer Wave Series, 308
trailing lobelia, 270
tree fern, 160
tree roots, 72–75
trees
    large trees, 168
    leaf size and abundance, 30
    qualities to consider when adding, 30
    removal, 35
    selected, 168–207
    shapes of, 30
*Tricyrtis*, 50, 274, 290
    'Sinonome', 54, 290
*Tricyrtis formosana*, 54
    'Dark Beauty', 290
    'Samurai', 290
*Tricyrtis hirta*, 290
*Trillium*, 38, 102, 272
*Trillium erectum*, 291
*Trillium grandiflorum*, 42, 291
*Trillium luteum*, 291, 292
tropical gardens, 118
tropical plants, 47, 118, 294–309
trumpet honeysuckle, 212
tuberous begonia, 297
tulip, 128, 291
*Tulipa*, 53
*Tulipa biflora*, 291
*Tulipa clusiana*, 291
*Tulipa orphanidea* Whittallii Group, 291
*Tulipa sylvestris*, 274, 291
*Tulipa turkestanica*, 291
tulip tree, 168
Turk's-cap lily, 269

turtlehead, 164, 244
twinleaf, 42, 67, 267

**U**
*Ulmus americana*, 11
umbrella leaf, 250
understory, 30, 43, 69, 150
upright wild ginger, 284
*Uvularia*, 277, 292
*Uvularia grandiflora*, 292

**V**
variegated butterbur, 279
variegated foliage, 157
variegated Virginia tovara, 279
*Veratrum*, 153
*Veratrum nigrum*, 48, 292
*Veratrum viride*, 292
vernal witchhazel, 189
viburnum, 207
*Viburnum*, 38, 50, 75, 207
*Viburnum nudum*, 207
*Viburnum rhytidophyllum*, 67, 207
*Viburnum tinus*, 207
*Vinca*, 83
*Vinca minor*, 293
vines, 78, 208–213
*Viola*, 41, 309
*Viola biflora*, 293
*Viola labradorica*, 293
*Viola pedata*, 293
violas, 309
*Viola sororia* 'Freckles', 293
*Viola striata*, 293
*Viola tricolor*, 309
*Viola ×wittrockiana*, 309
violet, 309
Virginia bluebells, 11, 42, 273
Virginia creeper, 212
Virginia spiderwort, 290
Virginia sweetspire, 159, 193
volcano mulch, 98

**W**
walled gardens, 124–125
walls, 32–33
water gardens, 120–123
watering, 47, 92–95
water sprouts, 79
wax begonia, 297
weeds, 47
Welsh poppy, 273
white baneberry, 229
white fringe tree, 181
white oak, 168
white wake-robin, 291
white wood aster, 254
whorled stonecrop, 286
wildflowers, 79

wild ginger, 237
wildlife, 144–146
wild sweet William, 280
willow oak, 168
windflower, 232
winter, 26, 54–59
winter aconite, 58, 67, 253
winterberry holly, 193
wintercreeper, 210
winter rose, 261
Winterthur Museum, Garden and Library, 106, 113, 184
wishbone flower, 308
*Wisteria*, 79
witchhazel, 189
    cultivars, 58
    'Rochester', 159
wood anemone, 233
wood fern, 67, 219
woodland forget-me-not, 274
woodland gardens, 106
woodland peony, 278
woodland phlox, 280
woodland stonecrop, 286
woodland tobacco, 159, 304
woodland tulip, 291
wood mulches, 98
wood poppy, 287
wood spurge, 254
Woronow's snowdrop, 256
Wyck Historic House, 33

**X**
xeric gardens, 115–117

**Y**
yellow corydalis, 247
Yellow Garden, 130
yellow wax bells, 48, 267
yew, 181, 205

**JENNY ROSE CAREY** is a renowned educator, historian, and author, and director at the Pennsylvania Horticultural Society's Meadowbrook Farm in Jenkintown. She previously worked at Temple University for over a decade, first as an adjunct professor in the Department of Landscape Architecture and Horticulture and then as director of the Ambler Arboretum.

Jenny Rose has been lecturing nationally and internationally for many years. She is an avid, hands-on gardener who has gardened in both England and the United States. Her Victorian property, Northview, contains diverse garden spaces, including a shade garden, moss garden, and a stumpery. Jenny Rose and her gardens have been featured on the PBS series *The Victory Garden*, in the *Wall Street Journal*, the *Philadelphia Inquirer*, *Green Scene* magazine, and the *Pennsylvania Gardener*.